Endplays In Bridge

ELIMINATIONS, SQUEEZES & COUPS

George Coffin

Dover Publications, Inc.
New York

Published in Canada by General Publishing Com-
pany, Ltd., 30 Lesmill Road, Don Mills, Toronto,
Ontario.
Published in the United Kingdom by Constable
and Company, Ltd., 10 Orange Street, London
WC2H 7EG.

This Dover edition, first published in 1981, is a
republication of *Endplays: Sixth Master Edition
of Eliminations, Squeezes, Coups* as published by
Duckworth and Company, London in 1975. Omitted
in the present edition are: a portrait drawing of
the author, an editorial cartoon, an "Endplays Hall
of Fame" and a letter to the author from A. R. H.

International Standard Book Number: 0-486-24230-7
Library of Congress Catalog Card Number: 81-69898

Manufactured in the United States of America
Dover Publications, Inc.
180 Varick Street
New York, N.Y. 10014

AUTHOR'S FOREWORD 1975

This book is the sixth revised edition of *Endplays,* being Book Four of *Bridge Play Four Classics.* It all stemmed from the author's copious articles on endplays, all published during 1931 in the then three English-language monthlies, *Bridge Magazine* edited by Milton C. Work, *Bridge Magazine of Great Britain* edited by A.E.Manning-Foster, and *Bridge World* founded and edited by the then czar of contract bridge, Ely Culbertson. These articles plus other new material made up the first edition of 64 pages in 1932 to which the author added 32 pages of new deals that fall in the second edition.This was an exhaustive collection of bridge endings, many hypothetical, which the author thought might occur in actual play. After 1932 the great amount of expert play not only more than fulfilled his anticipations but also unearthed many new endings, necessitating drastic additions and revisions. These more than doubled the size of the work, the third edition of the Ad Press in New York City in 1938, to 224 pages. Later Duckworth of London published and revised slightly the fourth edition in 1950 and the fifth edition in 1957. Both Duckworth editions were dedicated to my mother,Elizabeth Wood Coffin.

This new sixth edition required further minor revisions, mostly in updating the English and styling to conform to *The Bridge Writer's Manual* and in making a few corrections in technical terms. The author has retained some quaintness of 1938 like capital letters for honor cards, and most references to events in the world of bridge and personalities are of that era. Few of its bridge stars are living today.

Many bridge books barely touched on endplays, so the author invites you into his inner sanctum of many beautiful, rare and exotic plays to delight the bridge connoisseur. They will sharpen your game.

They also form the backbone of double dummy problems. Our book, *Double Dummy Bridge,*(Book Three in *Bridge Play Four Classics).* offers 300 problems. They supplement *Endplays.* You are invited to examine "The Great 88 Five-Card Endings" starting on page 17. There you will find old friends, some renamed. For example, the trump squeeze so-called from auction bridge days is really a *squeeze ruffout.* The *true trump squeeze* is No. 47 of the Great 88. Other writers use their own peculiar names and in England animal names such as *The Hedgehog* appear, perhaps imitating those gasoline guzzlers called *The Barracuda, The Cougar, The Jaguar,* et cetera. In any field of science names are important. Bridgers can thank the author and others for avoiding the standards of botany and zoology, Latin names!

American Contract Bridge League

The various editions of *Endplays* mark the birth and growth of the ACBL. Obviously the 1932 editions were prenatal. The ACBL referred to on page 80 had grown from some 8,000 players in 1947 to more than 53,000 in 1957. As of the period ending 31 October 1973 the ACBL reported 169,869 members, with annual dues upped from $1.00 to $5.00. Such is the growing interest in tourney bridge.

Frank K. Perkins wrote the foreword to the 1938 master edition (third). He won the New England championships nine times, and the Nationals once, wrote a daily bridge column for the *Boston Herald-Traveler* 1931 thru 1970 and two bridge books, *Vital Tricks* and *Contract Bridge Standards*. On *Endplays* he commented, "George Coffin was the first writer to appreciate the importance of endings, and the first edition of this book in 1932 was the pioneer in their serious classification. Tho not called a self-teacher, we believe that this 1932 edition was the best self-teacher ever published on the play of the hand. It made the reader think! The reader would work out the early play that led to the ending,- with the result that he became a good player *ipso facto*.

"Mr. Coffin plowed an almost virgin field in 1932. Other writers had touched on endings, and most later books cover the matter in some way. But no writer has even approached the author in his arrangement, clarity and completeness. The 1938 edition is the logical outgrowth of the original work, and it is a marvel of analysis and card sense. It deserves any superlative that can be applied.

"Mr. Coffin was so far ahead of other writers in this field that no nomenclature existed to cover the positions,-so new descriptive terms had to be coined.* Take the book in small doses. Unless you can follow diagrams easily and well, lay out the cards in order to follow the play."

The author expresses sincere thanks to Mr. Alfred P. Sheinwold for his untiring efforts in checking the galley proofs (in 1938), and killing those annoying errors that always creep into every bridge book.

*Most of Coffin's names have been adopted worldwide by writers on bridge and by the ACBL *Encyclopedia of Bridge*, third edition in 1 9 7 1, page 4 15 and its references,- Editor.

iv

CONTENTS AND CLASSIFICATION

•

DIVISION ONE

ELIMINATIONS, Endplays of Position

DIVISION TWO

Squeezes, Endplays of Mass

DIVISION THREE

COUPS, Endplays of Time

Introduction

ENDPLAY, as generally conceived, is forcing an opponent, cornered by lack of idle* cards at the end of the play of the hand, to lead, to discard, or to play at the sacrifice of one or more tricks which he would normally win if played earlier. Although an endplay situation usually occurs when all four hands are played down to a few cards, endplays sometimes embrace so many cards that a player is "endplayed" even on the opening lead! The great Philip Hal Sims ardently preaches that he always takes advantage of this latter phenomenon. He bids notrump initially in order to have the opening lead come up to his hand whenever it is replete with tenace combinations (which we call forks), even if he holds a good biddable six-card major suit!

Endplays are based on the principle of diminishing flexibility. The general hypothesis is that flexibility in play decreases directly with the number of cards left unplayed. This general statement, of course, applies only to endplays as a class. Each individual endplay hand does not follow this general pattern, but it has its own critical point at which the endplay occurs. Again, generally speaking, the more complex the endplay, the more cards it involves, and therefore the sooner the critical point is reached in actual play. But no ending, however complex, requires more than eight cards in each hand for complete expression. Endings based on more than

---

*Ely Culbertson differentiates idle cards from busy cards as cards which may be discarded without reducing the trick-taking value of the hand, that is, they are not potential trick-winners or essential guards to same.

eight cards, such as those rarities wherein an opponent is endplayed on the opening lead, are invariably based on duplicated massing. After superfluous preparatory plays and/or filling cards have been discounted, it consists of **eight cards or fewer**. Of course, extremely difficult double-dummy endings may be found exceeding the eight-card limit, but they are so rare as to be practically impossible to compose or to solve.

Naturally, the fewer essential busy cards required for an endplay, the simpler it is. Paradoxical as it may sound, simplicity in endings increases directly with variety. While it would seem that there would be more varieties based on complex combinations from a mathematical point of view according to the theory of combinations and permutations, variety in complexity diminishes rapidly as the eight-card maximum is reached, because more and more elements become impossible to compound or to combine.

Contrary to popular opinion, most endplays are so simple that even tyros could execute them if all the cards were exposed. The difficult part is counting opponents' hands so that their holdings are known when the players are all down to the last few cards. Many end positions, however, do not require careful counting of hands, because playing for the end position in question is often the only course open to win the desired number of tricks.

The Modern Theory of Cards

Endplays embrace closely the finest points of strategy of the opposing forces as they clash in their field. In no other part of the game is the basic structure of cards more apparent.

Bridge is like war and games of war, such as Chess and Checkers. They all originate from two concepts, to wit, the FORCES which struggle for supremacy, and the FIELD which is their scene of battle. The forces contain two structural elements, LEADERSHIP characterized by the honor cards, and MASS characterized by suit lengths. Likewise the field comprises TIME manifested by leads, and POSITION manifested by honor-card and suit relationships. It takes definite units of *time* to *lead masses* of soldiers from a given *position* into battle. In cards the honors may be considered as the commissioned officers, the spot cards as the enlisted men, the positions of these honor and suit masses around the Bridge table as tactical situations, and the time units (leads and plays) as charges and other manoeuvres of battle.

All endplays are divided into three large groups: negative, positive, and neutral. Eliminations are *negative* because one lead, that is, one time unit at the crucial point *loses* a trick; squeezes are *positive* because the crucial lead *gains* a trick; overruffing finesses (true coups) are *neutral* because they neither gain nor lose tricks not ordinarily available by normal trump finesses.

The first group, eliminations, is based primarily on the *leadership* element of cards manifested by tenace *positions,* forks, whose strength is based on the concession of a time unit in order to compel the proper adversary to lead up to the tenace or fork. For example, you make him lead away from a guarded King up to your Ace-Queen.

(As all tenaces and tenace positions are forks, or fourchettes, as they used to be called in the heyday of Whist, we use the term "fork" to denote the missing guarded high card of the tenace as well as the tenace itself. For example, with K-x against A-Q, both K-x and A-Q are called forks.)

The second great division of endplays, the squeezes, is based on the *mass* element of cards, manifested by *positive time units* or leads which destroy the adversary's potentially winning masses. Guarding two suits, two mass formations, the adversary is forced to lose control of one by a discard. As the name describes his deplorable situation, he is virtually squeezed. For example, holding ♠ A and ♡ K-Q he discards before the dummy holding ♠ K and ♡ A-J.

The coups, comprising the third great division of endplays, are called *endplays of time*. One avoids leading away from a fork in trumps by an unblocking manoeuvre, getting rid of superfluous trumps in normal time sequence without the gain or concession of time units. For example, one gets rid of the ♠ 2 holding ♠ A-Q-2 (trumps) when the adversary on the right holds ♠ K-3 in order to lead through and surely capture his King at the end when one's trumpless partner leads a plain suit. When winners are trumped with superfluous trumps, the coup is called "grand."

The above is the popularly conceived form of coups. Actually, the preliminary trump reducing is only an embellishment. It may be wanting. The basic coup enables a player, devoid of trumps, to lead a plain suit, often at the twelfth trick, in order to force second hand with ♠ K-3 (trumps) to trump, so that third hand may over-trump and score two tricks with ♠ A-Q.

To summarize, all endplays are split naturally into three great divisions by the three different kinds of basic plays, forcing an opponent to *lead,* to *discard,* or to *trump* at the sacrifice of one or more tricks.

Eliminations, endplays of position, make him lead.

Squeezes, endplays of mass, make him discard.

Coups, endplays of time, make him trump.

♠   ♡   ◇   ♣

DIVISION ONE

Eliminations—Endplays of Position

CHAPTER ONE

BASIC ELIMINATIONS

THE object of an elimination play is to force your opponent to make a lead that will cost him a trick. To develop the play, you *eliminate* certain cards from his hand in order to trap him perfectly when you throw him on lead.

There are three primary types of this elimination trap, which are called the three basic positions. In the *fork* or tenace position you force your opponent to lead up to some such tenace position as your Ace-Queen, when he holds over you the guarded King of the same suit. In the entry position you force an opponent to lead a suit of which you hold a winner that can not be otherwise scored for lack of entries. Generally, you use your opponent as *entry* to your partner's hand, when it is hopelessly void of entry cards from your own hand. While these two basic positions are both independent of a trump suit, the ruff-and-discard or *crossruff* position involves trumps, both in your partner's hand and in your own. You force your opponent to lead a suit, whereof you hold no card in your partner's hand or in your own hand, so that you can discard a losing card while your partner ruffs (trumps), or vice versa.

Those eliminations containing force-avoiding or coup positions properly constitute the special group of Ruffing Eliminations treated in Chapter Three. The latter two positions are secondary because they must be combined with at least one basic position in order to make an elimination occur. Hence, eliminations containing them are not true Compound Eliminations, because this group contains only eliminations made up of two or more of the three basic positions, or eliminations compounded with basic squeeze positions. While the crossruff position is really a ruffing elimination, it is a basic position and is therefore analyzed in this chapter.

[1]

First Basic Position

As the completion of an elimination play involves three steps, it is really the combination of three different plays in sequence. Its success is based on an adversary's leading away from a combination of cards that costs him a trick; this act is called the *leadaway*. For example:

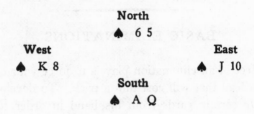

As West is on lead, he must lose his King of spades by leading away from it up to South's major tenace, or top fork as we call it. This position is the *leadaway*.

Throwing a player in the lead to force his leading away from such a disadvantageous position is called the *throwin*. Take the same example one lead earlier:

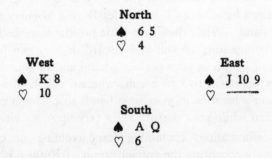

At notrump South *throws* West *in* with the heart to make him *lead away* from the King of spades.

But when a player *eliminates* or *strips out* cards which would otherwise afford the enemy an avenue of escape before throwing him in, the play is called an elimination or strip. Because it is shorter we use the term "strip" rather than "elimination" in naming end positions. Completing our endplay, still one lead earlier:

[2]

FORK STRIP

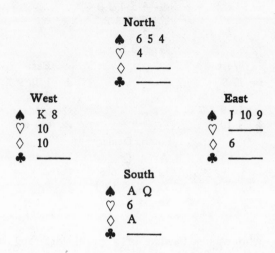

North
♠ 6 5 4
♡ 4
◇ ——
♣ ——

West
♠ K 8
♡ 10
◇ 10
♣ ——

East
♠ J 10 9
♡ ——
◇ 6
♣ ——

South
♠ A Q
♡ 6
◇ A
♣ ——

South eliminates or *strips* out West's diamond before throwing him in with the heart to force him to lead away from the fork in spades. This act makes the complete play a Fork Strip Throwin Leadaway, or simply a Fork Strip.

Note that if South leads the heart first, West can escape or *exit* from his predicament by leading the diamond to throw the undesired lead back to South. A *strip*, therefore, strips certain escape cards, or *exit* cards as they are technically called, from the adversary so that he cannot help losing a trick when thrown in the lead.

Checker players call the soul of all positional endplays "opposition." After the red cards have been played, whoever is to lead is forced to sacrifice his tenace position and to lose a trick. The "opposition" is said to be *against* the player who must lead at the cost of a trick, and to be *with* his opponent. Hence, the objective of elimination play is to throw the "opposition" against the enemy.

Composers of Bridge problems always start with a simple ending and work *backwards,* building up their problems card by card until the finished problem is produced. Likewise, we follow the same line to show you the stuff endplays are made of. Let us hark back to the original scene of the above endplay. The complete originally dealt hands are:

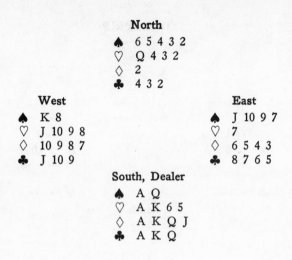

North
♠ 6 5 4 3 2
♡ Q 4 3 2
◇ 2
♣ 4 3 2

West
♠ K 8
♡ J 10 9 8
◇ 10 9 8 7
♣ J 10 9

East
♠ J 10 9 7
♡ 7
◇ 6 5 4 3
♣ 8 7 6 5

South, Dealer
♠ A Q
♡ A K 6 5
◇ A K Q J
♣ A K Q

South, who was somewhat of a prankster, rang in a "cold deck" with the idea of dealing someone a perfect hand of four Aces, four Kings, four Queens, and a Jack; but he did not arrange the cards perfectly, so that the King of spades and the Queen of hearts strayed from the fold. And, like all the bad birds that come home to roost, East's cut gave South the big hand. South decided not to temporize with forcing bids and bid six notrump, which call all passed.

West led the Jack of hearts which South won with his Ace. After winning all his diamond and club tricks, he played the King then Queen of hearts to enter his dummy hand, and finessed the Queen of spades. Of course, West pounced on this trick with his King and won his established heart trick, defeating the contract.

South's play was good until he led the spade. At that point he must instead lose the heart trick to West, thereby forcing West to lead away from his King of spades.

It should be noted that six hearts or six diamonds can also be made only by the same endplay.

Whenever you smoke a cigarette
It's your own life that you bet.

Jettison

When a player deliberately throws away a master card, a sure winner, in order to unblock its suit to avoid being thrown in and forced to lead to his disadvantage, he is throwing overboard cargo in order to save his ship from sinking. The nautical term for this act is to *jettison*. In Bridge essential unblocking by discarding a winner is called a jettison play. It is sometimes a vital feature in endplays.

JETTISON THROWIN

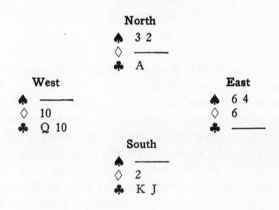

At notrumps South, requiring two tricks, leads a diamond to throw West in while North *jettisons* the Ace of clubs.

A minor variation of the first basic elimination position is the Strip Finesse, wherein the stripping process is employed to develop a finessing position at the end. In the Grand National Championships held by the United States Bridge Association in New York City in 1933, Norman Bonney was the only player to score three notrump on the following deal:

North, Dealer
♠ 4 3 2
♡ 7 5 2
◇ K 9 2
♣ 9 7 5 3

West
♠ K Q 9 8 5
♡ K 9 6
◇ 5
♣ J 10 8 4

East
♠ 7 6
♡ J 8 3
◇ J 8 7 6 3
♣ A Q 2

South
♠ A J 10
♡ A Q 10 4
◇ A Q 10 4
♣ K 6

After two passes Mr. Bonney, sitting South, optimistically bid three notrumps, against which West led the eightspot of spades. South's ten won, dummy's King of diamonds won, and the finesse of the ten of hearts forced West's King. West returned the King of spades, forcing South's Ace, and on the fourth round of hearts West falsecarded the eightspot of clubs to advertise possession of the Ace, but Mr. Bonney did not believe him. On the second round of diamonds West completed his echo in clubs by playing the fourspot, hoping to induce Mr. Bonney to think that West held the Ace of clubs, but Mr. Bonney still thought he was lying. On the third lead of diamonds West discarded a spade, and Mr. Bonney next put East in with a diamond. After winning another diamond trick East found himself stripped down to two clubs, the Ace-Queen. In desperation he led the Queen and Mr. Bonney jumped right up with his King for his ninth and game trick.

This ending is not exactly a Fork Strip, because it terminates in a regular finesse that has a fifty percent chance of losing. The stripping process simply compensates for dummy's lack of the necessary entries to lead toward the King of clubs,—it forces East to lead clubs for Mr. Bonney to finesse.

Second Basic Position

As their name implies, the Entry Eliminations make it possible to reenter the dummy, which is apparently devoid of entries, by means of forcing one adversary to put dummy in the lead. In all

examples South is the declarer and North the dummy, unless
otherwise stated.

ENTRY STRIP *

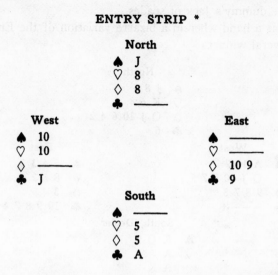

North
- ♠ J
- ♡ 8
- ◊ 8
- ♣ ———

West
- ♠ 10
- ♡ 10
- ◊ ———
- ♣ J

East
- ♠ ———
- ♡ ———
- ◊ 10 9
- ♣ 9

South
- ♠ ———
- ♡ 5
- ◊ 5
- ♣ A

At notrumps South, requiring two tricks, draws West's last
club to strip him of his last exit card, and throws West in with
the heart in order to materialize a trick from the dummy's spade.
This ending resulted from another prank gone wrong.

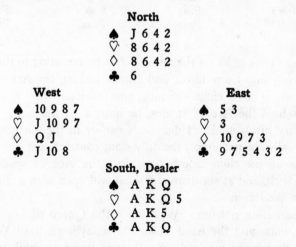

North
- ♠ J 6 4 2
- ♡ 8 6 4 2
- ◊ 8 6 4 2
- ♣ 6

West
- ♠ 10 9 8 7
- ♡ J 10 9 7
- ◊ Q J
- ♣ J 10 8

East
- ♠ 5 3
- ♡ 3
- ◊ 10 9 7 3
- ♣ 9 7 5 4 3 2

South, Dealer
- ♠ A K Q
- ♡ A K Q 5
- ◊ A K 5
- ♣ A K Q

Our hero playing South dealt and bid six notrumps, which call
everyone passed. West led the Jack of hearts, and South simply

*See footnote on page 9.

laid down all his winners to strip the hands, and threw West in with the heart at the twelfth trick, as shown above, in order to realize the dummy's Jack of spades.

Here is a hand wherein a bizarre variation of the Entry Strip scores several winners:

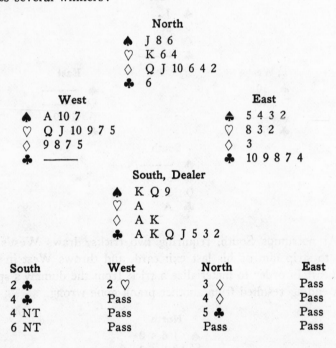

	North	
	♠ J 8 6	
	♡ K 6 4	
	◇ Q J 10 6 4 2	
	♣ 6	
West		**East**
♠ A 10 7		♠ 5 4 3 2
♡ Q J 10 9 7 5		♡ 8 3 2
◇ 9 8 7 5		◇ 3
♣ ———		♣ 10 9 8 7 4
	South, Dealer	
	♠ K Q 9	
	♡ A	
	◇ A K	
	♣ A K Q J 5 3 2	

South	West	North	East
2 ♣	2 ♡	3 ◇	Pass
4 ♣	Pass	4 ◇	Pass
4 NT	Pass	5 ♣	Pass
6 NT	Pass	Pass	Pass

South tries to locate the missing Ace by resorting to the popular Four Notrump Convention, and North, lacking the Ace of spades, signs off at five clubs. South now realizes that since North doesn't hold the Ace of spades, he must hold the King of hearts to justify his free bid of diamonds earlier in the auction. Hence South calls six notrump , the only slam contract that can be made, because at six clubs South must lose the Ace of spades and a trump trick, and at six diamonds East will open with a club, giving West a fatal ruff.

Against six notrump West leads the Queen of hearts, which South wins, and the hand looks like a laydown until West fails on the first high club lead. South runs two more club tricks and unblocks the diamonds by playing the Ace and King, leaving seven cards in each hand as follows:

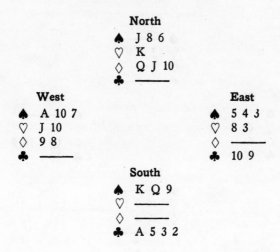

North
♠ J 8 6
♡ K
◊ Q J 10
♣ ——

West
♠ A 10 7
♡ J 10
◊ 9 8
♣ ——

East
♠ 5 4 3
♡ 8 3
◊ ——
♣ 10 9

South
♠ K Q 9
♡ ——
◊ ——
♣ A 5 3 2

South leads the King of spades to coax West to cover with the Ace and set up the Jack in dummy for an entry, but West knows his defence and passes the trick. South leads the Queen of spades, but again, West passes. South throws West in with the Ace of spades, and now the luckless West is locked in with no escape from North's good red cards.

Third Basic Position

The third basic position brings us into the realm of the Ruffing Eliminations, strip plays based on a trump suit. Besides the various Ruffing Eliminations analysed in Chapter Three, we have the basic trump-and-discard or crossruff type, which enables Declarer to discard a loser from one hand while trumping in his other hand. This play is given here, because it is truly basic.

From page 7. *Terence Reese calls an entry strip the stepping stone elimination because you use an opponent as a stepping stone to get your otherwise entryless partner on lead.*

CROSSRUFF STRIP

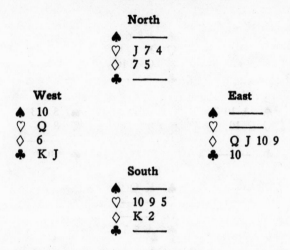

North
- ♠ —
- ♡ J 7 4
- ◇ 7 5
- ♣ —

West
- ♠ 10
- ♡ Q
- ◇ 6
- ♣ K J

East
- ♠ —
- ♡ —
- ◇ Q J 10 9
- ♣ 10

South
- ♠ —
- ♡ 10 9 5
- ◇ K 2
- ♣ —

Hearts are trumps and South, requiring four tricks, seems to be in a serious predicament with a trump loser and a diamond loser. South plays his high diamond to strip out West's only exit card, the l o w diamond. South next throws West in with a heart, and whichever black suit West leads causes East's apparently sure diamond trick to evaporate into thin air when North trumps the black suit led while South discards his otherwise losing diamond. Let's look at the original complete deal:

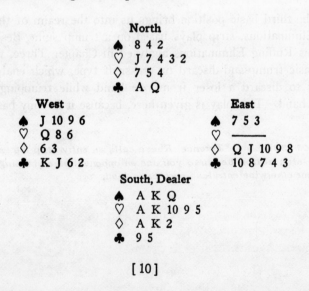

North
- ♠ 8 4 2
- ♡ J 7 4 3 2
- ◇ 7 5 4
- ♣ A Q

West
- ♠ J 10 9 6
- ♡ Q 8 6
- ◇ 6 3
- ♣ K J 6 2

East
- ♠ 7 5 3
- ♡ —
- ◇ Q J 10 9 8
- ♣ 10 8 7 4 3

South, Dealer
- ♠ A K Q
- ♡ A K 10 9 5
- ◇ A K 2
- ♣ 9 5

South deals and bids two hearts, North three hearts, South four clubs, an Asking Bid, North five clubs to show the Ace, and South six hearts, closing the auction.

West opens with the Jack of spades which South wins, and receives a rude jolt when he leads the King of hearts and finds Her Highness, the Queen, too well chaperoned to be caught. With no possible way of discarding his sure diamond loser on anything he can lead, his only chance to fulfill his contract is to find the King of clubs and not more than two diamonds with West. South wins two trump tricks, three spades, two clubs by finessing, and two diamonds before throwing West in with the Queen of hearts.

Crossruff Throwin

Saul Butters of Chelsea, Mass. discovered the third basic position neatly hidden in a tournament deal.

Note: for the same endplay in 1974, see *Double Dummy Bridge* page 172,- GSC.

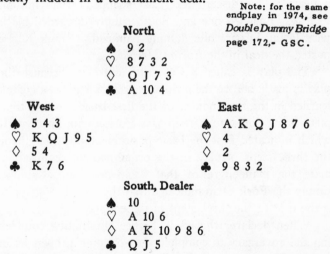

West led the King of hearts. With two heart losers and a spade loser game looked hopeless, but Mr. Butters followed bidding clues. West probably held five hearts and no spade picture .

With both sides vulnerable Saul Butters was playing South, and he bid one diamond. West called one heart, North two diamonds, East four spades, and South five diamonds, which contract he fulfilled.

[11]

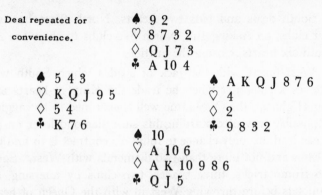

Deal repeated for convenience.

            ♠ 9 2
            ♡ 8 7 3 2
            ◇ Q J 7 3
            ♣ A 10 4
♠ 5 4 3   ♠ A K Q J 8 7 6
♡ K Q J 9 5   ♡ 4
◇ 5 4   ◇ 2
♣ K 7 6   ♣ 9 8 3 2
            ♠ 10
            ♡ A 10 6
            ◇ A K 10 9 8 6
            ♣ Q J 5

For the endplay to succeed, East had to hold only one heart and the quart major in spades. Hence South won the heart opening lead with the Ace, pulled two rounds of trumps, finessed clubs successfully for three tricks, and led a spade which East won with the Jack. East led the King of spades and South *discarded* a heart! This discard left East stripped of all but black cards to lead. East led one and South simply discarded his last otherwise losing heart while dummy trumped. Frank K. Perkins reported the deal in the *Boston Herald*.

The play is called a Crossruff Throwin, because the throwin play is made before the stripping process has been completed. We learned in the terminology of the first basic position that the complete name for a fork strip was Fork Strip Throwin Leadaway, which indicated first the basic position or positions involved, then the three steps of play in the order named, required to consummate the manoeuvre of that basic position. Calling the play simply the Fork Strip indicated that the complete stripping process is the first of the three steps of the endplay.

When declarer throws in before eliminating completely, forcing the adversary to complete the stripping proper, as in the deal above, the complete endplay is called a Throwin. Whichever of the three steps of the endplay occurs first, determines its generic name. By this token, if a player were endplayed on the opening lead, his unfortunate predicament would be called a Leadaway.

The term, Elimination, is used as a general name to indicate all or any of this family of endplays.

Here is a neat Crossruff Strip, wherein the vital endplay took place before all opponents' trumps had been exhausted.

North
♠ J 6 4 2
♡ Q 6
◇ Q 6 4 2
♣ A 6 4

West
♠ 10 8
♡ A K 10 8 5 3
◇ J 10 8
♣ K J

East
♠ Q 9 7
♡ 9 7 4 2
◇ 9 7
♣ Q 9 7 2

South, Dealer
♠ A K 5 3
♡ J
◇ A K 5 3
♣ 10 8 5 3

South	West	North	East
1 ♠	2 ♡	2 ♠	3 ♡
4 ♠	Pass	Pass	Pass

While South's jump rebid to four spades was optimistic, South relied on North for more strength than a mere courtesy raise over West's heart overcall; and as West was vulnerable, West didn't dare to venture to five hearts as a defensive measure.

West led the King then Ace of hearts, and South trumped. Four losing tricks seemed to confirm the optimism of South's bidding, but South had a good play for game, if he could pick up the Queen of spades or develop an endplay. South laid down the Ace-King of spades without felling the Queen, won three diamond tricks, and played the Ace then low in clubs, throwing West in. Denuded of everything but hearts, West of necessity had to lead one, whereon the dummy shed the losing club while South trumped.

While West could have unblocked the clubs by playing his King under the Ace, this play would have done his side no good. Had East won the second round of clubs with the Queen, he would have dropped West's jack and set up South's ten.

Furthermore, it would have done East no good to trump the third round of diamonds, because South could have thrown in West on the second round of clubs, regardless of what East returned.

This deal occurred in a "family game" at the A. Marshall Jones' in Fitzwilliam, New Hampshire, in August of 1937.

Defence Against Eliminations

Against perfect play there is no defence against a perfect elimination, but bluff tactics will sometimes cause declarer to slip. A Poker face and bold unhesitant discarding will go a long way to lead declarer astray.

"Endplays" Coffin Outwitted

Mrs. Francis Kendall of Belmont, Massachusetts, had the honor of succeeding at this chicanery, thereby winning top score in a club duplicate in this deal:

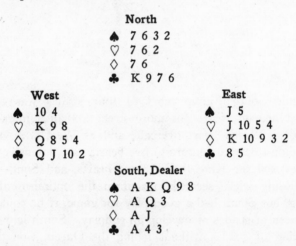

```
                    North
                 ♠ 7 6 3 2
                 ♡ 7 6 2
                 ◊ 7 6
                 ♣ K 9 7 6
     West                        East
  ♠ 10 4                      ♠ J 5
  ♡ K 9 8                     ♡ J 10 5 4
  ◊ Q 8 5 4                   ◊ K 10 9 3 2
  ♣ Q J 10 2                  ♣ 8 5
                 South, Dealer
                 ♠ A K Q 9 8
                 ♡ A Q 3
                 ◊ A J
                 ♣ A 4 3
```

We played the contract for three notrump at South, and Mrs. Kendall, playing West, led the Queen of clubs. South won the trick with the Ace and returned a low club to establish the tenth trick with dummy's nine. Mrs. Kendall split her equals, playing the tenspot, and dummy, devoid of side entries, ducked. Mrs. Kendall switched to the four of diamonds and Mr. Kendall, playing East, put up his King, forcing the Ace. Five spade tricks and two club tricks, by finessing the nine of clubs, followed. With South down to the Ace-Queen of hearts and the Jack of diamonds, dummy led a diamond, throwing Mrs. Kendall in with her marked Queen of diamonds, and South was annoyed when she produced another diamond, holding the contract down to four odd. It seemed that she had dared to bare her King of hearts!

CHAPTER TWO

IMPERFECT ELIMINATIONS—DEFENCE

As the name implies, Imperfect Eliminations are endings wherein the defence has available an avenue of escape. An Imperfect Elimination has a weak spot,—a hole through which the defence can slide out if the defence is on the alert. Imperfect Eliminations fall into two groups, the Exit Strips and the Pseudo or False Strips. In an Exit Strip an opponent has the opportunity to unblock the throwin suit so that his partner can gain the lead therein and kill the endplay, whereas in a False Strip the declarer depends solely on the adversary to make a mistake after he has been thrown in and to lead a suit that will give the declarer the vital extra trick he seeks.

An Exit Elimination is any strip that can be thwarted by unblocking, or exiting as it is called, whereby the stripped opponent can get rid of the entry card that would force him in to lead disastrously at the end.

EXIT FORK STRIP

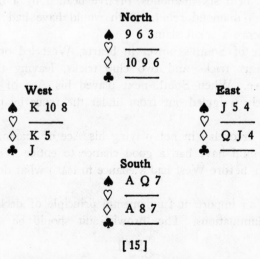

```
              North
              ♠ 9 6 3
              ♡ ———
              ◇ 10 9 6
              ♣ ———
West                          East
♠ K 10 8                      ♠ J 5 4
♡ ———                         ♡ ———
◇ K 5                         ◇ Q J 4
♣ J                           ♣ ———
              South
              ♠ A Q 7
              ♡ ———
              ◇ A 8 7
              ♣ ———
```

At notrump , South, requiring three tricks, leads the Ace of diamonds in order to strip the suit and throws West in with the King of diamonds and forces him to lead up to the Ace-Queen of spades, but wily West will have none of it and unblocks diamonds by throwing his King on South's Ace. Declarer, however, had not played his hand to best advantage from the start.

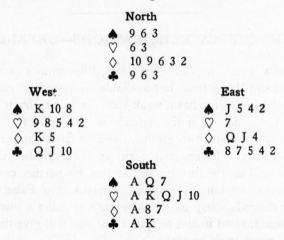

North
♠ 9 6 3
♡ 6 3
◊ 10 9 6 3 2
♣ 9 6 3

West
♠ K 10 8
♡ 9 8 5 4 2
◊ K 5
♣ Q J 10

East
♠ J 5 4 2
♡ 7
◊ Q J 4
♣ 8 7 5 4 2

South
♠ A Q 7
♡ A K Q J 10
◊ A 8 7
♣ A K

West dealt and passed, North passed, and East bid one notrump! South doubled, West redoubled, and North rescued him by calling two diamonds. South jumped to four notrump , revealing East's wretched psychic, and so everyone passed.

South's jump to four notrump was a definite slam attempt. Had North held six diamonds, or five headed by a high honor warranting a diamond rebid, South would have had a sporting chance to score a small slam.

Unaware of South's power in hearts, West led one. South ran five heart tricks and two club tricks, leaving the ending shown above. When South next played his Ace of diamonds, West blithely wriggled out from under the fence by playing his King.

South's error lay in not playing his Ace of diamonds earlier when he would have had a good chance to entice West to play low thereon, before West had a chance to learn what declarer was up to.

This is an important fundamental principle of declarer's play of Exit Eliminations. The throwin suit should be stripped as early as possible, before the defence has had a chance to size up the situation and unblock.

A unique double exit, where an adversary had to throw away four high cards in two throwin suits, was discovered by Walter Wyman of Arlington, Massachusetts, and it was described by Dick Frey in the January 1937 *Bridge World* as follows:

Double-Dummy Unblock

"George Coffin, who specializes in tongue-bursting titles for his coups, could probably think of a better one for this hand. But Walter Wyman, who played the defence with the South cards titles it merely 'The Four Nines'. Actually, it is a successful unblock in *two* suits, which rarity could have been important only because the hand, played at two diamonds, occurred in a duplicate game.

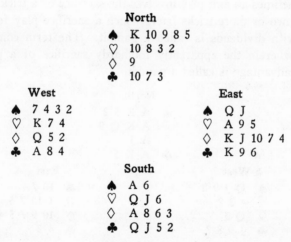

North
♠ K 10 9 8 5
♡ 10 8 3 2
◇ 9
♣ 10 7 3

West
♠ 7 4 3 2
♡ K 7 4
◇ Q 5 2
♣ A 8 4

East
♠ Q J
♡ A 9 5
◇ K J 10 7 4
♣ K 9 6

South
♠ A 6
♡ Q J 6
◇ A 8 6 3
♣ Q J 5 2

"South bid a club, North responded one spade. East overcalled with two diamonds concluding the bidding. Mr. Wyman opened the Ace and a low spade and North continued with a third round of the suit, which East ruffed with the Jack of diamonds, South discarded a club. A trump was led to dummy's Queen, and the drop of North's nine, followed by South's duck of the next diamond lead, established his Ace-eight as a tenace over declarer's King-seven.

"Declarer led a club to dummy's Ace, and South dropped the Jack. Foiled in this department, declarer cagily led the heart King, but again Mr. Wyman parted with a Jack.

"*Both* these unblocks were necessary. If South had carelessly dropped a small heart, satisfied that he had provided an exit card in clubs, declarer would have led a club and finessed the nine, removing the carefully created exit card and later freezing him in with a heart to lead away from his diamond tenace.

"Of course, having begun with his unblocking, South pitched both Queens away for the sheer artistry of it, and North, somewhat dazed by the access to trickdom of both his tens, nevertheless produced the required lead of the nine of spades at the proper moment, couping declarer's trumps."

This play is called the Double Fitzwilliam Coup. See "Eliminations Dubbed Coups" in Chapter Twenty, and the last deal in Chapter Fifteen.

Sometimes an exit play involves the sacrifice of a trick in order to win two or more tricks later. Such a sacrifice play for future gains with dividends is called a gambit. The term comes from Chess wherein the apparently foolhardy sacrifice of a piece for a later advantage is called a gambit.

North
♠ A K 5 2
♡ A K Q 9
♢ A J
♣ A K 5

West
♠ Q J 9 8
♡ 4 3 2
♢ Q 3
♣ J 9 8 7

East
♠ 10 7
♡ J 10 7 5
♢ 10 9 7 5 4
♣ 4 2

South, Dealer
♠ 6 4 3
♡ 8 6
♢ K 8 6 2
♣ Q 10 6 3

South dealt and passed, North bid two spades, South two notrump , North three hearts, South three notrump , North four notrumps to invite a slam, and South, with two face cards heretofore unrevealed by his signoff bidding, jumped to six notrump

West led the seven of clubs which coasted to South's ten. West's choice of opening leads was atrocious. He jeopardized a probable club winner when he had a harmless heart opening. South finessed the Jack of diamonds in dummy and played all dummy's high cards hoping to throw in East, played by Mrs. H. Spaulding Coffin of New York City, with a heart and make her lead a diamond so that South could realize his two tricks. But Mrs. Coffin knew her defence and jettisoned her heart winner, making the dummy's nine of hearts good, but leaving the dummy locked in with two losing spade tricks at the end!

While Mrs. Coffin's brilliant defence is highly commendable, South played badly. His diamond finesse was asinine, because he would have lost all chance to fulfill his contract had the finesse failed. South should have ducked a spade at Trick Two and developed an automatic squeeze. See Chapter Six for further analysis of this deal.

Another Jettison Exit

While Mrs. Coffin's play was excellent, it was pretty well marked at the end of the hand. An obscure jettison exit has been the source of much profit to bettors in the deal given below.

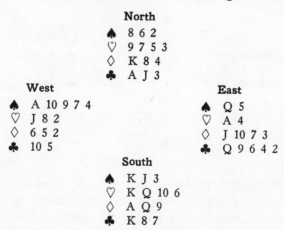

North
♠ 8 6 2
♡ 9 7 5 3
◇ K 8 4
♣ A J 3

West
♠ A 10 9 7 4
♡ J 8 2
◇ 6 5 2
♣ 10 5

East
♠ Q 5
♡ A 4
◇ J 10 7 3
♣ Q 9 6 4 2

South
♠ K J 3
♡ K Q 10 6
◇ A Q 9
♣ K 8 7

You are shown the deal and given from five to thirty minutes to decide whether you can make three notrump , playing South, or can defeat this contract, playing defensively. Suppose you wager that you can make it.

[19]

West leads the ten of spades, and you let East's Queen win. East returns a spade and your Jack forces the Ace. Everything looks fine. As you have to lead toward the King-Queen of hearts only once to win three heart tricks, you need only one entry to dummy. Thus you will win a spade trick, three hearts, three diamonds, and two clubs, making nine tricks easily.

But note what happens when West leads another spade on which East jettisons the Ace of hearts! Try and make three no-trump now!

Robert Neville published this hand in the New York *Herald Tribune,* and Richard L. Frey subsequently described it in the *Bridge World Magazine.*

An Exit Elimination is an imperfect strip, but a Pseudo or False Elimination is in fact no elimination at all. Based on deception, it makes a player think that he is stripped and induces him to make a mistake that will cost him a trick.

FALSE ELIMINATION

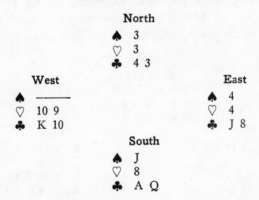

North
♠ 3
♡ 3
♣ 4 3

West
♠ ———
♡ 10 9
♣ K 10

East
♠ 4
♡ 4
♣ J 8

South
♠ J
♡ 8
♣ A Q

Spades are trumps and South, desiring three tricks, pitches West in with the heart. Now West, who at this point knows the heart situation, may be at a loss to know what to lead if he does not know the club and trump situation. He thinks leading back a heart will give South a discard while North trumps, but he does not know that East can overtrump the dummy, killing South's winning discard. Hence, a club lead looks like the proper play to West, as he hopes that East holds the Ace or Queen of clubs.

The proper defence against the same kind of False Elimination may be based on giving declarer a useless ruff and discard.

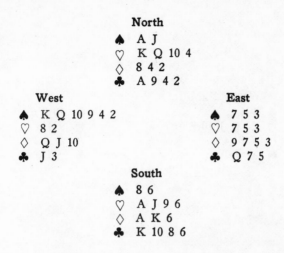

North
- ♠ A J
- ♡ K Q 10 4
- ◊ 8 4 2
- ♣ A 9 4 2

West
- ♠ K Q 10 9 4 2
- ♡ 8 2
- ◊ Q J 10
- ♣ J 3

East
- ♠ 7 5 3
- ♡ 7 5 3
- ◊ 9 7 5 3
- ♣ Q 7 5

South
- ♠ 8 6
- ♡ A J 9 6
- ◊ A K 6
- ♣ K 10 8 6

South dealt and bid one heart, West one spade, North three hearts, East passed, and South bid four hearts, closing the auction.

West led the King of spades, and the heart game was a lay-down, but as the game was match point duplicate, an extra trick for South was valuable. Declarer won the spade lead in dummy, ran three rounds of trumps, and threw West in the lead on the third round of diamonds. Of course, a third round spade lead is harmless, because it doesn't give two discards while dummy trumps, but West, scared by the ruff and discard bugaboo, fell into the trap and opened clubs, which was fatal for the club trick which his side should have won. North won West's Jack of clubs lead with the Ace and finessed the Nine   through East's Queen, thereby making an extra trick for five odd.

A False Elimination sometimes helps declarer to eliminate making a guess in finessing.

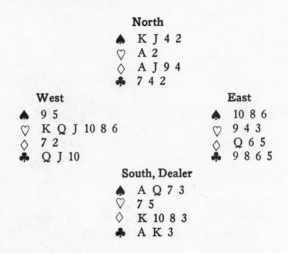

North
♠ K J 4 2
♡ A 2
♦ A J 9 4
♣ 7 4 2

West
♠ 9 5
♡ K Q J 10 8 6
♦ 7 2
♣ Q J 10

East
♠ 10 8 6
♡ 9 4 3
♦ Q 6 5
♣ 9 8 6 5

South, Dealer
♠ A Q 7 3
♡ 7 5
♦ K 10 8 3
♣ A K 3

Perley Weatherbee of Portland, Maine, playing South in the New England Pair Championships, dealt and bid one spade. West overcalled at two hearts, North three spades, and South closed the auction at four spades.

West led the King of hearts, forcing dummy's Ace, and South won three trump leads to exhaust all adverse trumps. At this point the majority of other declarers assumed that West held the Queen of diamonds as a part of the heart overcall and finessed diamonds the wrong way up to East, thus winning only ten tricks. But Mr. Weatherbee threw West in the lead on the third round of clubs. Fearing a ruff and discard if he led hearts, West led a diamond, thereby eliminating the necessity for South to guess the diamond situation. Had West returned a heart instead, North would have trumped while South discarded a diamond, but this play would have done South no good, as he still would have had to guess the diamond finesse. Frank K. Perkins, who kibitzed this play, described it in the *Boston Herald*.

CHAPTER THREE

RUFFING ELIMINATIONS

As THEIR name suggests, the Ruffing Eliminations involve a trump suit. In this classification, a feature of play in trumps is always secondary to the basic elimination position. While the Crossruff Strip is, strictly speaking, a ruffing elimination, it is definitely a basic position and therefore it is not classified in this special group. The secondary elements in trumps in the Ruffing Eliminations are of two types, the force-avoiding type and the trump-reducing type. In a force-avoiding elimination you refuse to trump winners led by an opponent, lest you damagingly shorten your own trumps, until he spends his strength and is forced to lead to your advantage. In a trump-reducing elimination you purposely shorten your own trumps as a part of the stripping process preparatory to the endplay. As this trump-reducing feature is frequently involved in the True Coups, trump-reducing eliminations are often confused with coups, and there are several endplays wherein the basic coup and elimination positions are so combined with trump-reducing preparation that it is hard to tell whether they are eliminations or True Coups.

As the element of avoiding a force usually occurs early in the play, it rarely appears involved with elimination and it is not usually thought of in conjunction with an endplay.

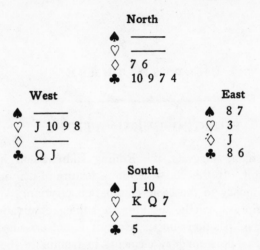

North
- ♠ ——
- ♡ ——
- ◇ 7 6
- ♣ 10 9 7 4

West
- ♠ ——
- ♡ J 10 9 8
- ◇ ——
- ♣ Q J

East
- ♠ 8 7
- ♡ 3
- ◇ J
- ♣ 8 6

South
- ♠ J 10
- ♡ K Q 7
- ◇ ——
- ♣ 5

Spades are trumps and South needs four tricks. This looks easy, but unfortunately *North has the lead.* The dummy leads a club to throw West in, and West leads another club. If East had only one trump, or surely two or more hearts with his two trumps, South could trump, and cash three more tricks. But as South can not stand the force, he must discard a low heart on the second club lead to insure four tricks. For the sake of simplicity, this elimination is shown after the stripping has been completed.

It should be noted that if the Queen and Jack of hearts are interchanged, South wins the same number of tricks because West has to lead up to South's top fork in hearts at the end. Under these conditions the endplay would be titled Force-Avoiding Fork Throwin.

DOUBLE TROUBLE

South opened two notrump
   And North next made it four.
Seven notrump South jump bid;
   They had the tricks galore.

West doubled, North redoubled;
   It sounded like an odd stack.
By mistake some dimwit had
   Dealt out a pinochle pack!

The original hands from a club duplicate follow:

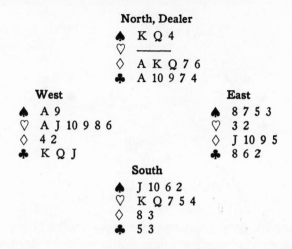

North, Dealer
♠ K Q 4
♡ ——
◇ A K Q 7 6
♣ A 10 9 7 4

West
♠ A 9
♡ A J 10 9 8 6
◇ 4 2
♣ K Q J

East
♠ 8 7 5 3
♡ 3 2
◇ J 10 9 5
♣ 8 6 2

South
♠ J 10 6 2
♡ K Q 7 5 4
◇ 8 3
♣ 5 3

North dealt and bid one diamond, South one heart pleasing West who passed; North three clubs, and South three spades. North, figuring the plain suit stoppers would protect South's advertised abbreviated trump suit from premature forces, raised South to four spades, and West doubled, closing the auction.

Thinking he could give East a ruff, West opened with the Ace of hearts which the dummy trumped low, and the picture looked quite rosy for declarer. Dummy led a trump which West won with his Ace, and West led the King of clubs driving out dummy's Ace. Dummy pulled another trump and won three diamond tricks, eliminating diamonds from West, on which South discarded a low heart. South now made the safety play of leading a club from dummy, which West won, and South let West win another club trick, forcing him to lead a heart at the end. Thus South lost only two club tricks and the Ace of trumps, thereby winning a top score at four spades, because the deal will produce only nine tricks at notrump.

FORCE-AVOIDING CROSSRUFF THROWIN

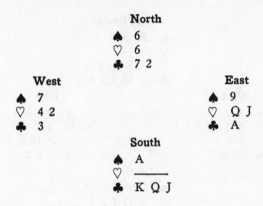

North
- ♠ 6
- ♡ 6
- ♣ 7 2

West
- ♠ 7
- ♡ 4 2
- ♣ 3

East
- ♠ 9
- ♡ Q J
- ♣ A

South
- ♠ A
- ♡
- ♣ K Q J

At spades, South, requiring two tricks, leads a club to drive out East's Ace. As leading a trump would make the last three tricks easy for South, East must lead a heart. To insure two tricks, South must discard a good club and wait for the second heart lead which dummy can trump.

In the trump reducing eliminations the trump reducing feature may be deployed so that the opponents' finessing power in trumps is demoted one trick.

FORCED-FORK STRIP

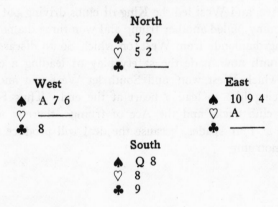

North
- ♠ 5 2
- ♡ 5 2
- ♣

West
- ♠ A 7 6
- ♡ ———
- ♣ 8

East
- ♠ 10 9 4
- ♡ A
- ♣ ———

South
- ♠ Q 8
- ♡ 8
- ♣ 9

With spades trumps South leads his high club, and North trumps with the five of spades to make East trump high with an equal, thereby promoting South's trumps to the rank of second fork (tenace minor), which is good for a trick with the opponents in the lead.

When a player reduces his own excess length in trumps by trumping his partner's plain suit winner, the stripping may be called Grand Coup.

GRAND COUP FORK STRIP

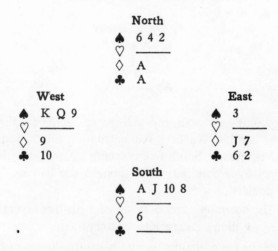

North
♠ 6 4 2
♡ ——
◇ A
♣ A

West
♠ K Q 9
♡ ——
◇ 9
♣ 10

East
♠ 3
♡ ——
◇ J 7
♣ 6 2

South
♠ A J 10 8
♡ ——
◇ 6
♣ ——

Spades are trumps and South, requiring four tricks, puts North in with the Ace of diamonds, and South trumps the Ace of clubs. This play reduces his trumps to the same number as West's, and South leads a low trump to win two of the last three tricks against West's King-Queen-nine held over him.

Point of View
When you or I make a misplay
It's observed a hand we blew.

If an expert goofs the same way,
They say, "He took a wrong view."

By George S. Coffin
in *Bridge Mother Goose*
[27]

This odd ending came from a spectacular hand we played recently in a rubber game.

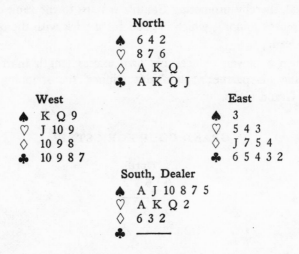

North
♠ 6 4 2
♡ 8 7 6
◇ A K Q
♣ A K Q J

West
♠ K Q 9
♡ J 10 9
◇ 10 9 8
♣ 10 9 8 7

East
♠ 3
♡ 5 4 3
◇ J 7 5 4
♣ 6 5 4 3 2

South, Dealer
♠ A J 10 8 7 5
♡ A K Q 2
◇ 6 3 2
♣ ———

Playing South we dealt and bid one spade, North three clubs, South three spades, North three notrump , South four hearts, North four notrump , South five notrump , North six spades, and West, played by a fair lady who thought she had us "hooked," obligingly doubled.

While six notrump was a laydown with the favorable heart distribution, we didn't escape into that contract.

West led the ten of diamonds, and when the dummy was spread, she smiled smugly at her two trump tricks that she felt sure would come home wagging their tails behind them. With all the plain suit winners in our two hands the texture of West's double was obvious, at least K-Q-x in spades, so that normal play for a drop in spades was out of the question. We smiled as we remembered what Philip Hal Sims once said about "sucker doubles," and wondered if we could fulfill our contract. Dummy won the diamond opening, and we discarded a low heart on a club. We trumped a club, ran three heart tricks, reentered dummy with a diamond and trumped a club, and reentered dummy again in diamonds and trumped the last club. When we led the Jack of spades, the face of the fair damsel on our left became red, and she gave us a practical demonstration of how artistically she could swear when she saw how the tables had been turned.

SOMETHING FOR NOTHING

But when a declarer can force an opponent to trump with his sure winning trump tricks declarer's plain suit losers, surely declarer is getting something for nothing. In the following deal declarer developed a pretty ending by repeating this bizarre coup!

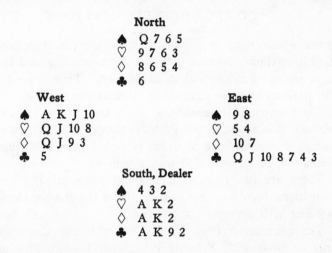

North
♠ Q 7 6 5
♡ 9 7 6 3
♢ 8 6 5 4
♣ 6

West
♠ A K J 10
♡ Q J 10 8
♢ Q J 9 3
♣ 5

East
♠ 9 8
♡ 5 4
♢ 10 7
♣ Q J 10 8 7 4 3

South, Dealer
♠ 4 3 2
♡ A K 2
♢ A K 2
♣ A K 9 2

While South holds six honor-tricks, he also holds six losing tricks. Therefore he must start the auction at one club, because more honor-tricks than losers are required for an opening bid of two. West doubles for a takeout, North passes, and East, with five trump tricks apparently sure and a hand with no future, passes for penalties, and South passes also.

West opens with the King of spades and continues with the Ace, on which tricks East plays the nine then eightspot, to show that he holds no more spades and can trump the third round of the suit. West leads another spade whereon dummy plays the Queen to force East's advertised length in trumps. When East leads back a heart or a diamond, South cashes his four red tricks and leads a losing red card to force East to trump. East leads the Queen of clubs, which South wins and forces East to trump a red suit again. When East leads the Jack of clubs, South ducks, thereby making his Ace-nine top fork over East's ten-eightspot, giving South his contract for seven tricks!

CHAPTER FOUR

COMPOUND ELIMINATIONS

THE eliminations in the last chapter are not true Compound Eliminations, because both the force-avoiding and coup elements are not fundamental to elimination. They depend upon a basic position in order to make the elimination possible.

The Compound Eliminations derive their name from the fact that each elimination in this group is compounded of two or more *basic positions,* any one of which is capable of making up a true elimination, or compounded with a squeeze.

There are two types of Compound Eliminations: the simple eliminations involving one opponent and the double eliminations involving both opponents at the end.

The commonest type of elimination is the Crossruff Fork Strip, or what Mrs. Prescott Warren of Boston, Massachusetts is pleased to call the Work Elimination, after that Grand Old Man of Bridge, the late Milton C. Work. He doted on it and wrote it up in his books and newspaper columns almost to the exclusion of all other endplays. It is quite common.

CROSSRUFF FORK STRIP

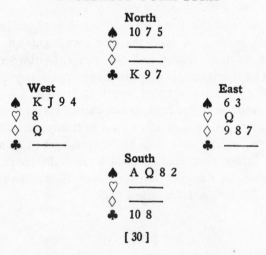

```
                      North
                   ♠  10 7 5
                   ♡  ——
                   ◇  ——
                   ♣  K 9 7

     West                           East
  ♠  K J 9 4                      ♠  6 3
  ♡  8                            ♡  Q
  ◇  Q                            ◇  9 8 7
  ♣  ——                           ♣  ——

                      South
                   ♠  A Q 8 2
                   ♡  ——
                   ◇  ——
                   ♣  10 8
```

[30]

Requiring five tricks with clubs trumps, South has the lead in dummy. He leads the ten of spades. Whatever honor East might play would be promptly covered, but as East plays low, the ten of spades runs to the Jack, and all the King's horses can not prevent South from winning the last five tricks. West has the unpleasant choice of leading up to South's A-Q *fork* in spades or of leading a red card, allowing South to discard his losing spade in dummy while he trumps in his own hand, that is, to *crossruff*.

This ending came from a hand well played by Charles W. Taintor, 2nd, of Cambridge, Massachusetts, as follows:

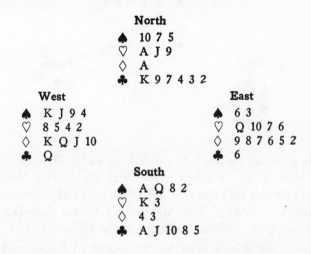

North
- ♠ 10 7 5
- ♡ A J 9
- ◇ A
- ♣ K 9 7 4 3 2

West
- ♠ K J 9 4
- ♡ 8 5 4 2
- ◇ K Q J 10
- ♣ Q

East
- ♠ 6 3
- ♡ Q 10 7 6
- ◇ 9 8 7 6 5 2
- ♣ 6

South
- ♠ A Q 8 2
- ♡ K 3
- ◇ 4 3
- ♣ A J 10 8 5

Sitting South, Mr. Taintor played the contract at six clubs, against which West opened with the King of diamonds. To insure his contract against any possible adverse distribution, Mr. Taintor exhausted the opponents' trumps, eliminated the red suits from his two hands by trumping back and forth, and finessed the ten of spades from the dummy when down to the ending shown above.

It should be noted that the development of this endplay is marked at the outset. Sometimes the endplay does not heave into sight until a few bad suit splits makes its use the last resort to fulfill an apparently hopeless looking contract. Frank K. Perkins illustrated this principle in his *Boston Herald* column as follows:

North
- ♠ 10 6 5 3 2
- ♡ A 6 2
- ◇ A 6
- ♣ K 6 2

West
- ♠ ——
- ♡ Q J 10 7 5
- ◇ J 8 5 2
- ♣ J 9 8 3

East
- ♠ Q J 9
- ♡ 9 8 4 3
- ◇ K 10 9 3
- ♣ 7 5

South, Dealer
- ♠ A K 8 7 4
- ♡ K
- ◇ Q 7 4
- ♣ A Q 10 4

South	North
1 ♠	3 ♠
4 ◇ ?	4 NT
5 ♣ ?	5 NT
6 ◇ ?	6 ♠

The question marks indicate Asking Bids. The decision between bidding six or seven spades was decided by North's inability to control both the first and second lead of diamonds. For an analysis of Asking Bids, see Coffin's Pocket Self-Teacher or consult any other reliable textbook on the subject. *

Against six spades West led the Queen of hearts, and South regretted not chancing the grand slam call on the probability of picking up the Jack of clubs so that the dummy could discard the losing diamond on the fourth round of clubs. After winning the heart opening lead with the King, South played his two high trumps. West's chicane trump holding confirmed South's original conservatism in stopping at six spades. South played the King of clubs, discarded a low diamond on the Ace of hearts, trumped a heart, and ran two more club tricks, receiving in that suit another rude jolt when East failed to follow suit on the third round.

After discovering two unlucky divisions in the black suits, several South players proved to be "quitters," and they resigned themselves, like fatalists, to a one-trick set. One South player, however, believing that the red suits might be lucky, threw East

*See *Encyclopedia of Bridge,*
1971 edition, page 14.

in the lead with a spade and prayed that East held the King of diamonds.

In the Compound Eliminations involving one opponent, there are four combinations of three basic positions, to wit, the fork and crossruff positions just shown, fork and entry positions, crossruff and entry positions, and all three positions compounded in one endplay.

ENTRY FORK STRIP

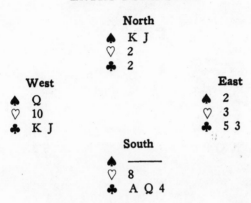

North
♠ K J
♡ 2
♣ 2

West
♠ Q
♡ 10
♣ K J

East
♠ 2
♡ 3
♣ 5 3

South
♠ ———
♡ 8
♣ A Q 4

At notrump South, needing three tricks, throws West in with the heart in order to make him lead clubs up to South's fourchette holding or to put North in for two spade tricks. Here's a variation wherein the fork and entry elements are compounded in one suit:

FORK-ENTRY STRIP

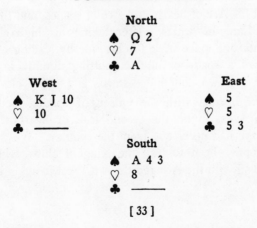

North
♠ Q 2
♡ 7
♣ A

West
♠ K J 10
♡ 10
♣ ———

East
♠ 5
♡ 5
♣ 5 3

South
♠ A 4 3
♡ 8
♣ ———

At notrump , South, wishing three tricks, pitches West in with
the heart to force him to lead spades and make the Queen in
dummy an entry for bringing in the Ace of clubs.

While the majority of endplays occur toward the end of the
hand, sometimes they take place early in the play. The more
the elements are compounded, the earlier the ending is apt to
take place. Note how this happens in the Two-Entry Fork Strip
below:

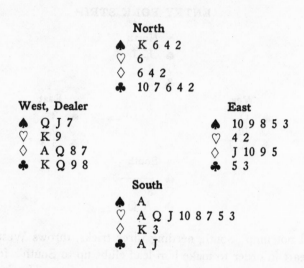

North
♠ K 6 4 2
♡ 6
♢ 6 4 2
♣ 10 7 6 4 2

West, Dealer
♠ Q J 7
♡ K 9
♢ A Q 8 7
♣ K Q 9 8

East
♠ 10 9 8 5 3
♡ 4 2
♢ J 10 9 5
♣ 5 3

South
♠ A
♡ A Q J 10 8 7 5 3
♢ K 3
♣ A J

West dealt and bid one diamond, North and East passed, and
South, the author, playing in a social game, jumped to four hearts,
buying the contract.

West led the King of clubs which South won with his Ace.
South played his Ace of hearts and Ace of spades, and threw West
in with the King of hearts. After taking his high club, West
could win only one more trick for his side by leading a diamond.
If he returned a spade or a club, putting dummy in the lead,
South would get two diamond discards and enjoy eleven tricks.

Had West opened with the Queen of spades, South would
have thrown West in on the second lead of hearts, and West
would still have had no escape from the endplay. West's best defence would have been to lead the King of clubs, which South
would have won with the Ace and thrown West in again by returning his club.

North
♠ 3
♡ 7
♢ K
♣ 4 3

West
♠ ———
♡ Q 10
♢ Q J 10
♣ ———

East
♠ ———
♡ ———
♢ 9 8 6
♣ K Q

South
♠ J 10 9
♡ 8
♢ ———
♣ 2

With spades trumps, South wants four tricks and throws West in with the heart, making him lead a diamond giving South a club discard, or lead a heart allowing South to discard the same club while North trumps. Here is the endplay involving all three basic positions:

Carrying partner,- one named Joey.

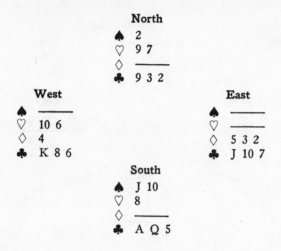

Spades are trumps, and South, wanting four tricks, puts West in with the heart to make him return a heart for South to discard a club on, to lead a diamond for the club discard while North trumps, or to lead up to South's club fork. As this endplay involves three suits, it might readily be called a Triple Elimination!

Split Eliminations

An elimination is said to be split whenever either opponent is forced to sacrifice a trick by leading away from a suit commonly held by both opponents. To be more precise, a split elimination is based on a split guard. For an analysis of guards, see Chapter Eleven.

BALANCED SPLIT GUARD

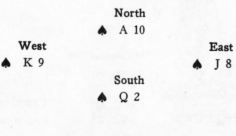

If either West or East has the lead, North and South are sure to win both tricks by proper finessing. If West leads low, North passes to South's Queen; if East leads low, South plays low to force West's King. This combination was pivotal in a hand from a tournament directed by Mrs. Glenham Jones in Brattleboro, Vermont.

TWO FORK STRIP

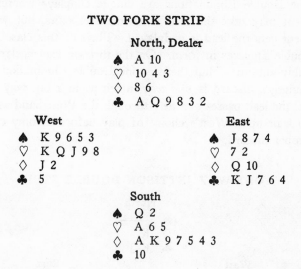

North, Dealer
♠ A 10
♡ 10 4 3
◇ 8 6
♣ A Q 9 8 3 2

West
♠ K 9 6 5 3
♡ K Q J 9 8
◇ J 2
♣ 5

East
♠ J 8 7 4
♡ 7 2
◇ Q 10
♣ K J 7 6 4

South
♠ Q 2
♡ A 6 5
◇ A K 9 7 5 4 3
♣ 10

North dealt and bid one club, South one diamond, West one spade, North two clubs, and South five diamonds, closing the auction.

The contract was defeated at every table, but it can be made in two different ways.

West opens with the King of hearts. In order to fulfill the contract by one line of play, South holds up his Ace of hearts. West next leads the Jack of hearts which South wins with the Ace. South pulls trumps in two leads and finesses the Queen of clubs. East wins the club finesse with the King, but he has been fork stripped in two suits. He can't lead clubs without giving South two discards; and if he leads a low spade, South plays low to force West's King.

If South wins the opening lead of the King of hearts, he can fulfill his contract by a squeeze strip against West. Declarer pulls trumps in two leads, plays the Ace of clubs and trumps a club, and runs all his trumps, forcing West to shed all his hearts but two to

[37]

guard his King of spades. At the end South loses two heart tricks to West, finally making him lead away from and lose his King of spades.

Double Eliminations

The Double Eliminations are unique endplays wherein either opponent may take the lead when declarer exits, but whichever opponent gets the lead is endplayed. Plays of this class resemble the double squeezes in form. On the throwin lead declarer's play is doubly automatic, but there is one Double Elimination wherein the dummy's discard is *one way*, much as in a one-way squeeze, that is, the lead passes *one way* through the West hand as dummy has to wait upon West's choice of play before dummy can make the proper discard.

ONE-WAY JETTISON DOUBLE STRIP

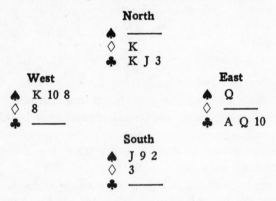

At notrump South, wanting two tricks, leads a low spade. When East wins, he has to lead up to North's King of clubs, and the King of diamonds wins also. If West wins the spade trick, North must *jettison* his top diamond, and, after West wins with his now good diamond, he has to lead up to South's top fork in spades.

Jettison is a good old fashioned nautical term, meaning to throw overboard the valuable cargo of a floundering ship in order to save the ship from sinking in a storm. This is exactly what happens when North throws overboard his good King of diamonds to keep his King-Jack of clubs from sinking the ship.

FORK DOUBLE STRIP

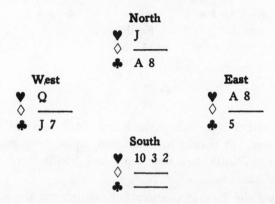

North
♥ J
◊ ——
♣ A 8

West
♥ Q
◊ ——
♣ J 7

East
♥ A 8
◊ ——
♣ 5

South
♥ 10 3 2
◊ ——
♣ ——

There is no trump and South, requiring two tricks, leads the Jack of hearts from dummy. East must pass the trick or else his side will win only one trick, and West is forced to underlead his club tenace at the end. While East and West hold two winners between them, proper entry back and forth to realize them is blocked.

This pretty ending was made by Norman Bonney of Boston, Mass. and shown in his book, "The Russell System," written jointly with Carlton. Russell of Brookline, Mass. Here is the original deal:

North, Dealer
- ♠ Q 9 7
- ♡ J 9 7 5
- ◇ K 8
- ♣ A K Q 8

West
- ♠ 6 5
- ♡ Q 6
- ◇ J 10 9 6 3
- ♣ J 10 7 6

East
- ♠ K J 3 2
- ♡ A 8 4
- ◇ A 7 2
- ♣ 5 4 2

South
- ♠ A 10 8 4
- ♡ K 10 3 2
- ◇ Q 5 4
- ♣ 9 3

With neither side vulnerable North dealt and bid one club. East, too weak to double for a takeout, called one spade, South one notrump, North two notrump , and South three notrump closing the auction.

West led the Jack of diamonds, North played the King, East the Ace, and South, played by Mr. Bonney, held up his Queen until the third round to eliminate East's diamonds. While the contract of three notrump is now a sorry looking affair, East's spade overcall, indicating most of the adverse high card strength, offered substantial hope of shutting out West's established diamonds. Bonney led the nine of clubs. When West dropped the six, Mr. Bonney correctly suspected that West held J-10-7-6 in clubs as the 5, 4, and 2 had not yet appeared. But courage failed Bonney, and he played the Queen from dummy. He led the seven of spades which East ducked, and it won the trick. Bonney led the Queen of spades which the King and Ace covered in turn. When Bonney led the eightspot of spades, West discarded one of his established diamonds. This discard is the key play of the deal that enabled Bonney to count the distribution and to ascertain the location of all the important missing high cards. West must have held the originally suspected J-10-7-6 of clubs, and his two hearts can not include the Ace, or he would have discarded a low heart. East won the spade trick and cannily led a low heart to get West in with the Queen, but Bonney jumped right up with his King. Bonney ran his spade, squeezing the last diamond from West, who had to guard hearts and clubs. Bonney shed a heart from dummy. He led a low club and West split his equals, playing the ten to force North's King, leaving the ending shown above that produced three notrump. Now Bonney led the Jack of hearts and it was all over except the weeping and wailing by the defence. We consider this one of Mr. Bonney's most remarkable hands.

CROSSRUFF DOUBLE STRIP

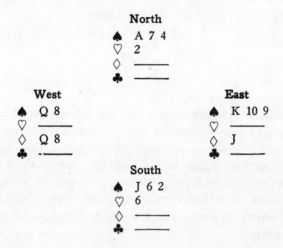

North
♠ A 7 4
♡ 2
♢ ——
♣ ——

West
♠ Q 8
♡ ——
♢ Q 8
♣ ——

East
♠ K 10 9
♡ ——
♢ J
♣ ——

South
♠ J 6 2
♡ 6
♢ ——
♣ ——

With hearts trumps North plays the Ace of spades. West can not unblock by underplaying the Queen without enabling South to set up the Jack, and on the second spade lead East can not put up the King for the same reason. Hence the exit in spades is blocked, and West, thrown in with the Queen of spades, must lead a diamond, enabling South to make his trumps separately.

In the early editions of *Endplays* this ending was labelled the Blocked-Exit Crossruff Strip on account of the way the spade suit was blocked so that West couldn't exit without sacrificing his trick sooner.

Another fork double strip was played in a famous Whist hand. Compare the play at Contract Bridge given below with the play at Whist given in Chapter Nineteen.

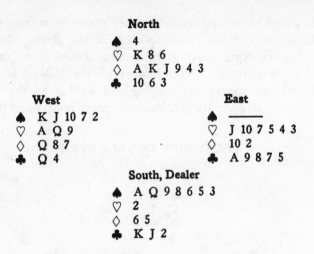

North
- ♠ 4
- ♡ K 8 6
- ♢ A K J 9 4 3
- ♣ 10 6 3

West
- ♠ K J 10 7 2
- ♡ A Q 9
- ♢ Q 8 7
- ♣ Q 4

East
- ♠ ———
- ♡ J 10 7 5 4 3
- ♢ 10 2
- ♣ A 9 8 7 5

South, Dealer
- ♠ A Q 9 8 6 5 3
- ♡ 2
- ♢ 6 5
- ♣ K J 2

The diamond suit, which was the key side suit at Whist, was the game trump suit at Contract Bridge. South dealt and bid one spade, West made a waiting pass, North called two diamonds, South two spades, North three diamonds, South three spades, North four spades, whereupon West came out of ambush and doubled. South ran to five diamonds, and West, realizing that his double wasn't so smart, was completely cowed by his grievous error and passed.

East led a low heart which West headed by the Ace and returned the Queen, hoping to shorten dummy's trumps. North passed and dummy cut. North finessed the Jack of diamonds, pulled all adverse trumps and West's last heart, and led a low club. East signalled with the seven to show the Ace, a foolhardy play, and North now diagnosed the situation correctly, regardless of East's signal. As West had produced the Ace-Queen of hearts and the Queen of diamonds, and was marked with at least K-J-x in spades, he would have doubled five diamonds had he held the Ace of clubs also. Hence dummy hopped up with the King of clubs leaving this ending:

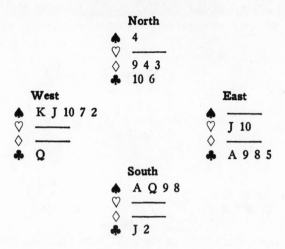

North
♠ 4
♡ ———
◇ 9 4 3
♣ 10 6

West
♠ K J 10 7 2
♡ ———
◇ ———
♣ Q

East
♠ ———
♡ J 10
◇ ———
♣ A 9 8 5

South
♠ A Q 9 8
♡ ———
◇ ———
♣ J 2

Declarer now lost his only club trick, or two tricks in all, including the Ace of hearts lost earlier. West was endplayed in spades and East couldn't overtake the Queen of clubs with his Ace lest he set up that extra trick for Declarer in clubs.

Stop Press: A Dogfight!

The series of plays and counter plays ending in a *repeat strip* in the deal below made a delightful dogfight:

♠ A K 10 4
♡ J 6 3
◇ 8 7 4
♣ 6 5 4

♠ 8 7 5
♡ 9 5
◇ A 9 3
♣ 10 9 8 7 3

♠ Q 9 6 2
♡ Q 10 8 2
◇ 6 2
♣ K Q J

♠ J 3
♡ A K 7 4
◇ K Q J 10 5
♣ A 2

South dealt and opened 1 ♡, North replied 1 ♠: South rebid 2 ◇ and North raised to 3 ◇, then South said 3 N T and bought the contract, The partners were using canapé bids. These marked South with four hearts and five diamonds.

West led his ♣ 10 and South held up his ♣ A, but he had to take it on East's club return. *(Concluded on page 44)*

The majority of double eliminations are based on a middle suit which is blocked, but the 1937 Bridge Olympic Hand No. 15 is based on two identical middle suits, neither of which was blocked.

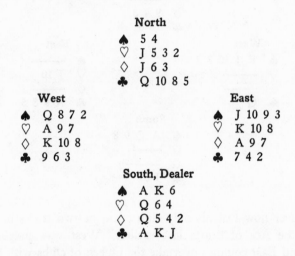

North
♠ 5 4
♡ J 5 3 2
◊ J 6 3
♣ Q 10 8 5

West
♠ Q 8 7 2
♡ A 9 7
◊ K 10 8
♣ 9 6 3

East
♠ J 10 9 3
♡ K 10 8
◊ A 9 7
♣ 7 4 2

South, Dealer
♠ A K 6
♡ Q 6 4
◊ Q 5 4 2
♣ A K J

South bid one notrump and all passed. West led the deuce of spades, marking him with a four-card suit. Declarer won the trick with the Ace, ran four club tricks, and played the King then low in spades in order to force the opponents to open the red suits and yield the odd trick to declarer. Obviously, declarer can not open either red suit himself without losing three tricks therein.

The contract is hopeless unless clubs split 4-4 or East has ♣ K-Q-J dry as here to block the suit. So South pushed his high diamonds and West held up his ace twice while East petered in order to show two diamonds only. If South now leads another diamond to West's ace, East jettisons his blocking club picture in order to let West run clubs and break the contract.

But South smelled this jettison play coming, so he had to hope for both the ♠ Q and ♡ Q to lie East. South quit his diamonds, led his ♠ J to the ♠ K to unblock then he boldly threw East on lead with dummy's last club. East returned a low heart that South let ride around to dummy's jack, then South lost the fourth heart lead to East to force a spade lead for South's ninth trick. P. F. Saunders first wrote up this pretty deal on page 38 of January 1974 *Bridge Magazine*. Thank you, Sir, for such a lovely running dogfight!

CHAPTER FIVE

REPEATING ELIMINATIONS

As the name suggests, the Repeating Eliminations, or progressive Eliminations as they are sometimes called, are combination endplays wherein one elimination follows another. They are freaks, pure and simple, and are analagous to the four-legged chicken and the two-headed calf.

REPEATING STRIP

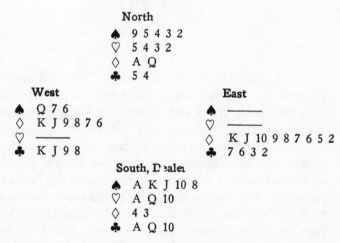

North
♠ 9 5 4 3 2
♡ 5 4 3 2
◇ A Q
♣ 5 4

West
♠ Q 7 6
◇ K J 9 8 7 6
♡ ——
♣ K J 9 8

East
♠ ——
♡ ——
◇ K J 10 9 8 7 6 5 2
♣ 7 6 3 2

South, Dealer
♠ A K J 10 8
♡ A Q 10
◇ 4 3
♣ A Q 10

South deals and bids one spade, West two hearts, North two spades, East jumps to five diamonds, and South calls five spades, whereupon West doubles, closing the auction.

South's ten of hearts wins West's opening eightspot. South throws West in on the third round of spades. West leads another heart, and South throws West in again on the fourth round of hearts, using the Ace of diamonds to enter dummy for this second elimination.

If West leads a club at Trick Five, Declarer eliminates this suit from his own two hands, and throws East in on the second round of diamonds.

The only repeating strip we encountered in actual play had a strange twist. Both throwin manoeuvres were made in the same suit!

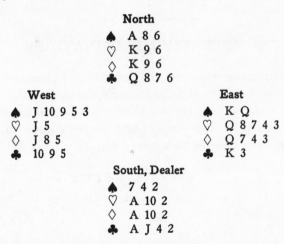

North
♠ A 8 6
♡ K 9 6
◇ K 9 6
♣ Q 8 7 6

West
♠ J 10 9 5 3
♡ J 5
◇ J 8 5
♣ 10 9 5

East
♠ K Q
♡ Q 8 7 4 3
◇ Q 7 4 3
♣ K 3

South, Dealer
♠ 7 4 2
♡ A 10 2
◇ A 10 2
♣ A J 4 2

South, played by my father, Sturgis Coffin of Fitzwilliam, New Hampshire, staggered into a weird contract of five clubs, which, with four losing tricks and a finesse and a drop, doesn't seem to have a Chinaman's chance. Of course, three notrump is the logical contract, and it requires some luck to be fulfilled.

Playing West against five clubs we led the Jack of spades, which the dummy's Ace won. South finessed the Jack of clubs and played the Ace, felling East's King. Declarer next lost a spade trick to East, who returned a heart. Declarer played low and our Jack forced the dummy's King. Declarer pulled the last adverse trump with the Queen of clubs, finessed the ten of hearts and played the Ace, and threw me in with another spade. Realizing a spade lead would be fatal, because it would allow the dummy to trump while South shed his diamond loser, I led a low diamond thereby giving declarer three diamond tricks and his contract.

My father thought the hand was a great joke and "ribbed" us for presenting him with two tricks in the red suits.

The hand has a unique trap. If declarer pulls three rounds of trumps immediately, East can jettison his blocking spade and defeat the contract. Frank K. Perkins published the hand in the *Boston Herald* as a double dummy problem!

By the inherent nature of cards, you will find in the chapters on squeezes that a squeeze can be repeated only once, because it is limited by four suits. Some basic elimination positions, however, can be repeated several times in one deal, because tenace positions can be almost indefinitely pyramided. Such a combination of three or more progressive throwins is called the Continuous Elimination. If the number of cards of a suit or suits were infinite, the Continuous Elimination could also be an infinite Perpetual Elimination.

JACOB'S LADDER

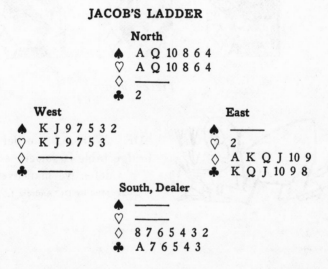

North
♠ A Q 10 8 6 4
♡ A Q 10 8 6 4
◇ ——
♣ 2

West
♠ K J 9 7 5 3 2
♡ K J 9 7 5 3
◇ ——
♣ ——

East
♠ ——
♡ 2
◇ A K Q J 10 9
♣ K Q J 10 9 8

South, Dealer
♠ ——
♡ ——
◇ 8 7 6 5 4 3 2
♣ A 7 6 5 4 3

The deal is from one of the famous Pitt stories, wherein Samuel Pitt, playing South in a terrible nightmare, has to fulfill a contract of three notrump redoubled, or else have his head chopped off on the Guillotine Block.

West leads the seven of spades. Seven from eleven leaves four, and as dummy holds four cards higher than the seven, by the Rule of Eleven the eightspot is marked to win the trick. It does, and East discards the Ace of diamonds, screaming to West to lead a diamond. Eventually hearts have to be led, so why not now? Dummy leads the Queen of hearts in order to reduce as much as possible East's chance of getting the lead and at the same time retaining first round control of the suit with the Ace. West

wins with the King and leads another spade, dummy leads the
ten of hearts, and West and dummy toss the lead back and forth,
until dummy wins seven tricks, when East, who is Pitt's threatening executioner, gets squeezed and gives up the ghost!

Tierce minor

"Dr. Watson, murder at the
bridge table is sometimes the only
defensive maneuver."

(Suggested by Dr. Andrew J. Torrielli)

Origin of the Squeeze

Before 1910 the term, squeeze, was probably unknown; and
the play was technically called in whist and in early bridge the
"forced discard." Similar names might be compress, jam, crunch,
crush and squash, et cetera; and future writers may use these to
separate such squeeze compounds as *squeeze suitout, squeeze
ruffout, squeeze strip, squeeze finesse* and so on where the
squeeze is only a preparatory play.

DIVISION TWO

Squeezes - Endplays of Mass

THE FABULOUS FIFTY-TWO

By James Pipes

A poor motherless chile was one day travellin' an' got lonesome so he was outside a city sittin' down lookin' thru the Fifty-Two which was the only Bible he had.

The mayor of the city came along and saw th' boy. He looked at him an' said "It is a sentence to be caught gamblin' on the highway."

But the li'l boy answered "I'm not gamblin' 'cause Papa always taught me w'en I was alone ter read th' Bible."

The Mayor said, "Yes, but that is not a Bible, but a pack of cards."

Then the l'il boy shook his head an' said, "Oh, yes, it is too th' Bible."

"Well," said the Mayor, "You jus' prove it th' Bible an' not a pack of cards an' it won't be a crime 'gainst you."

♠ 2 *"Hah," shouted the li'l boy, "You look here: w'en I lay down the deuce it reminds me th' Father, Son.*

♡ 3 *"An' w'en I see the trey it reminds me Father, Son, Holy Ghost.*

♢ 4 *"An' th' fo' spot is fo' evangilists Matt, Mark, Luke and John.*

♣ 5 *"Now the five spot is five w'at was wise an' five w'at was foolish, th' five wise virgins that took* °il *an' the five foolish virgins that took no* °il.

♢ 6 *An' he played another card an' said, "Now this here six-spot remind me that God made heaven an' earth in six days.*

♡ 7 *"An' this here seven tell me that on th' seventh day He rested.*

♠ 8 *"W'en I see th' eight spot it reminds me eight people was saved w'en th' worl' was 'stroyed, Noah an' his wife, Sham, Ham, an' Japeth an' their wives.*

♡ 9 *"I see the nine spot fall an' know it was ten persons had th' leprosy an uncurable disease where people was put out in hedges with nine-inch brim hats ter mark their plight an' out of the ten only one returned thanks an' Jesus asked 'But where are the nine?'" Then the li'l boy preached Luke seventeen, number eleven to the Mayor.*

♢ 10 *"Now," he said, "Behold th' ten spot an' I knew God gave Moses th' Ten on Mount Sinai." So he preached again to the Mayor an' spoke of Exodus number twenty.*

♡ J *As he played another card he said, "Oh, the jack, you know is the devil met Christ on th' pinacle of a mountain an' tol' him he would give him all th' kingdoms but Christ said, 'Get thee behind me Satan for it is writ thou shalt not tempt the Lawd but Him only thou serve.'" Then he preached Luke fo', third and eight to the Mayor.*

♣ Q *"Lo, here is the queen an' she tell me it was th' Queen of Sheba w'at come to the uttermos' part of Jerusalem to tes' the wisdom of Solomon an' said to Solomon 'I've seen the settin' of thy servants an' the incense they send up in thy temple but my own eyes have seen Thy greatness an' yet th' half is not tol' me.'"*

♢ K *Now the li'l boy played another card and said, "Oh, w'en I see the king it reminds me one King of Glory."*

♡ A *"And the ace remind me it's only one god."*

(Concluded on page 65.)

CHAPTER SIX

BASIC SQUEEZES

E VERY True Squeeze takes advantage of the fact that two hands can hold more cards than one hand, and therefore their greater *mass* has the one hand in a vise, making it discard to the breaking point *and* breaking it. Many players, not realizing this, fail to squeeze, because they lead all but one trump. In other words, like a skittish jumper, they gleefully canter up to the hurdles, then suddenly refuse,—they lead trumps to the breaking point, then refuse to part with that last trump. It's leading the last trump that damages opponents.

The squeeze position depends on three elements: a quick *entry* into the opposite friendly hand for bringing in another suit or suits that can not be held in the forcing hand for want of card space; a *forcing card,* which is a winner (often that last trump), led to *force* an opponent to discard, or rather, to "disguard" a busy* suit; and *guards,* by which are meant the busy* cards, master cards and/or suit stoppers. If you suspect a squeeze ending, look for these three elements, Entry, Forcing Card, and Guards.

While squeeze positions do exist when a quick entry is wanting, they are not True Squeezes, but are Squeeze Strips. See Chapter Fifteen.

The forcing card implies two other elements unnecessarily stressed by minor writers, to wit, "assumption" and "projection." By the former is meant that a player *assumes* that the guards are properly located with one opponent to insure the success of the squeeze, and plays the squeeze accordingly. If the guards fail to appear as desired, nothing is lost by trying to squeeze, and a

---

*Ely Culbertson differentiates idle cards from busy cards as cards which may be discarded without reducing the trick-taking value of the hand, that is, they are not potential trick-winners or essential guards to same.

chance to gain a trick has not been overlooked. In that case the forcing card turned out not to be a forcing card at all, because it forced nothing. By "projection" is meant projecting the squeeze position forward by eliminating all idle* cards, but here again, if leading the forcing card brings down only idle discards from opponents, the forcing card is not forcing anything. *In order to be forcing, the forcing card must force an opponent to "disguard" a busy suit,* freeing a trick therein for you.

E F G Formula

In other words, you must break down the guards and force an imprisoned card's way to trick-winning freedom. To remember these three vital elements, simply imagine that you are breaking jail. To ENTER freedom, FORCE the GUARDS! E F G !

According to the projection theory, the partnership hands must be able to win all but the one trick they are trying to develop by the squeeze. By this token, if you hold more than one losing trick, you must lose a trick early in the play in order to develop the squeeze. This principle is fundamental. The only variation is when you may develop two extra tricks by a repeated squeeze, in which case you must adjust your winners to number two less than the total number left unplayed.

First Basic Position

The Rotary or One-way Squeezes depend on the rotary order of discarding to pass *one way* through second then third hand. The turn to discard can pass *one way through only one opponent,* because the partner of the forcing leader can not elect his discard until the defender has discarded, and therefore in the one-way position it is impossible to squeeze the other defender, because the forcing leader's partner is squeezed first.

---

*See footnote at bottom of page 51.

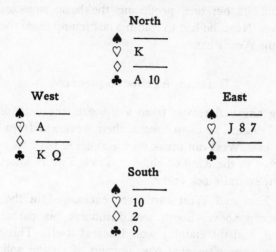

North

♠ ——————
♡ K
◊ ——————
♣ A 10

West

♠ ——————
♡ A
◊ ——————
♣ K Q

East

♠ ——————
♡ J 8 7
◊ ——————
♣ ——————

South

♠ ——————
♡ 10
◊ 2
♣ 9

Diamonds are trumps and South, requiring all three tricks, leads his last trump. West has the unpleasant choice of discarding before North. Whichever mass he breaks is wrong.

This endplay came from a classic hand played by Al Parrott back in 1925 before the days of Contract.

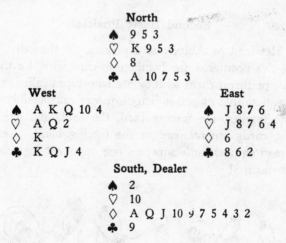

North

♠ 9 5 3
♡ K 9 5 3
◊ 8
♣ A 10 7 5 3

West

♠ A K Q 10 4
♡ A Q 2
◊ K
♣ K Q J 4

East

♠ J 8 7 6
♡ J 8 7 6 4
◊ 6
♣ 8 6 2

South, Dealer

♠ 2
♡ 10
◊ A Q J 10 9 7 5 4 3 2
♣ 9

Parrott playing South dealt and bid five diamonds, West five spades, playing North we bid six diamonds, and West doubled; correct bidding at either Auction or Contract. West led the King of spades, following with the Queen. South trumped and ran all his diamonds but one, producing the basic squeeze position shown above. Next, he had to lead his last trump to do the damage and break up West's hand.

Defence Against Squeezes

Lacking any real escape from a squeeze, the defending partners should discard so as to conceal their weakness from declarer. But in this case West can break up the squeeze position effectively if he switches to the King of clubs at Trick Two to knock out the Ace, dummy's vital quick entry.

If the East and West cards are exchanged in the one-way squeeze shown above, South would squeeze his partner before fourth hand, and the endplay would defeat itself. This condition is caused by *isomerism,* that phenomenon of similar solid objects that makes it impossible for us to put a left-handed glove on the right hand. Hence, if you render the True Squeeze useless by switching the East and West hands, or find it hopeless because they are already switched, you have what we call the Isomeric Squeeze.

Second Basic Position

The Retained or Automatic Squeezes, on the other hand, do not have this positional disadvantage to cope with, for the squeezing cards, or threat cards as they are sometimes called, are not all in one hand so that no self-inflicted squeeze can possibly exist. As the name implies, the forcing card, the lead, and one or more squeezing cards are *retained* in the forcing hand. Leading the forcing card *automatically* squeezes one opponent regardless of the order of discard!

Two
Mixed
Pairs

[54]

AUTOMATIC SQUEEZE

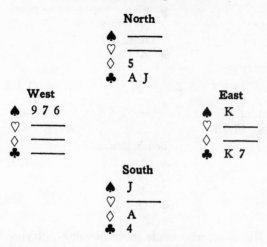

North
♠ ——
♡ ——
◇ 5
♣ A J

West
♠ 9 7 6
♡ ——
◇ ——
♣ ——

East
♠ K
♡ ——
◇ ——
♣ K 7

South
♠ J
♡ ——
◇ A
♣ 4

There is no trump and South, wanting all three tricks, plays his Ace of diamonds. The control of the situation is *retained* because South still has the lead and the Jack of Spades, should East elect to discard his King of spades. For the success of this automatic squeeze, it makes no difference whether East or West holds the black suit honors, but these cards must be massed all in one adverse hand. Of course, in this particular case, there would be a winning finesse against the King of clubs if West held it, but if the defensive club holding were King-Queen, there would be no alternative play.

Hence, the Automatic Squeeze is polyisomeric, because it functions equally well in both its isomers. It follows, therefore, that the Automatic Squeeze has *twice as good a chance* of scoring as the One-way Squeeze, because the former has a choice of *two* opponents to victimize, whereas the latter has only one.

The complete deal came from the New England Championships held in Boston by the Boston Chess Club in 1935.

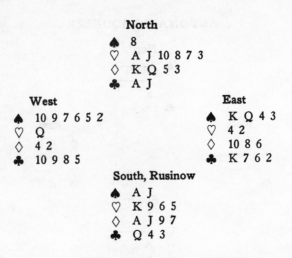

North
- ♠ 8
- ♡ A J 10 8 7 3
- ◇ K Q 5 3
- ♣ A J

West
- ♠ 10 9 7 6 5 2
- ♡ Q
- ◇ 4 2
- ♣ 10 9 8 5

East
- ♠ K Q 4 3
- ♡ 4 2
- ◇ 10 8 6
- ♣ K 7 6 2

South, Rusinow
- ♠ A J
- ♡ K 9 6 5
- ◇ A J 9 7
- ♣ Q 4 3

Sydney Rusinow, who made seven notrump playing South for a clean top score on this deal, needs little introduction to Bridge players. He has won two national championships, and the New England Championships in 1935, when he played this famous hand in Boston. We are proud to quote his statement, "I learned how to play Bridge from Endplays," referring to earlier editions of this work, and therefore we are only too glad to submit his hand in his honor.

Against Rusinow's contract of seven notrump West opened with the ten of spades, and East's Queen forced the Ace. Declarer ran six heart tricks in dummy, discarding the Queen and a low club from his own hand in order to unblock for a possible club finesse at the end. He won the fourth round of diamonds in his own hand, automatically squeezing East.

Poor defence made the squeeze a "sure bet" play for Mr. Rusinow. West foolishly discarded all his clubs, enabling Mr. Rusinow to count opponents' clubs down to two. When Mr. Rusinow led his last diamond and East discarded a club, the deserted King was marked alone. Had West kept one or two clubs, Mr. Rusinow would have been forced to guess at the end whether to play the Ace of clubs or to finesse the Jack.

At other tables, only six hearts or six notrump were made, because the club finesse lost. It takes the same squeeze to produce seven hearts, but seven diamonds was bid and laid down at one table without a finesse, because the heart suit offers two club discards. The deal illustrates that much harped-on principle that a trump suit, divided four and four between partners, will produce more tricks than a trump suit of eight or more cards unevenly divided between partners, because the 4-4 suit offers no discard when the other suit is trumps. While the grand slam in this case can be made at either contract of seven hearts or of seven diamonds, at best, the play for the grand slam trick at hearts is uncertain.

Mrs. Charles Geissler of Boston, Mass., a leading "Master Teacher" of New England, demonstrated her ability to execute an automatic squeeze at one of her own Tuesday evening tournaments.

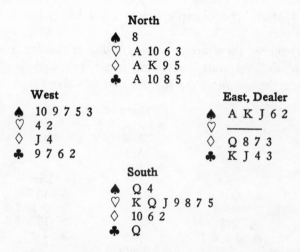

North
- ♠ 8
- ♡ A 10 6 3
- ◇ A K 9 5
- ♣ A 10 8 5

West
- ♠ 10 9 7 5 3
- ♡ 4 2
- ◇ J 4
- ♣ 9 7 6 2

East, Dealer
- ♠ A K J 6 2
- ♡ ———
- ◇ Q 8 7 3
- ♣ K J 4 3

South
- ♠ Q 4
- ♡ K Q J 9 8 7 5
- ◇ 10 6 2
- ♣ Q

East dealt and bid one spade, Mrs. Geissler playing South jumped to three hearts, and playing West we called three notrump as a psychic measure to bluff opponents out of calling their game or possible slam. North didn't bother to double us, but bid four notrump to show real strength and to tell his partner that my bid was "the bunk." East passed, South called five hearts, and North called six hearts, closing the auction.

West led the five of spades which East won with his King. East switched to a low diamond, and West's Jack forced dummy's King. Properly diagnosing the Queen of diamonds and the King-Jack of clubs with East for his opening bid, Mrs. Geissler pulled trumps in two leads, trumped her spade in dummy, played dummy's King of diamonds to unblock the diamonds (Vienna Coup) for the forthcoming automatic squeeze, and ran down all her trumps, forcing East to discard down to the Queen of diamonds and the King-Jack of clubs with still an impossible discard to make. Had East shed his last diamond, South's ten   would have become good. So East let go a club, hoping West held Q-x in clubs, and dummy's Ace and ten of clubs won the last two tricks. The deal was originally published by us in *Leisure Magazine,* July, 1937.

Important: Had Mrs. Geissler failed to take dummy's King of diamonds, her last heart lead would have squeezed dummy instead of fourth hand. She unblocked diamonds to establish her ten as a squeeze card, retained in her own hand for the automatic squeeze. This Vienna Coup play is not necessary to squeeze second hand, who discards before third hand, but it is a good safety play.

Whenever there are too many losing tricks for a squeeze to operate, declarer must lose his idle tricks early sometimes, in order to bring the victim of the squeeze into effective range.

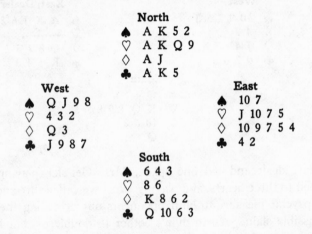

```
                         North
                         ♠ A K 5 2
                         ♡ A K Q 9
                         ◊ A J
                         ♣ A K 5
        West                              East
        ♠ Q J 9 8                         ♠ 10 7
        ♡ 4 3 2                           ♡ J 10 7 5
        ◊ Q 3                             ◊ 10 9 7 5 4
        ♣ J 9 8 7                         ♣ 4 2
                         South
                         ♠ 6 4 3
                         ♡ 8 6
                         ◊ K 8 6 2
                         ♣ Q 10 6 3
```

South plays at six notrump , and wins West's club opening with the ten.   As declarer has only eleven winners, two in spades, three hearts, two diamonds, and four clubs, he loses a spade trick immediately to reduce his hands to only one losing trick. If opponents' spades break three and three, declarer scores his slam without further ado; but as they split four and two, declarer prepares his cards for a simple squeeze anyway. West wins the spade trick and returns another club. Dummy runs two club tricks, two spades, a heart, and a diamond; and South wins the second round of diamonds with the King, leaving:

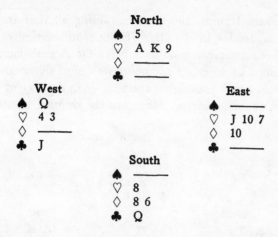

North
♠ 5
♡ A K 9
◇ —
♣ —

West
♠ Q
♡ 4 3
◇ —
♣ J

East
♠ —
♡ J 10 7
◇ 10
♣ —

South
♠ —
♡ 8
◇ 8 6
♣ Q

South cashes his club trick, squeezing East automatically. East discards the ten of hearts, but that play doesn't fool South who wins his last three tricks with dummy's hearts.

Compare this correct play with the incorrect play that declarer followed, as shown in Chapter Two, page 18.

Third Basic Position

The third basic squeeze position is the trump squeeze, so called because one or more trump cards are vital in order to trump out a suit and establish it, if opponents unguard that suit. Basic trump squeezes are always automatic.

TRUMP SQUEEZE *

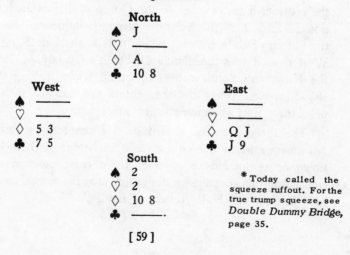

North
♠ J
♡ —
◇ A
♣ 10 8

West
♠ —
♡ —
◇ 5 3
♣ 7 5

East
♠ —
♡ —
◇ Q J
♣ J 9

South
♠ 2
♡ 2
◇ 10 8
♣ —.

* Today called the squeeze ruffout. For the true trump squeeze, see *Double Dummy Bridge*, page 35.

Hearts are trumps, and South, wanting all four tricks, plays the Jack of spades in dummy. East is automatically squeezed. If East sheds a diamond, dummy plays the Ace of diamonds and South trumps in, to enjoy his now established diamond. If East sheds a club, South establishes the ten   in dummy by trumping the eightspot immediately. Here are the original hands:

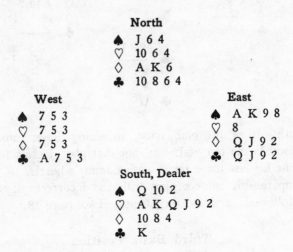

```
                    North
                    ♠ J 6 4
                    ♡ 10 6 4
                    ◇ A K 6
                    ♣ 10 8 6 4
    West                            East
    ♠ 7 5 3                         ♠ A K 9 8
    ♡ 7 5 3                         ♡ 8
    ◇ 7 5 3                         ◇ Q J 9 2
    ♣ A 7 5 3                       ♣ Q J 9 2
                South, Dealer
                    ♠ Q 10 2
                    ♡ A K Q J 9 2
                    ◇ 10 8 4
                    ♣ K
```

South deals and bids three hearts which call North raises to four hearts and all pass.

West pitches the seven of spades, the top of nothing, which East catches with the King. East returns the Ace of spades whereon South underplays his Queen to unblock. East can defeat the contract if he switches to the Queen of diamonds, but temptation to lead through declarer's strength influences East to lead the Queen of clubs instead, which falls to the lone King and Ace. West now attacks the diamonds, but it's too late. Dummy plays the King, and South runs five trump tricks leaving the ending shown above. When declarer enters the dummy with the Jack of spades, East is automatically squeezed.

The three squeezes shown in this chapter are purely basic. All other squeezes are either slight variations of these basic positions, or compounds of two or more basic positions. And in concluding this chapter, we might add that the simple basic squeeze hold is truly the Half Nelson of Bridge!

CHAPTER SEVEN

BASIC SQUEEZE VARIATIONS

A s WE learned in Chapter Six, every squeeze is based on three elements, a *quick entry* to partner's hand, a *forcing card* to lead, and threat cards menacing opponents' *guards*. The usual order of play is to lead the *forcing card,* to break the opponent's *guards,* and to play partner's *quick entry* in order to run any winners established by the squeezed opponent's discard. In the common arrangement of these elements, one or more threat cards accompany the quick entry, menacing a defender's second round (or later) guard.

A basic variation without trumps requires two quick entries. Whenever one quick entry to a player's own hand is a singleton, its suit must be represented by at least two cards in the partner's hand, in which case there must be another quick entry in another suit to partner's hand also. This arrangement is fundamental to the basic trump squeeze just analysed. The notrump analogy is called the Criss-Cross Squeeze, because a quick entry is similarly required in each partnership hand in order to facilitate entry back and forth in criss-cross fashion.

Three low trumps

CRISS-CROSS SQUEEZE (AUTOMATIC)

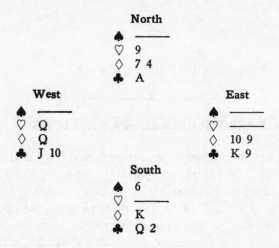

North
- ♠ ——
- ♡ 9
- ◊ 7 4
- ♣ A

West
- ♠ ——
- ♡ Q
- ◊ Q
- ♣ J 10

East
- ♠ ——
- ♡ ——
- ◊ 10 9
- ♣ K 9

South
- ♠ 6
- ♡ ——
- ◊ K
- ♣ Q 2

With spades trumps South, requiring all four tricks, led his last trump, and established the fourth trick for himself in whichever suit East unguarded. This bizarre position is much like the Criss-Cross Repeating Squeeze shown in Chapter Ten.

This endplay was made by Ely Culbertson in the famous Lenz-Culbertson match held several years ago in New York City. The complete deal is a historical comedy of errors in which Mr. Culbertson played the part of *héro comedien*. See page 89.

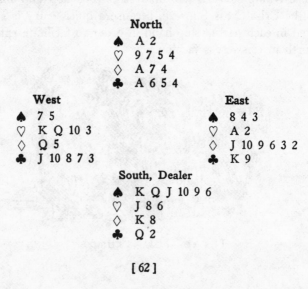

North
- ♠ A 2
- ♡ 9 7 5 4
- ◊ A 7 4
- ♣ A 6 5 4

West
- ♠ 7 5
- ♡ K Q 10 3
- ◊ Q 5
- ♣ J 10 8 7 3

East
- ♠ 8 4 3
- ♡ A 2
- ◊ J 10 9 6 3 2
- ♣ K 9

South, Dealer
- ♠ K Q J 10 9 6
- ♡ J 8 6
- ◊ K 8
- ♣ Q 2

Culbertson, playing South, dealt, and, not seeing the King of diamonds naughtily hiding with perverse stickiness behind the eight-spot,   passed. West passed and North bid one notrump (they bid one notrump on three bare aces in those days!), and South, still unwittingly gazing at twelve cards only, bid two spades, buying the contract.

Modern bidding would probably develop thus: South one spade, North two clubs forcing for one round, South two spades, North two notrump , and South three notrump , which bid is a laydown, or four spades.

Against two spades West led the King of hearts, which Sidney S. Lenz, playing East, overtook with his Ace to unblock and returned the deuce, which West's ten   won, and East trumped West's low return lead of the suit. East led the Jack of diamonds, which South won with dummy's Ace. South led six rounds of trumps, automatically squeezing East at the end. Mr. Culbertson, however, had a safer way of making four spades by playing for a double squeeze. See Culbertson's Lucky Squeeze in Chapter Nine.

In another more common arrangement of criss-cross entries, the entries exist in the same suit, accounting for the term "inverted squeeze" used by minor writers to denote something that apparently looks upside down. Leonard B. Meyer of New York, a former Chess player of note, just qualified in a major tournament on the last board of the session by grace of such a squeeze, afterwards reproduced by Frank K. Perkins in the *Boston Herald*.

Coffin says: When I talk about the health evils of smoking, you may not like it. But you know that I am dead right!

Smoking cigarettes at the bridge table has become such a big problem that around 1971 the American Contract Bridge League inaugurated no-smoking sections experimentally and they became an instant success.

In May of 1937 I ran the world's first no-smoking bridge tournament, the Spring *Appleblossom* New England Championships in Fitzwilliam NH. After each hour of play I called "Take ten," and the smokers streamed out of the antique Wren town hall to "take ten" (or more) puffs. After this country tournament of two sessions for 64 players ended, I received five complaints.

I also received five commendations for running a clean-air game! Let's not croak from smoke. It's the wrong endplay to make!

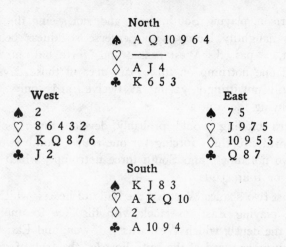

North
♠ A Q 10 9 6 4
♡ ——
◇ A J 4
♣ K 6 5 3

West
♠ 2
♡ 8 6 4 3 2
◇ K Q 8 7 6
♣ J 2

East
♠ 7 5
♡ J 9 7 5
◇ 10 9 5 3
♣ Q 8 7

South
♠ K J 8 3
♡ A K Q 10
◇ 2
♣ A 10 9 4

After much strong bidding, North arrived at the proper lay-down contract of seven spades, but as Meyer was too far behind to qualify unless he won a top score, he "shot the works" and gambled on calling seven notrump.

Against seven notrump West led the King of diamonds, which dummy's Ace won. Dummy ran six spade tricks on which South shed two clubs, and the last spade lead automatically squeezed East when down to four hearts and three clubs.

In another minor variation of the two-entry squeeze, the two opposite entries are both in the same suit, thus enabling an auto-matic squeeze to develop whenever the forcing card and the quick entry, accompanied by its squeeze card, are all in one hand.

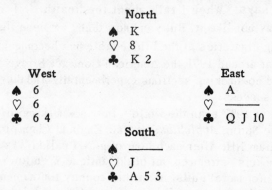

North
♠ K
♡ 8
♣ K 2

West
♠ 6
♡ 6
♣ 6 4

East
♠ A
♡ ——
♣ Q J 10

South
♠ ——
♡ J
♣ A 5 3

At notrump South leads his good heart in order to win four tricks,

It often happens that a player has all the remaining tricks, but lack of entries makes it impossible to realize on them. A squeeze ending will sometimes make up for this dearth of entries.

OVERTAKING AUTOMATIC SQUEEZE

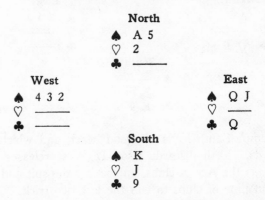

At notrump South holds three winners in his two hands, but the unfortunate spade situation would make it impossible for him to capture more than two tricks, if the heart lead did not squeeze East automatically. If East elects to discard a spade, North overtakes South's King in order to win the last trick with the five of spades. An Overtaking Squeeze may be either automatic as above, or one-way; but the Jettison Squeezes, based on a reverse overtaking idea, are always one-way.

THE FABULOUS FIFTY-TWO
(Concluded from page 50)

♠ K Q J   ♡ K Q J   ◇ K Q J   ♣ K Q J

"An', Mister Mayor, th' twelve w'at is called face cards is twelve months in a year, an' twelve at Last Supper with Jesus.

◇ 3   ♣ 6   ♡ 5

"The three hunnert sixty-five* spots on my fifty-two cards remind me of three hunert sixty-five days in a year and the fifty-two cards remind me it's fifty-two weeks an' fifty-two Sundays in a year."

"Now, sir, kin I go free?"

"Boy," the Mayor said, "You is free born!"

---

* Apparently 365 is arrived at by counting jack as 11 pips, queen as 12 and king as 13; but this brings the total to 364, not 365. Presumably the joker is also counted, as one pip, bringing the total to the desired 365, except on leap year (29 Feb) when the joker is not used.—Editor

JETTISON SQUEEZE

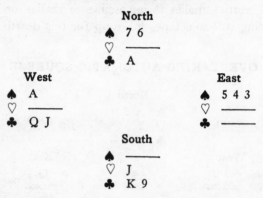

North
♠ 7 6
♡ —
♣ A

West
♠ A
♡ —
♣ Q J

East
♠ 5 4 3
♡ —
♣ —

South
♠ —
♡ J
♣ K 9

At notrump South leads his good heart, and whichever suit West discards, North discards also. If West releases his club, North *jettisons* the Ace of clubs, unblocking the suit and enabling the King and nine of clubs to win the last two tricks.

This jettison manoeuvre may be repeated. Take the above endplay one move earlier:

REPEATED-JETTISON SQUEEZE

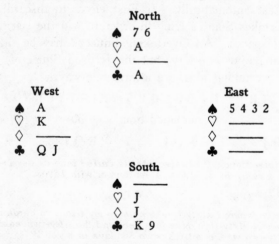

North
♠ 7 6
♡ A
◇ —
♣ A

West
♠ A
♡ K
◇ —
♣ Q J

East
♠ 5 4 3 2
♡ —
◇ —
♣ —

South
♠ —
♡ J
◇ J
♣ K 9

South first leads the Jack of diamonds. Whichever suit, hearts or clubs, West discards, North discards also. West's best defence is to discard a heart, whereupon, as before, South cashes his now good Jack of hearts to repeat the jettison squeeze.

Preparatory Squeeze

As the name suggests, a Preparatory Squeeze *prepares* the ground for another play that takes place *after* the squeeze itself has been completed. The play following the squeeze may be another squeeze, a strip, or a simple play like suiting out (establishing a suit by straight leads), or finessing.

ONE-WAY SQUEEZE SUITOUT

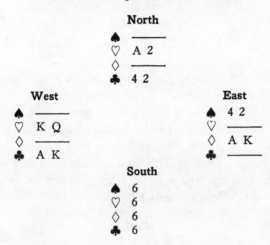

North
♠ ———
♡ A 2
◇ ———
♣ 4 2

West
♠ ———
♡ K Q
◇ ———
♣ A K

East
♠ 4 2
♡ ———
◇ A K
♣ ———

South
♠ 6
♡ 6
◇ 6
♣ 6

At notrump South, requiring three tricks, leads his good six of spades, forcing West to discard a good club. Next South sets up or *suits out* a club trick. Note that this squeeze defies the hidebound rule laid down by minor writers, that one always requires all but one trick in order to squeeze successfully. While this preliminary endplay has two apparent losers at the outset, the unique Automatic Squeeze Suitout below has three losers.

ESCAPE

It was gruesome for my twosome;
I landed in four spades doubled.
I was sure to endure
A set of five greatly troubled.

At the finish, it was sinnish,
West had three cards and I had one.
I got off free of penalty;
The misdeal rule was so much fun!

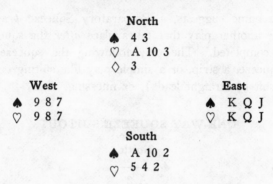

North
♠ 4 3
♡ A 10 3
◇ 3

West
♠ 9 8 7
♡ 9 8 7

East
♠ K Q J
♡ K Q J

South
♠ A 10 2
♡ 5 4 2

Diamonds are trumps, and North, wanting four tricks, leads his diamond, on which South sheds a heart. East is automatically squeezed. Whichever suit East pares down to two cards, South loses a trick therein immediately, establishing its ten   for the fourth trick. Of course, this ending is rare because it depends on finding tierce minor in both vital suits massed in one adverse hand. This endplay comes from a hand shown us by Emanuel Lasker, former World's Chess Champion.

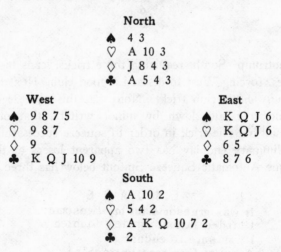

North
♠ 4 3
♡ A 10 3
◇ J 8 4 3
♣ A 5 4 3

West
♠ 9 8 7 5
♡ 9 8 7
◇ 9
♣ K Q J 10 9

East
♠ K Q J 6
♡ K Q J 6
◇ 6 5
♣ 8 7 6

South
♠ A 10 2
♡ 5 4 2
◇ A K Q 10 7 2
♣ 2

East dealt and bid one spade, Lasker playing South doubled, West two clubs, North doubled, East two hearts, South jumped to four diamonds, and North bid five diamonds, closing the auction.

West led the King of clubs, and the hand looks impossible for more than ten tricks even by the wildest stretch of the imagination. Mr. Lasker won the trick with dummy's Ace, trumped a club in his own hand with a top diamond, overtook the ten of diamonds with the Jack, trumped another club in his own hand with an honor, overtook the seven of diamonds with dummy's eightspot, and trumped the last club in his own hand with his last trump honor to unblock trumps. Two more diamond leads squeezed East automatically, and South set up his game-going trick in whichever major suit East weakened.

The deal is one of those fantastic affairs where many adverse cards had to be placed exactly in order to make game possible. South had to find third round control of both major suits held by one opponent exclusively,—the adversary to be squeezed had to hold in both suits either the three missing honors of each suit, or his partner couldn't hold more than two cards thereof,—and in addition the nine of trumps had to fall on the first trump lead! P. Hal Sims used to say that no matter how impossible a hand may look, assume that certain key cards will be placed so that you can make your contract, and you will be surprised how many times your foresight will be rewarded. Mr. Lasker considered this hand so difficult that he published it as a double dummy problem!

Queen doubleton, Russian style

A squeeze can prepare the way for a finesse ending. Usually the squeeze is compounded, but a simple squeeze finesse follows:

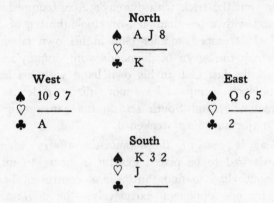

North
♠ A J 8
♡ —
♣ K

West
♠ 10 9 7
♡ —
♣ A

East
♠ Q 6 5
♡ —
♣ 2

South
♠ K 3 2
♡ J
♣ —

At notrump South, requiring all four tricks, leads his good heart. West must shed a spade and North his now useless club, leaving East's Queen of spades defenceless when North gets in with the King and leads the Jack to finesse. If East covers, West's ten and nine drop and the eightspot becomes good on the third round of the suit. This is based on a *scoop finesse*.

A squeeze strip is an elimination play that has been prepared by a squeeze play. Contrary to what has been said about the rarity of this type of ending, it appears with surprising frequency.

SQUEEZE FORK STRIP

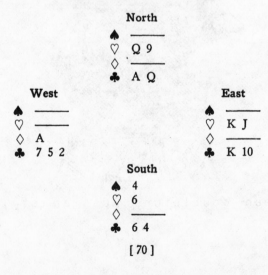

North
♠ —
♡ Q 9
◇ —
♣ A Q

West
♠ —
♡ —
◇ A
♣ 7 5 2

East
♠ —
♡ K J
◇ —
♣ K 10

South
♠ 4
♡ 6
◇ —
♣ 6 4

[70]

Spades are trumps and South, wishing three tricks, leads his last spade on which dummy sheds a low heart. East must discard a heart to guard the King of clubs, and South throws East in with a heart to make him lead up to dummy's Ace-Queen of clubs. Note the pretty way this ending became marked and was developed in the original deal.

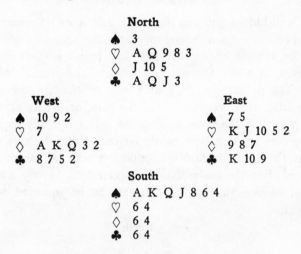

North
♠ 3
♡ A Q 9 8 3
◇ J 10 5
♣ A Q J 3

West
♠ 10 9 2
♡ 7
◇ A K Q 3 2
♣ 8 7 5 2

East
♠ 7 5
♡ K J 10 5 2
◇ 9 8 7
♣ K 10 9

South
♠ A K Q J 8 6 4
♡ 6 4
◇ 6 4
♣ 6 4

South deals and bids three spades, West passes, North bids four hearts, and East doubles. East's action is not aimed at defeating four hearts, because he knows only too well that South will shift back to his safe and solid spade suit, but East wants to inform his partner that he can take care of hearts defensively with a probable trick on the side, so that West can double four spades on a couple of tricks. South rebids to four spades. West, now properly advised by East's delicate informatory double, doubles for penalties, and all pass.

West leads the King then Queen of diamonds, and as East refuses to echo by playing his seven then eightspot, showing the nine also, West shifts to the seven of hearts. As East doubled four hearts, he must hold the two missing Kings and dummy's finesses are both losers. Declarer, therefore, plays dummy's Ace of hearts and runs all his trumps, forcing East to discard down to the lone King of hearts and the King-ten of clubs. Declarer then throws East in with a heart, forcing him to lead up to dummy's Ace-Queen of clubs.

West's defence was too wooden to obtain the best result. He should have switched to his singleton heart at Trick Two to defeat the contract.

Further examples of preparatory squeezes will be given in Chapter Fifteen.

Hidden Squeezes

A well hidden squeeze is usually a Prepared Squeeze wherein some preliminary manoeuvre prepares the squeeze ending. It is just the reverse of the arrangement found in the Preparatory Squeezes, in which the squeeze prepares the ground for another play. The preparation play of a hidden squeeze may be a long range affair that occurs early in the play, or it may occur on the trick preceding the squeeze, as below. It frequently happens that the squeeze position is so neatly concealed that declarer misses it. Declarer's failure to find one opponent with all the proper high cards is often the basis of this concealment. Merely transferring control of one suit to the opponent to be squeezed solves the problem.

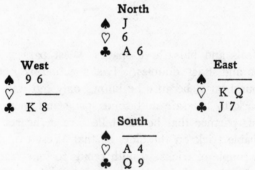

At notrump South, wishing all four tricks, leads the Queen of clubs, in order to *transfer* club control to East, who is squeezed one way by North's lead of the Jack of spades. This method of hiding a squeeze is a favorite trick of the problem composers. Note that if North has the lead originally, he can win all four tricks by a Squeeze Pick-up.

Mr. Oswald Jacoby, whom we rated as the all-American Bridge Champion in the January 1937 issue of *Judge Magazine*, made a beautiful transferred squeeze combined with a Vienna Coup (see Coups) on this deal:

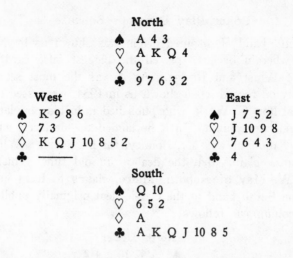

North
♠ A 4 3
♡ A K Q 4
◇ 9
♣ 9 7 6 3 2

West
♠ K 9 8 6
♡ 7 3
◇ K Q J 10 8 5 2
♣ —

East
♠ J 7 5 2
♡ J 10 9 8
◇ 7 6 4 3
♣ 4

South
♠ Q 10
♡ 6 5 2
◇ A
♣ A K Q J 10 8 5

Playing South, Mr. Jacoby dealt and bid one club, West jumped to four diamonds, North six clubs, and South seven clubs, closing the wholesale auction.

West led the King of diamonds, calling South's Ace. As West's jump bid indicated great length in diamonds, probably seven at least, accompanied by the King of spades, West was well marked to hold fewer hearts than East, and therefore the heart suit stood little chance of breaking three and three for declarer. Therefore, if declarer is to squeeze out his thirteenth trick, he must place adverse control of both hearts and spades in one adverse hand. Obviously, nothing can be done about transferring heart control, but if West holds the King of spades and East the Jack, declarer can transfer the control of spades to East by leading the Queen of spades and forcing West to cover. Hence Mr. Jacoby won a trump trick and led the Queen of spades, intending to let it run if West failed to cover, but West covered and the dummy's Ace won the trick. This manoeuvre also accomplished the second purpose of unblocking the spade suit, and establishing a spade winner with an opponent in preparation to squeeze it out later, a play called the Vienna Coup. Mr. Jacoby next ran all his trumps, keeping in dummy ♡ A-K-Q-4, in his own hand ♠ 10 and ♡ 6-5-2, and East, guarding these two suits with ♠ J and ♡ J-10-9-8, had an impossible discard to make. The late Louis H. Watson published this deal in his fine book, *Watson on the Play of the Hand at Contract Bridge.*

Poker Play Develops Squeeze

A pretty hand of disputed origin was shown us by Norman Bonney, wherein declarer played the biggest false card in the history of Whist and Bridge. As it was the most sensational Poker play on record when shown us in 1934, we passed it on to the late Milton C. Work, who published it in his popular newspaper syndicate column. In it he lauded the declarer, whom he mistakenly thought was Mr. Bonney, for his genius. While Mr. Bonney now claims that the deal is an old time Whist hand, Charles W. May of Auburn, Maine, claims to have held and played the South hand in the classic deal originally published in Work's column, as follows:

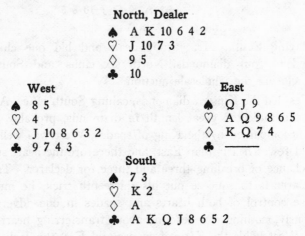

```
                    North, Dealer
                    ♠ A K 10 6 4 2
                    ♡ J 10 7 3
                    ◇ 9 5
                    ♣ 10

        West                            East
        ♠ 8 5                           ♠ Q J 9
        ♡ 4                             ♡ A Q 9 8 6 5
        ◇ J 10 8 6 3 2                  ◇ K Q 7 4
        ♣ 9 7 4 3                       ♣ ——

                    South
                    ♠ 7 3
                    ♡ K 2
                    ◇ A
                    ♣ A K Q J 8 6 5 2
```

With both sides vulnerable, North dealt and bid one spade, East, holding freakish distribution, conservatively overcalled at only two hearts, and Mr. Bonney, in his typical dramatic style, jumped to six clubs. This bid coasted around to East, who doubled it, and Mr. Bonney promptly redoubled, closing the auction.

West led the four of hearts and East played his Ace. Seeing the trey and deuce of hearts in his own two hands, Mr. Bonney realized that the opening heart lead, the four, was a singleton, and that his King of hearts would surely be trumped by West, defeating the contract. Hence Mr. Bonney produced his elephantine false card by nonchalantly tossing his King of hearts on the Ace immediately!

As this Poker play made East think that West held the deuce of hearts, East switched to the King of diamonds, giving Mr. Bonney his small slam. When Mr. Bonney led his last club, keeping the A-K-10 of spades in dummy, East, down to the Q-J-9 of spades and the only high heart, was automatically squeezed. Still under the delusion that his partner held the deuce of hearts, East discarded his last heart, giving Mr. Bonney the immense satisfaction of winning his vital slam trick with this lowly card!

Futile Defence

Undertrumping to avoid a squeeze has been lauded as fine defensive play by minor writers, but we have found that this line of defence is futile to ward off a True Squeeze. Undertrumping only postpones the evil moment when Old Hiram Squeeze comes around like the much hated tax collector.

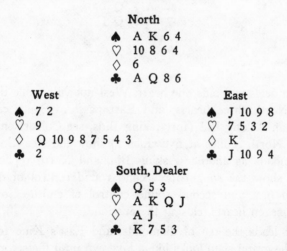

```
                    North
                 ♠  A K 6 4
                 ♡  10 8 6 4
                 ◇  6
                 ♣  A Q 8 6
    West                          East
 ♠  7 2                        ♠  J 10 9 8
 ♡  9                          ♡  7 5 3 2
 ◇  Q 10 9 8 7 5 4 3           ◇  K
 ♣  2                          ♣  J 10 9 4
                 South, Dealer
                 ♠  Q 5 3
                 ♡  A K Q J
                 ◇  A J
                 ♣  K 7 5 3
```

South dealt and bid one heart, West not vulnerable jumped to four diamonds, North optimistically leaped to six hearts, and South, holding solid trumps and the Ace of diamonds, could not resist bidding seven hearts, closing the auction.

West led the ten of diamonds, and East's King forced the Ace. After winning two trump leads, South carefully trumped high the Jack of diamonds in dummy, and lo and behold, East discarded a low trump! According to the original author of this hand, this "clever play avoided a squeeze in the black suits and defeated the contract." Actually, East merely put off the evil moment of the automatic squeeze when South led his last trump.

But let's mix the cards around a bit so that we can see what the author of the original deal was really trying to prove.

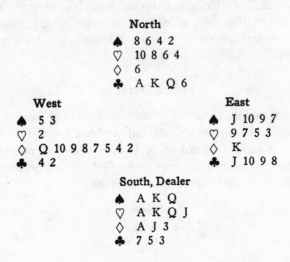

North
♠ 8 6 4 2
♡ 10 8 6 4
♢ 6
♣ A K Q 6

West
♠ 5 3
♡ 2
♢ Q 10 9 8 7 5 4 2
♣ 4 2

East
♠ J 10 9 7
♡ 9 7 5 3
♢ K
♣ J 10 9 8

South, Dealer
♠ A K Q
♡ A K Q J
♢ A J 3
♣ 7 5 3

South deals and bids one heart, West not vulnerable three diamonds, North three hearts, and East passes. South calls four clubs as an Asking Bid (for Asking Bids, see Culbertson's "Gold Book"), North replies at five clubs to show the Ace, South calls five diamonds as another Asking Bid, and North replies at six clubs to show the sought-for second round control of diamonds and both first and second round control of clubs. South now ventures seven hearts, closing the auction.

West leads the ten of diamonds, and East's King forces the Ace. The grand slam looks like a laydown until the second trump lead reveals East's ability to overtrump one diamond ruff by dummy. Therefore, declarer must set up a black suit thirteener for one diamond discard. Dummy trumps high a diamond, and East *undertrumps*. Two more trump leads by South now reveal why East's underruffing play is a winner. Declarer's last trump lead completely emasculates the dummy, forced to discard before East. The squeeze is isomeric and the contract is defeated.

False Squeezes

While the False Squeezes, or Pseudo Squeezes as they are also called, have no real squeeze position, the unfortunate adversary is deceived into thinking one exists.

FALSE AUTOMATIC SQUEEZE

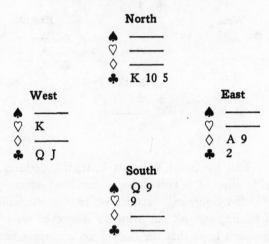

```
                   North
                ♠ ─────
                ♡ ─────
                ◇ ─────
                ♣ K 10 5
    West                        East
 ♠ ─────                      ♠ ─────
 ♡ K                          ♡ ─────
 ◇ ─────                      ◇ A 9
 ♣ Q J                        ♣ 2
                   South
                ♠ Q 9
                ♡ 9
                ◇ ─────
                ♣ ─────
```

When South leads a good spade at notrump, West, fearing the clubs in the North hand, discards the high heart. West fears the next best heart and a club are with South for the automatic squeeze position, and hopes South holds a club and a diamond.

In another variation of the False Squeezes, an opponent makes a wrong discard that enables a real squeeze to develop against his side. A good example of this will be shown in Chapter Fourteen on Defence in Squeezes.

MONEY BRIDGE
My partner's a jolly good fellow,
Though often he sticks out his neck.
He pays no heed to what I bellow,
So we end up by writing a check.

The Discard Guessing Squeeze does not even simulate a squeeze, because no possible squeeze position can exist. It is based on some such ending as the one below:

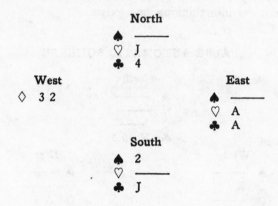

```
                        North
                        ♠ ——
                        ♡ J
                        ♣ 4
West                                        East
◇ 3 2                                       ♠ ——
                                            ♡ A
                                            ♣ A
                        South
                        ♠ 2
                        ♡ ——
                        ♣ J
```

A spade lead by South compels East, the declarer, to *guess* which Ace to discard. This squeeze has been jocosely referred to as the "Coffin Squeeze," because we have consistently made a practice of leading out all our winners whenever we hold a sure loser, on the slim hope that the "dope" on our right or left might discard wrongly. And we have been pleasantly surprised at the number of tricks that we have pilfered this way!

"In all the bridge-game places,
The rats get at the aces."

Chain smokers and fat players die young:

Coffin's Law

Squeezed by Protest

An induced Coffin Squeeze was stillborn in the Pair Finals, 10 October 1937, in the Northeastern Championships of the then newly formed American Bridge Association, held in Boston, Mass. by the Towne Club.

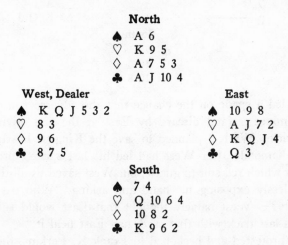

North
♠ A 6
♡ K 9 5
♢ A 7 5 3
♣ A J 10 4

West, Dealer
♠ K Q J 5 3 2
♡ 8 3
♢ 9 6
♣ 8 7 5

East
♠ 10 9 8
♡ A J 7 2
♢ K Q J 4
♣ Q 3

South
♠ 7 4
♡ Q 10 6 4
♢ 10 8 2
♣ K 9 6 2

The bidding, both sides vulnerable.

West	North	East	South
Pass	1 ♢	Pass	1 NT
Pass	Pass	Double	All pass

West's pass of East's Takeout Double was dangerous, because East delayed his double, indicating not more than three honor-tricks. But West, lured by six easy spade tricks if East held the guarded Ace, couldn't resist the temptation to pass for penalties.

West led the King of spades. Playing South as declarer, we saw that the contract was probably easy to fulfill if the Queen of clubs could be picked up. We won the spade opening with the Ace, and led a low heart which the Queen won. Placing the Queen of clubs with East by his double, we took dummy's Ace of clubs and led the Jack to finesse, but the drop of the Queen made four club tricks easy. We cashed our seventh trick with the Ace of diamonds to make sure of our doubled contract for a probable top score, leaving this situation:

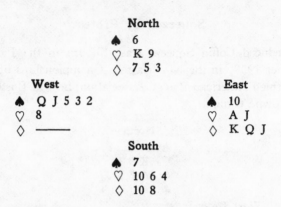

North
- ♠ 6
- ♡ K 9
- ♢ 7 5 3

West
- ♠ Q J 5 3 2
- ♡ 8
- ♢ ———

East
- ♠ 10
- ♡ A J
- ♢ K Q J

South
- ♠ 7
- ♡ 10 6 4
- ♢ 10 8

We led a spade on the chance that the adverse run of spades might induce a fatal discard by East at the end, giving us an extra trick. We had planned to save the King of hearts and the ten of diamonds after West had led his last spade, forcing East to *guess* which red suit to guard; but West saved us all the trouble by carelessly exposing his hand and asking, "Who has the Ace of hearts?" West naively thought that East would surely have won the last trick with that card, had East held it.

We protested and beckoned to Frank K. Perkins, then directing the tournament. His decision awarded us the disputed extra trick!

New Bridge League

The newly formed American Bridge Association was mentioned on page 79. It is the amalgamation of the former American Bridge League and the United States Bridge Association, two rival bodies which held "national" tournaments without mutual recognition. They buried harmful jealousies and unified championship Bridge in the Eastern United States under one organization, whose objects are high ethical standards and equitable geographic representation. The new A.B.A. should recognize or absorb the Pacific Bridge League on the West Coast.

The Northeastern Championships, from which the above deal was cited, was the first tournament of the new association.

Just as this book was about to go to press, the American Bridge Association was found to be the name of an organization of colored players. Hence the name of the new joint organization had to be changed to the American Contract Bridge League.

CHAPTER EIGHT

BASIC DOUBLE SQUEEZES

THE Compound Squeezes comprise that realm of endplays in which every squeeze is a part of another squeeze, or of an elimination, or a coup. One compound squeeze form is the Double Squeeze, so called because it operates on both opponents, forcing one to discard so as to make discarding disastrous for the other. It is in effect a single squeeze in three suits, depending on the discarding of *both* adversaries for its success. One suit common to both opponents, called the *middle suit,* is the backbone of the Double Squeeze, because it occupies the central position straddling them, and it also supplies the quick entry or entries vital to the squeeze. One two-suit squeeze of one opponent follows another two-suit squeeze of the other, often progressively during the play to the same trick.

First Basic Position

We learned in Chapter Six that the three basic squeeze positions were the one-way squeeze, the automatic squeeze, and the trump squeeze.* Likewise there are three basic forms of the double squeeze, which are the double squeeze variations of the above. While the automatic squeeze is the most common basic squeeze, the most common double squeeze is the

---

* Now called the squeeze ruffout. The true trump squeeze is a rare esoteric ending. See *Double Dummy Bridge,* page 35.

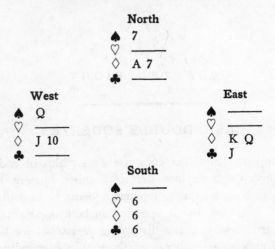

North

♠ 7
♡ ———
◇ A 7
♣ ———

West

♠ Q
♡ ———
◇ J 10
♣ ———

East

♠ ———
♡ ———
◇ K Q
♣ J

South

♠ ———
♡ 6
◇ 6
♣ 6

Hearts are trumps and South, requiring all three tricks, leads his heart. West, squeezed one way, must shed a diamond in order to keep North's spade covered, North discards his now useless spade, and East is squeezed automatically. East must control clubs, and he can't discard a diamond, because his partner has only one diamond left. Note that in this compound the first squeeze is one-way, while the second is purely automatic.

This endplay came from a deal played in a large tournament at which only one pair in twenty made the grand slam, although nearly everybody bid it.

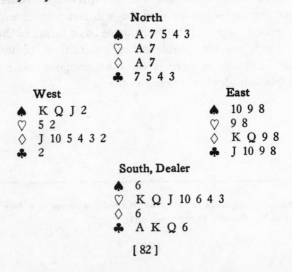

North

♠ A 7 5 4 3
♡ A 7
◇ A 7
♣ 7 5 4 3

West

♠ K Q J 2
♡ 5 2
◇ J 10 5 4 3 2
♣ 2

East

♠ 10 9 8
♡ 9 8
◇ K Q 9 8
♣ J 10 9 8

South, Dealer

♠ 6
♡ K Q J 10 6 4 3
◇ 6
♣ A K Q 6

South dealt with both sides vulnerable and -bid three hearts. West and East always passed. North bid three spades, South four diamonds as an Asking Bid, North five notrump to show three Aces, and as this was all South wanted to hear, he jumped to seven hearts.

West led the King of spades, driving out dummy's Ace. The contract looks like a pianola. Wherever the contract failed, two rounds of trumps were pulled, and declarer had a rude awakening when clubs failed to tumble well. Declarer ran all his trumps to develop the squeeze, but East, seeing the double squeeze ending coming, dropped all his diamonds like hot potatoes, trusting West to hold them, while East kept control of both black suits. Hence fine defence defeated the contract.

The one wise declarer made a remarkable safety play, the preparation play for the double squeeze. In order to protect himself against the possible poor division of adverse clubs, declarer won the first trick with the Ace of spades and *immediately* trumped a spade. He won the second round of hearts with dummy's Ace and trumped another spade, pulling all East's, thereby cutting off East's escape from the double-squeeze ending. Declarer ran three club tricks, then all his trumps, squeezing West one way down to one diamond, then East automatically.

Second Basic Position

In the Automatic Double Squeeze, both squeezing operations are simultaneously automatic. Even if either defender be given the opportunity to discard before his partner, they have no escape, because, whichever defender discards first, leaves his partner in trouble.

AUTOMATIC DOUBLE SQUEEZE

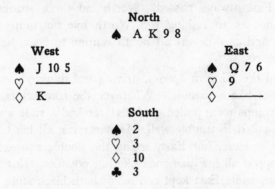

North
♠ A K 9 8

West
♠ J 10 5
♡ ——
◇ K

East
♠ Q 7 6
♡ 9
◇ ——

South
♠ 2
♡ 3
◇ 10
♣ 3

At notrump South, requiring all four tricks, leads his good club on which North sheds a spade. East and West are both squeezed simultaneously. Neither can shed his top red card, and both cannot discard spades.

This particular squeeze is very rare, because the forcing card and both pinning cards must all be massed in the forcing hand, an arrangement necessitating, for lack of card space, a "recessed" entry suit to partner's hand, that is, a suit containing a singleton in the forcing hand opposite two or more quick tricks.

This is the only double automatic we have ever found in actual play, which appeared at Bonnie Oaks Inn and Camps at Fairlee, Vermont, 27 July 1936, when we acted as Bridge host there.

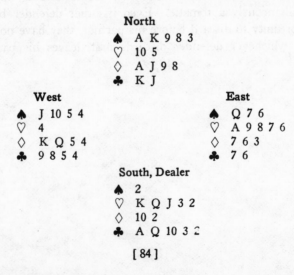

North
♠ A K 9 8 3
♡ 10 5
◇ A J 9 8
♣ K J

West
♠ J 10 5 4
♡ 4
◇ K Q 5 4
♣ 9 8 5 4

East
♠ Q 7 6
♡ A 9 8 7 6
◇ 7 6 3
♣ 7 6

South, Dealer
♠ 2
♡ K Q J 3 2
◇ 10 2
♣ A Q 10 3 2

[84]

South dealt and bid one heart, playing North we bid two spades, South three clubs, North three diamonds, South three hearts, and North six notrump , which call East unwisely doubled, ending the auction.

With all suits bid against him, East opened with the seven of clubs in order to push the lead *through* a bid suit, and North won. The ten of hearts drove out East's Ace, and East led another club, which North won. North played the Ace of diamonds to unblock the forthcoming double squeeze, a manoeuvre called the Vienna Coup. South ran three heart tricks and three club tricks, automatically squeezing both distressed opponents out of their otherwise slam-saving trick.

The most famous Automatic Double Squeeze in Bridge History occurred in the following classic deal originally published by Ernest Bergholt in his book, *Royal Auction Bridge*.

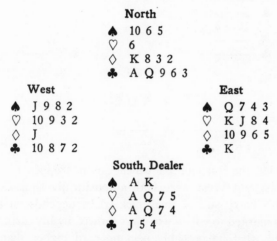

North
- ♠ 10 6 5
- ♡ 6
- ◊ K 8 3 2
- ♣ A Q 9 6 3

West
- ♠ J 9 8 2
- ♡ 10 9 3 2
- ◊ J
- ♣ 10 8 7 2

East
- ♠ Q 7 4 3
- ♡ K J 8 4
- ◊ 10 9 6 5
- ♣ K

South, Dealer
- ♠ A K
- ♡ A Q 7 5
- ◊ A Q 7 4
- ♣ J 5 4

At Auction Bridge South bid one notrump and all passed. This is Ernest Bergholt's bidding, and we don't guarantee it. When the deal was played in a local Contract game of prepared hands, at one table the bidding went thus: South one diamond, North three diamonds, and South jumped to six notrump , closing the auction. We don't guarantee this bidding either.

West led the deuce of spades and East put up the Queen, marking West's original lead from four headed by the Jack. South won and played the Ace of diamonds, and West failed on the King play. This renounce was the key play that revealed the adverse distribution and unlocked the door to grand slam for declarer. It marked West with four low hearts and four low clubs, as with four headed by a King or five or more of either suit, he would have led it originally in preference to the weaker Jack-high spade suit. Declarer played the Ace of clubs to catch East's now marked lone King, returned to his own hand with the Jack of clubs, played the Queen of diamonds, and the Ace of spades to unblock the forthcoming squeeze position (Vienna Coup), and ran two club tricks, finessing the nine. leaving:

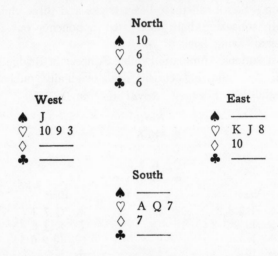

North
♠ 10
♡ 6
◇ 8
♣ 6

West
♠ J
♡ 10 9 3
◇ ———
♣ ———

East
♠ ———
♡ K J 8
◇ 10
♣ ———

South
♠ ———
♡ A Q 7
◇ 7
♣ ———

North led the last club on which South dropped his idle diamond. East and West were both automatically squeezed. Note that South's entry suit of two quick tricks depends on a finesse, which was marked to win when West showed by his early renounce in diamonds that he probably held no card higher than a Jack.

Third Basic Position

Like the single trump squeeze, the Double Trump Squeeze is purely automatic. *

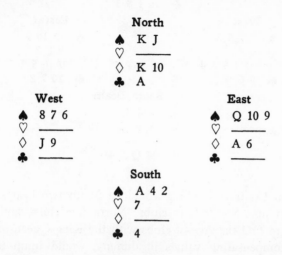

```
                        North
                      ♠ K J
                      ♡ ——
                      ◊ K 10
                      ♣ A
        West                              East
      ♠ 8 7 6                           ♠ Q 10 9
      ♡ ——                              ♡ ——
      ◊ J 9                             ◊ A 6
      ♣ ——                              ♣ ——
                        South
                      ♠ A 4 2
                      ♡ 7
                      ◊ ——
                      ♣ 4
```

Hearts are trumps and South, wanting all five tricks, leads a club. West must discard a spade, as shedding a diamond would enable North to lead the King through East's Ace and make or set up a diamond trick depending on the cover. Now East cannot discard a spade, and blanking the Ace of diamonds makes the King a winner, after South trumps a low diamond.

Had North the lead, East would have had to discard a spade and leave West without defence. This rare and exotic endplay came from a classic deal of early Auction Bridge days.

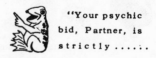

"Your psychic bid, Partner, is strictly .....:.

* In 1975 called the *double squeeze ruffout.*

North
- ♠ K J 5
- ♡ 5 3
- ◇ K 10 7 3
- ♣ A J 8 3

West
- ♠ 8 7 6 3
- ♡ 6 4
- ◇ Q J 9 8 4
- ♣ 9 6

East
- ♠ Q 10 9
- ♡ 9 8 2
- ◇ A 6 5 2
- ♣ 10 7 2

South, Dealer
- ♠ A 4 2
- ♡ A K Q J 10 7
- ◇ ——
- ♣ K Q 5 4

Modern Contract bidding would be South two hearts, North three notrump., South four clubs, North five clubs, and South, expecting to find the Ace of clubs with the King-Queen of spades or with compensating values in dummy, would jump to seven hearts, which contract requires the double trump squeeze to fulfill.

West led the Queen of diamonds and the problem was to catch the Queen of spades. The finesse of the Jack offered only a 50% chance to win, but, to play for the double trump squeeze made the contract sure. Dummy had to *refuse* to cover the Queen of diamonds. Declarer trumped her, ran four trump tricks, and won the fourth round of clubs in dummy, effecting the squeeze. And in concluding we might add that, since the double squeeze is the perfect hold of both opponents, it is truly the Full Nelson of Bridge!

. . . for the birds ! "

CHAPTER NINE

DOUBLE SQUEEZE VARIATIONS

Douche squeezes appear in actual play under widely diversified conditions, and therefore occur in various forms. Trying to develop a double squeeze instead of a single squeeze is sometimes a good safety play, because it includes more possible adverse distributions.

Culbertson's Lucky Squeeze

Note carefully in the first diagram of Chapter Seven how Ely Culbertson played a Criss-Cross Squeeze in his famous match against Sidney S. Lenz. We repeat the hand here: (See page 62.)

```
                    North
                 ♠  A 2
                 ♡  9 7 5 4
                 ◊  A 7 4
                 ♣  A 6 5 4
        West                        East
     ♠  7 5                      ♠  8 4 3
     ♡  K Q 10 3                 ♡  A 2
     ◊  Q 5                      ◊  J 10 9 6 3 2
     ♣  J 10 8 7 3               ♣  K 9
                    South
                 ♠  K Q J 10 9 6
                 ♡  J 8 6
                 ◊  K 8
                 ♣  Q 2
```

Against two spades, South's final call, the defence ran three heart tricks and led a diamond. Had West held three, four, or five diamonds, he could have guarded diamonds and hearts, defeating the criss-cross squeeze. Declarer should have played for the one-way double squeeze position to guard against this contingency. Instead of winning the diamond trick with the dummy's Ace, he should have won it in his own hand with the *King,* and next played dummy's Ace of clubs to unblock for the forthcoming squeeze position (Vienna Coup). Now diamonds would have become the middle suit of the double squeeze. Had East held the King of clubs, running all the trumps could not have failed to squeeze automatically, after West had been squeezed one way in his marked high heart control and down to one diamond, in case he had held more than two diamonds originally.

Either-Or Squeeze

Another variety of a selective single squeeze, having no possibility of being double, is based solely on concealment of forces. It is called the Either-Or Squeeze, because its play squeezes *either* West *or* East. It is exactly like a double squeeze in form and play, except that there are only enough adverse cards of the middle suit for one opponent to guard it, and hence only one opponent is squeezed. Declarer counts opponents' hands carefully in order to determine which opponent he is to squeeze at the end.

North
♠ Q 7 5 3 2
♡ 5
◇ K 7 5
♣ A Q 7 5

South, Dealer
♠ K
♡ A K Q J 10 9 8
◇ A 9 8 3 2
♣ ————

With both sides vulnerable South, played by Norman Bonney at Mrs. Charles Geissler's Duplicate in Boston, Mass., dealt and bid one heart, West one spade, North one notrump, and East two clubs. South called two diamonds, North three diamonds, and South jumped to six hearts without further ado, closing the auction.

West led the Ace of spades, then the six of clubs. Another losing trick in diamonds threatened the contract, because the Queen of spades and the Ace of clubs offered declarer only two diamond discards, and he needed three. Of course, declarer might have tried to finesse the Queen of clubs, but that play was doomed to lose, because opponents' vulnerable overcalling with few high cards marked opponents with great length in their bid suits, and East was practically certain to hold the King of clubs.

But the marked location of the adverse black suits opened the way for an either-or squeeze,—declarer was able to squeeze *either* West *or* East, depending upon whichever adversary held three or more diamonds. Dummy won Trick Two with the Ace of clubs. South trumped a low spade as a safety measure, to strip East down to one spade at most in case East happened to hold three originally (actually he held only one), and South ran all but one trump, leaving this situation:

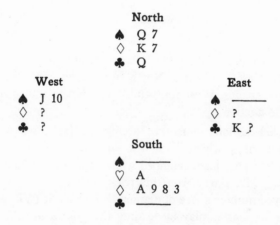

```
                    North
                 ♠  Q 7
                 ◇  K 7
                 ♣  Q
    West                          East
 ♠  J 10                       ♠  ————
 ◇  ?                          ◇  ?
 ♣  ?                          ♣  K ?
                    South
                 ♠  ————
                 ♡  A
                 ◇  A 9 8 3
                 ♣  ————
```

When South led his last trump, West was squeezed only if he then held three diamonds, because he would have had to give up a diamond to defend spades. But West discarded a club, showing he was not squeezed, North discarded his low spade now revealed useless, and East a club. East held the King of clubs and three diamonds, according to declarer's count. Dummy captured the lead with the King of diamonds, and led the Queen of spades, really squeezing East. He had to discard his King of clubs, or break diamonds.

Mr. John F. Barry, former president of the Boston Chess Club, Chess Editor of the *Boston Evening Transcript,* and Chess player of note, showed us a one-way double squeeze that had to be developed by transferring control of one suit across the table to the proper opponent's hand.

North
- ♠ K 9 3
- ♡ A 7 2
- ◇ A 10 4 2
- ♣ Q 9 2

West
- ♠ A 6 2
- ♡ J 8 6 5 4
- ◇ 6
- ♣ J 6 4 3

East
- ♠ 8
- ♡ Q 10 9
- ◇ Q J 5 3
- ♣ A K 8 7 5

South
- ♠ Q J 10 7 5 4
- ♡ K 3
- ◇ K 9 8 7
- ♣ 10

With both sides vulnerable East dealt and bid one club, South one spade, West two hearts, North two spades, East three hearts, South three spades, West four clubs, and North four spades, concluding the auction.

West led his lone diamond, forcing the Jack then King. Mr. Barry led a trump which West won with his Ace. West put East in with a low club lead, trumped a diamond return, and switched to a heart. Mr. Barry won this trick with his King, led trumps twice, played dummy's Ace of diamonds to unblock (Vienna Coup), and made his master play by leading the *Queen* of clubs, forcing East to cover. South trumped and thus established the Jack of clubs as the top club with West, where it could be used to make West discard down to one heart at the end.

As East was marked with the high diamonds during the play and with the Ace-King of clubs for his club bid, transferring the control of clubs to West by leading dummy's Queen was a beautiful play to make the game.

We have seen and played quite a number of the basic variety of the one-way double squeeze, but we have seen a different form requiring a double entry on two occasions only. The first one was played by D. Lenox Barnes of Fitzwilliam, New Hampshire.

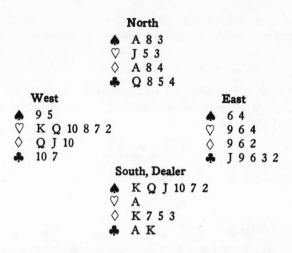

North
♠ A 8 3
♡ J 5 3
◇ A 8 4
♣ Q 8 5 4

West
♠ 9 5
♡ K Q 10 8 7 2
◇ Q J 10
♣ 10 7

East
♠ 6 4
♡ 9 6 4
◇ 9 6 2
♣ J 9 6 3 2

South, Dealer
♠ K Q J 10 7 2
♡ A
◇ K 7 5 3
♣ A K

Mr. Barnes playing South dealt and bid two spades. Playing North we jumped to four notrump and South called seven spades closing the auction.

West's opening lead of the King of hearts went to South's Ace. South led trumps twice, clubs twice, entered dummy with a trump, discarded a low diamond on the Queen of clubs, trumped a low heart, and led a trump leaving:

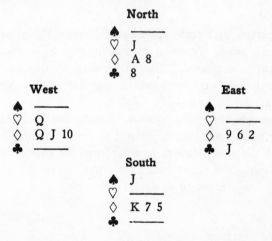

North
♠ ———
♡ J
◇ A 8
♣ 8

West
♠ ———
♡ Q
◇ Q J 10
♣ ———

East
♠ ———
♡ ———
◇ 9 6 2
♣ J

South
♠ J
♡ ———
◇ K 7 5
♣ ———

The two single pinning cards, the Jack of hearts and the eight-spot of clubs, are both in one hand, and the forcing card with the quick entry and squeezing card in the other. This inverted arrangement of the elements requires two quick entries, one in each hand, which is characteristic of this Double-Entry Double Squeeze (One-Way). South led his last spade squeezing a diamond out of West, dummy shed the now useless pinning heart, and East gave up the ghost.

The 1937 New England Championship held by the Boston Chess Club in Boston, Mass., produced the identical endplay in the Open Pairs event.

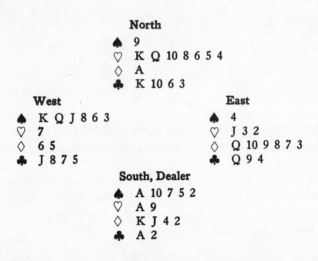

```
                          North
                       ♠ 9
                       ♡ K Q 10 8 6 5 4
                       ◇ A
                       ♣ K 10 6 3
           West                          East
        ♠ K Q J 8 6 3                 ♠ 4
        ♡ 7                           ♡ J 3 2
        ◇ 6 5                         ◇ Q 10 9 8 7 3
        ♣ J 8 7 5                     ♣ Q 9 4
                      South, Dealer
                       ♠ A 10 7 5 2
                       ♡ A 9
                       ◇ K J 4 2
                       ♣ A 2
```

South, played by Gerald Kalesky of Newton, Mass., dealt and bid one spade, which pleased Jack Kushner of Springfield, Mass. playing West who passed. Harold Druker of Brookline, Mass. playing North bid two hearts and Edgar Tierney of Springfield, originator of the famous TNT Club and TNT System (Tierney No Trump) playing East, passed. South bid three diamonds, North four hearts, and South jumped to six notrump , closing the auction. While seven hearts is a laydown by reason of South's ability to trump the third round of clubs, seven notrump produces a much better score at match point play.

Hoping to establish the setting trick in spades, West opened with the King which South won with his Ace. Declarer played the Ace of diamonds, Ace of hearts, King of diamonds and led all but one heart leaving:

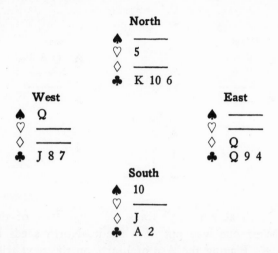

North
♠ ——
♡ 5
◇ ——
♣ K 10 6

West
♠ Q
♡ ——
◇ ——
♣ J 8 7

East
♠ ——
♡ ——
◇ Q
♣ Q 9 4

South
♠ 10
♡ ——
◇ J
♣ A 2

When North led the last heart, East had to discard a club in order to protect diamonds, South discarded his now useless diamond, and West was automatically squeezed.

When the preparatory squeeze occurs on a trick previous to the final squeeze trick, the squeeze is termed split, because the two squeezing leads have split the endplay into two separate operations. The inverted arrangement of the elements renders this splitting of the double squeeze into two separate plays necessary.

A Bridge Writer's Blooper

Around 1960 an enterprising Swedish bridge player launched a new monthly bridge magazine *in English*, hoping to invade the British Empire market. Unfortunately his bits of broken English crept into print and one day I spied the following:

"Mrs. Hans Kjellstrom*, the well-known Swedish national player, visited the United States for a year and spent most of her time playing the bridge tournaments. Having won enough points to join the ranks of life masters, in the American Contract Bridge League she became a life mistress."

* Name fictitious.

SPLIT ONE-WAY DOUBLE SQUEEZE

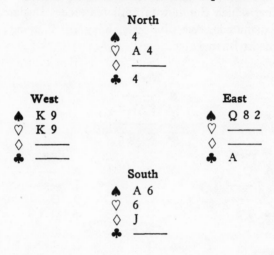

North
♠ 4
♡ A 4
◇ —
♣ 4

West
♠ K 9
♡ K 9
◇ —
♣ —

East
♠ Q 8 2
♡ —
◇ —
♣ A

South
♠ A 6
♡ 6
◇ J
♣ —

When South at notrump leads his good Jack of diamonds squeezing West one way out of a spade, North sheds his now useless heart. Playing the Ace of hearts on the next trick automatically squeezes East.

Inversion of the elements of the Double Automatic Squeeze, as in the One-way Double Squeezes, may split the play into two leads.

SPLIT AUTOMATIC DOUBLE SQUEEZE

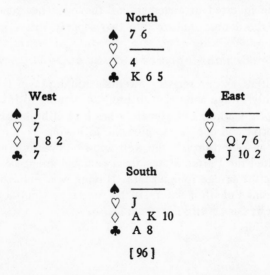

North
♠ 7 6
♡
◇ 4
♣ K 6 5

West
♠ J
♡ 7
◇ J 8 2
♣ 7

East
♠ —
♡ —
◇ Q 7 6
♣ J 10 2

South
♠ —
♡ J
◇ A K 10
♣ A 8

Requiring all six tricks, South led his good heart at notrump , on which North shed a spade, in order to make East disgorge a diamond to protect clubs. The play of the Ace then King of clubs automatically squeezed West. This remarkable play was made by none less than the famous writer, Ben Ames Williams, in this deal:

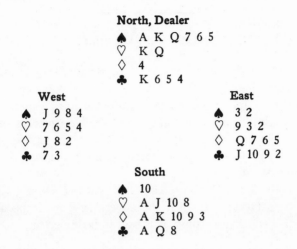

North, Dealer
♠ A K Q 7 6 5
♡ K Q
◇ 4
♣ K 6 5 4

West
♠ J 9 8 4
♡ 7 6 5 4
◇ J 8 2
♣ 7 3

East
♠ 3 2
♡ 9 3 2
◇ Q 7 6 5
♣ J 10 9 2

South
♠ 10
♡ A J 10 8
◇ A K 10 9 3
♣ A Q 8

In a rubber game "somewhere in Maine" North dealt and bid one spade, and Mr. Williams playing South immediately kited to six notrump . North bid seven spades and Mr. Williams returned to notrump at seven odd, closing the short and sweet bidding.

West led the four of hearts which dummy's Queen won, and three winning spade leads found West with a stopper. South shed two diamonds and East a heart. The King of hearts, Queen of clubs, and ten of hearts won the next three tricks, leaving the above described squeeze ending yielding seven notrump . Frank K. Perkins described this hand in the *Boston Herald*.

Dead Wrong by Coffin

Here lies the body of a bridge sneak. Often he'd take a quick sly peek.
He met foul play by a knife long; now he's as dead as he was wrong.

CHAPTER TEN

TRIPLE SQUEEZES

SINCE the early days of Auction Bridge the term, Triple Squeeze, has denoted a squeeze of one opponent guarding three suits. Triple Squeezes constitute the third general type of squeezes. Unlike the basic single and double squeezes on which they are founded, they may produce two extra tricks progressively when the opponent is squeezed again by the lead of the suit which he first "disguarded."

When the Triple Squeeze can thus win two extra tricks, it is said to be perfect; but when the adversary can escape a second squeeze by proper discarding, it is said to be imperfect.

TRIPLE SQUEEZE

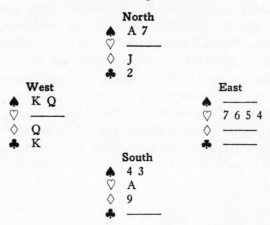

```
                    North
                  ♠ A 7
                  ♡ ―――
                  ◇ J
                  ♣ 2
      West                        East
    ♠ K Q                       ♠ ―――
    ♡ ―――                       ♡ 7 6 5 4
    ◇ Q                         ◇ ―――
    ♣ K                         ♣ ―――
                    South
                  ♠ 4 3
                  ♡ A
                  ◇ 9
                  ♣ ―――
```

When South leads the high heart at notrump , West must accept an automatic squeeze in a black suit in order to win a diamond trick, and to prevent South from operating a one-way squeeze with his nine of diamonds.

The Perfect Triple Squeezes do not offer the squeezed adversary this opportunity of saving a trick by his proper choice of discard. They are called Progressive,* or more accurately, Repeating Squeezes. The term Criss-Cross refers to the criss-cross play back and forth between the North and South hands.

CRISS-CROSS REPEATING SQUEEZE

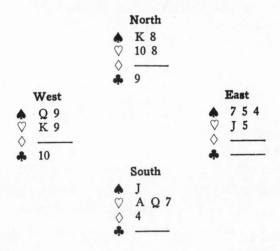

```
                        North
                     ♠  K 8
                     ♡  10 8
                     ◇  ——
                     ♣  9
        West                              East
     ♠  Q 9                             ♠  7 5 4
     ♡  K 9                             ♡  J 5
     ◇  ——                              ◇  ——
     ♣  10                              ♣  ——
                        South
                     ♠  J
                     ♡  A Q 7
                     ◇  4
                     ♣  ——
```

When South, requiring all five tricks at notrump , leads the good diamond, West can not avoid a second automatic squeeze regardless of what he discards. North discards a heart. If West sheds his club, playing the King of spades and the now good nine of clubs from dummy squeezes West again automatically. If West disgorges a spade, the second round of spades in dummy squeezes West again. And if West blanks his King of hearts, South cashes his two extra tricks in hearts immediately.

---

* Not progressive any more for in a progressive squeeze, the first squeezing lead promotes no trick, only prepares the position for the genuine squeeze that is to come later.— Editor.

The New Hampshire Wonder

The newspapers reported this remarkable squeeze in the New Hampshire State Championship Finals held at Manchester, N. H. 13 February 1937. This tournament was the last round of play conducted by the then newly formed New Hampshire Bridge Association, for which we directed 13 elimination games throughout the state wherein 408 players participated, with a 27-table Mitchell semi-final and a 12-table Howell final, in which the hand below is a historic masterpiece.

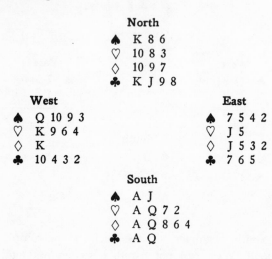

```
                    North
                 ♠ K 8 6
                 ♡ 10 8 3
                 ◇ 10 9 7
                 ♣ K J 9 8
     West                        East
  ♠ Q 10 9 3                  ♠ 7 5 4 2
  ♡ K 9 6 4                   ♡ J 5
  ◇ K                         ◇ J 5 3 2
  ♣ 10 4 3 2                  ♣ 7 6 5
                    South
                 ♠ A J
                 ♡ A Q 7 2
                 ◇ A Q 8 6 4
                 ♣ A Q
```

Mr. C. Carlton Coffin of Nashua playing South was partnered with Oscar L. Tacy, also of the "Gate City," when they won the New Hampshire Championships. According to the newspaper story a correspondent prepared for us, Mr. Coffin staggered into an optimistic contract of six notrump , but we learned afterwards that our correspondent had yarned a little, because Mr. Coffin had properly stopped at three notrump .

The hand, however, contains a beautiful series of plays culminating in the squeeze ending shown above. West led the ten of spades, and when dummy went down, South noted that an overtaking play in clubs, at the sacrifice of a club trick, was necessary to win three club tricks unless,—and here came the first beautiful play of the hand,—the dummy had a spade entry. South realized that if he won the spade opening with the Jack, a club trick would have to be sacrificed to score all dummy's black suit winners. But if South sacrificed his spade trick by winning the spade opening with his Ace, the forfeit would be counterbalanced by his ability to score four club tricks. In other words, *it made no difference in the number of tricks declarer could win in the black suits whether he played the Jack or Ace of spades on the opening lead,* but the play of the Ace retained more flexibility for the future development of the hand, offering *two* lines of entry to dummy instead of only one. South played the Ace of spades.

Declarer next observed that he couldn't get the lead in the dummy twice for the double finesse without badly impoverishing the black suits. So, instead of sacrificing a sure black suit winner in the slim hope of getting it back in diamonds, he made a beautiful safety play,—he laid down the Ace of diamonds!

And imagine his delight when the bare King tumbled from West! East made some crack to West here about holding up his cards. But declarer didn't let this good fortune relax his vigilance in play. He made his third fine play and unblocked the diamond suit by playing dummy's ninespot! The hand was too good to be true. The now marked finesse against the Jack of diamonds would bring home twelve tricks. South thought that he hated to be greedy and wish for another, and yet—

He played the Ace of clubs, overtook the Queen with dummy's King and cashed the Jack, hoping to drop the tenspot, but luck failed him in this department, and he discarded a heart. The ten, eightspot, then Queen of diamonds won the next three tricks as expected, while West petered in discarding two hearts, and shed a spade.

Mr. Coffin hardly expected a squeeze to develop, but was prepared in case it did. Down to the ending shown in the first diagram, he led the last diamond, on which West elected to shed a spade after much squirming, trusting his partner to defend spades. Mr. Coffin played the King then eightspot of spades, intending to finesse the Queen of hearts for his thirteenth trick, but West's agonizing squirms gave the whole show away when he discarded a heart, and Mr. Coffin played his Ace of hearts, picking up West's blanked King!

MILQUETOAST SQUEEZE

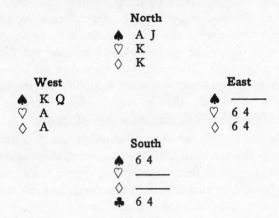

North
- ♠ A J
- ♡ K
- ◇ K

West
- ♠ K Q
- ♡ A
- ◇ A

East
- ♠ ———
- ♡ 6 4
- ◇ 6 4

South
- ♠ 6 4
- ♡ ———
- ◇ ———
- ♣ 6 4

Mr. Milquetoast, that timid soul of the cartoons, would miss many squeezes because he would lack the courage to lead his last trump in order to wreck his adversary's hand. But if he were playing South with clubs trumps in the above situation, he would squeeze out his extra trick by leading his next to last trump!

Squeezes rarely arise wherein two extra tricks are developed on one lead. They are called double-trick squeezes, and one extra trick can sometimes be established and won anyway by straight leads without the squeeze, but not in this case:

DOUBLE-TRICK TRIPLE SQUEEZE

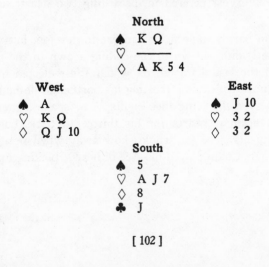

North
- ♠ K Q
- ♡ ———
- ◇ A K 5 4

West
- ♠ A
- ♡ K Q
- ◇ Q J 10

East
- ♠ J 10
- ♡ 3 2
- ◇ 3 2

South
- ♠ 5
- ♡ A J 7
- ◇ 8
- ♣ J

In order to win all six tricks at notrump, South leads his good club. Squeezed in three suits, West must immediately yield in one suit two crucial tricks.

Two-Trick Threats

You may have observed that the basic feature of the Double-Trick Triple Squeeze is its complete saturation with two-trick threats in all three squeezed suits. Usually the two-trick threat involves only one suit, or is wanting, and in the latter case the triple squeeze is almost never automatic. Triplication of the two-trick threat, as in the Double-Trick Triple Squeeze, is so rare that we have never seen it in actual play. The example given above is hypothetical. Likewise, duplication of the two-trick threat is so phenomenal that the only case on record is a classic Whist revival from double dummy play,—the

GREAT VIENNA COUP

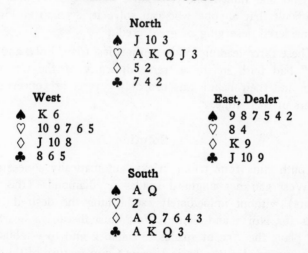

                    North
                ♠ J 10 3
                ♡ A K Q J 3
                ◇ 5 2
                ♣ 7 4 2

    West   East, Dealer
♠ K 6   ♠ 9 8 7 5 4 2
♡ 10 9 7 6 5   ♡ 8 4
◇ J 10 8   ◇ K 9
♣ 8 6 5   ♣ J 10 9

                    South
                ♠ A Q
                ♡ 2
                ◇ A Q 7 6 4 3
                ♣ A K Q 3

Clubs are trumps and South leads. North and South must win all *thirteen* tricks against any defence by East and West.

Stop! Before reading further, try to solve it.

The Great Vienna Coup is the grandfather of all Vienna Coups. About 1864 James Clay, leading Whist authority of his time, first introduced this problem in his books as follows:

"I may permit myself to present to my readers one of the most beautiful problems I have ever seen. It occurred a few months back in actual play in Vienna, (Austria), and at Double Dummy. Its story runs thus: The most celebrated player in Vienna had to play hands North and South. As soon as the cards were exposed, he exclaimed, 'Why, I shall make all 13 tricks.' This appeared impossible to the bystanders. . . . Large bets were made against the accomplishment of the feat, which was, however, performed; and it became evident that, if hands North and South are rightly played, hands East and West are utterly helpless, and, in spite of (their) guarded suits, must lose all 13 tricks."

The Great Vienna Coup was a difficult problem for Whist players of Clay's time. Henry Jones, a popular Whist writer generally known by his *nom de plume* "Cavendish," worked three days on it without finding the solution, only to stumble on it by accident. William Pole in his *Philosophy of Whist* wrote, "Problems in Double Dummy are sometimes given as puzzles for solution, and one famed one especially, called the 'Vienna Coup,' is so difficult that anyone who can solve it, even after long study, is considered deserving of great credit."

These three leading Whist authorities, Clay, Pole, and "Cavendish," had faith in the extreme difficulty of the Great Vienna Coup, and their belief was probably correct as concerned Whist players of their time.

Solution

South runs four trump tricks, automatically squeezing West. As West can not unguard spades or diamonds (the two-trick threats) without immediately establishing the desired two extra tricks for North and South, West must discard a heart. South next plays the Ace of spades to unblock and to establish West's King as a winner, the basic Vienna Coup feature of the play, and North runs five heart tricks, automatically squeezing West at the end.

Triple Squeeze Term Substantiated

Several modern authorities, feeling that "Triple Squeeze" is a misnomer for the above endplays, claim that "they ain't no sech animule." Since a double squeeze is a squeeze of two opponents, there can never be a triple squeeze, because there are never three opponents, they argue.* This, of course, may be true in four-handed Bridge, but they overlook entirely the possibilities for triple squeezes, according to their own interpretation, in five-handed and six-handed Bridge in which there are three opponents. For official rules of these games, see Coffin's Pocket Self-Teacher of Contract, Culbertson System and "Four Aces" System. #

The standard use of the term, "Triple," as applied to squeezes of one opponent guarding three suits, since the early Auction Bridge days is, however, accurately descriptive. Close analysis reveals the fact that squeezing a player in three suits, which we shall call suit A, suit B, and suit C, is really a triple squeeze, because *three distinct squeezes occur simultaneously;* one squeeze in suit A and suit B, another squeeze in suit A and suit C, and a *third* squeeze in suit B and suit C. By the same token, two squeezes take place in a double squeeze, one squeeze in suit A and suit B, and the second squeeze in suit B again (the common or middle suit as it is called) and in suit C. The fact that a double squeeze involves two opponents is merely incidental.

Here is a Perfect Triple Squeeze deal that involves some pretty play on declarer's part.

---

* Some of my very bad partners have made me feel at times as if I had three opponents. - Editor.

Long out of print. So instead see *Natural Big Club,* page 191.

North
♠ 9 5
♡ 8 6 3 2
◇ K 8 6 5
♣ K 8 5

West
♠ K J 10 2
♡ A K Q 9
◇ 9 4
♣ Q J 10

East
♠ 8 7 6 4 3
♡ 7 5 4
◇ 7
♣ 6 4 3 2

South, Dealer
♠ A Q
♡ J 10
◇ A Q J 10 3 2
♣ A 9 7

South deals and bids one diamond, West doubles, North calls two diamonds, and East passes. South jumps to five diamonds to score his 100 in honors instead of calling three notrump, West doubles, and all pass.

West leads the King, Queen, then Ace of hearts which South trumps. Curiously enough, South can win ten tricks by a Work Elimination (see Chapter Four, first page), by leading trumps twice, trumping a heart, and throwing West in on the third round of clubs.

This deal is an adaptation from a hand given on page 366 of the 1926 edition of "Auction Bridge Complete" by the late Milton C. Work to illustrate his favorite endplay, the crossruff fork strip. In the original deal hearts were trumps so that only four by cards were necessary to score game, and in the adapted deal above the eightspot and nine of clubs were interchanged to make the triple squeeze perfect, so that it could develop *two extra tricks*. Considering the fact that West's double marks West with the King of spades and probably the Queen-Jack-ten of clubs in his hand, trying the triple squeeze offers the best chance to win eleven tricks, and it also retains the chance to make one extra trick by a squeeze strip, if East holds a club honor doubly guarded.

After trumping the third round of hearts which West opened and continued, South leads four rounds of trumps, leaving:

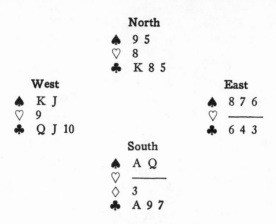

North
- ♠ 9 5
- ♡ 8
- ♣ K 8 5

West
- ♠ K J
- ♡ 9
- ♣ Q J 10

East
- ♠ 8 7 6
- ♡ ———
- ♣ 6 4 3

South
- ♠ A Q
- ♡ ———
- ◇ 3
- ♣ A 9 7

When South leads his last diamond, West has a threefold choice of discards, all fatal.

1. Should West discard a spade, the Ace dropping the King is followed by the Queen, squeezing him again in clubs and hearts.

2. Should West shed the heart, the Ace and King of clubs win, to unblock for the final squeeze position (Vienna Coup), followed by the eightspot of hearts, squeezing him again in spades and clubs.

3. Should West discard a club, South must lead the Ace then *nine* of clubs so that the eightspot in dummy will retain the lead on the third round of the suit, permitting the heart to win should West elect to discard his nine of hearts in a futile attempt to guard his King of spades.

The original three-headed Bridge Monster was based on a one-sided arrangement of the elements of a perfect triple squeeze, wherein all the squeeze cards and the forcing card were retained in one hand.

In the *Encyclopedia of Bridge*,*Ely Culbertson writes, "The following hand was called a three-headed Bridge Monster by George S. Coffin, who first described it in *The Bridge World*."

---

*In this first edition of *Encyclopedia of Bridge* published in 1935, s e e page 173 where the monster overleaf appears along with several other antique "wax figures" of monster hands. This deal was alleged to have appeared naturally in 1970 and reported in a mid-western-newspaper bridge column, We suspect that one of the four players witnessing the deal was a joker.- Editor.

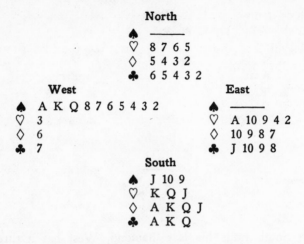

North
♠ ——
♡ 8 7 6 5
◇ 5 4 3 2
♣ 6 5 4 3 2

West
♠ A K Q 8 7 6 5 4 3 2
♡ 3
◇ 6
♣ 7

East
♠ ——
♡ A 10 9 4 2
◇ 10 9 8 7
♣ J 10 9 8

South
♠ J 10 9
♡ K Q J
◇ A K Q J
♣ A K Q

When South is out of the room East stacks the hand, and all but South participate in the practical joke. East deals the stacked cards, after reversing the pick-up to leave them as they were before they were cut, so that South will be sure to get the right hand. South bids three notrump which call all pass. If South should open the bidding at two diamonds, West passes and North bids two spades in order to jockey South into a final notrump contract, where he is purposely left.

West runs nine tricks, forcing South, squirming in agony, to part with all his lovely face cards save the King-Queen of hearts and two Aces.

REPEATING SQUEEZE

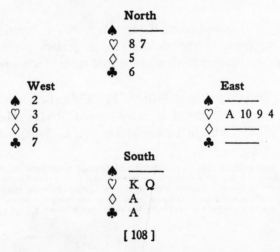

North
♠ ——
♡ 8 7
◇ 5
♣ 6

West
♠ 2
♡ 3
◇ 6
♣ 7

East
♠ ——
♡ A 10 9 4
◇ ——
♣ ——

South
♠ ——
♡ K Q
◇ A
♣ A

South certainly expects to salvage two tricks, but he can't help losing all thirteen. The last spade lead forces South to disgorge an Ace lest all East's hearts become good, and West leads a winner in the disarmed suit, squeezing South again.

The shoe was on the other foot in the next deal in which the same squeeze ending was preceded by some plain and fancy jettison plays. The deal came from one of the famous Pitt stories.

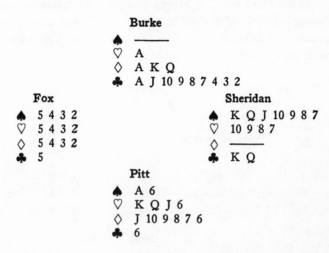

Burke
♠ —
♡ A
◊ A K Q
♣ A J 10 9 8 7 4 3 2

Fox
♠ 5 4 3 2
♡ 5 4 3 2
◊ 5 4 3 2
♣ 5

Sheridan
♠ K Q J 10 9 8 7
♡ 10 9 8 7
◊ —
♣ K Q

Pitt
♠ A 6
♡ K Q J 6
◊ J 10 9 8 7 6
♣ 6

After heavy bidding wherein Sheridan rebid his spades, Pitt arrived at seven diamonds, but the rascal Sheridan, not vulnerable, made a sacrifice stab at seven spades. Nothing daunted, Pitt called seven notrump , closing the bizarre auction.

Fox led the deuce of spades, and the contract was a sorry looking affair. While the clubs can be established in one lead, losing the lead once will let Sheridan in for a run of spade tricks. Therefore, to make sure of eleven tricks, Pitt had to jettison the Ace of hearts immediately, "or else—!" Pitt won the spade opening and ran three heart tricks whereon the dummy next jettisoned its three top diamonds, and the last diamond lead automatically did a rushing squeeze business with Sheridan with a repeat order!

Devil's Delight

This repeating squeeze may become perpetual, if the position can be expanded, so that one extra trick can be won for each extra suit added. Only automatic squeeze can be perpetual. As the lead is retained in one hand, the equeeze might be called the Perpetual Retained Squeeze.

As the story goes, an ardent Bridge fan dreamt he was in Hell, playing against Mephistopheles. In each extra suit the unfortunate East held the Ace, Mephistopheles playing South held the King, and North another spade as follows:

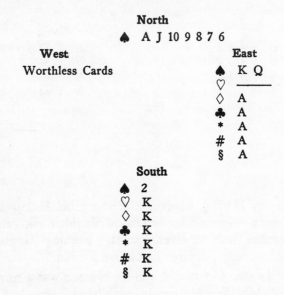

When His Blasphemy led the King of hearts, East, forced to guard spades to shut out all the rest of the tricks therein, had to discard an Ace, and for each Ace that East disgorged His Blasphemy played the King of the same suit *ad infinitum!* Thus East with his long string of Aces could not win a single trick! And that was the Hell of it!!

CHAPTER ELEVEN

ANALYSIS OF GUARDS

B EFORE going further, a detailed analysis of the defensive guards in squeeze positions is in order. As you may have noticed from the simple squeezes discussed so far, two different forms of guards have appeared, *simple guards* and *entry guards*. By a simple guard is meant the adverse master card of one of the squeezer's suits. For example, North holds the five of spades and West the King of spades, which are the last two spades. By an entry guard is meant the same combination as above, *headed* by the top card of its suit, a quick entry into either friendly hand, as North holding ♠ A-2 and West ♠ K-Q, wherein South holds a spade but East holds no more than one spade. The entry guard is just the simple guard topped by a quick entry card. Every quick or true squeeze requires one entry guard and at least one other guard.

In an inverted combination of a simple guard and a quick entry, the quick entry is a *singleton* opposite two low cards in the partner's hand, acting as a second round threat, as below.

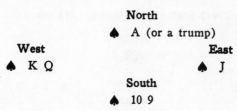

                    North
                    ♠ A (or a trump)
    West   **East**
    ♠ K Q   ♠ J
                    South
                    ♠ 10 9

This awkward arrangement usually necessitates its duplication in any true squeeze without trumps, as in the criss-cross squeezes. See Chapter Seven.

The three basic types of guards are *single* as above, *double,* and *split.* A single guard is based on single mass control by one opponent, such as in the simple and entry guards analysed above. A double guard is based on a double mass control by opponents, wherein *either* opponent alone may guard the suit, leaving his partner free to discard therefrom. Note below:

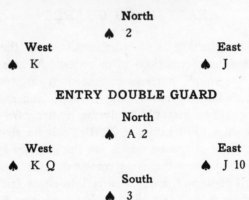

DOUBLE GUARD

North
♠ 2

West
♠ K

East
♠ J

ENTRY DOUBLE GUARD

North
♠ A 2

West
♠ K Q

East
♠ J 10

South
♠ 3

Obviously this type of guard is the strongest and most difficult for declarer to buck, because either opponent may escape the squeeze trap by letting his partner protect the doubly guarded suit.

The entry double guard has two common variations based on duplicated massing. One is based on two quick entries, one in each partnership hand as follows:

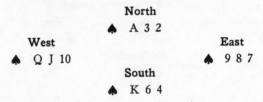

TWO-ENTRY DOUBLE GUARD

North
♠ A 3 2

West
♠ Q J 10

East
♠ 9 8 7

South
♠ K 6 4

In this arrangement declarer playing South can discard a low spade from either hand without impairing the strength of the position, in order to leave room to save a squeeze card or forcing card.

The other variation is the deep or double guard based on a "recessed" suit, so called because two quick entries opposite a singleton add depth to the power of the combination by giving the singleton hand room for *two* squeeze cards, or for a forcing card and a squeeze card.

DEEP DOUBLE GUARD

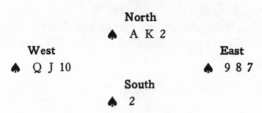

North
♠ A K 2

West
♠ Q J 10

East
♠ 9 8 7

South
♠ 2

This position forms the backbone of double automatic squeezes.

While both single and double guards are based on simple mass control, a *split guard* so straddles both opponents defending themselves against unbalanced rank promotion in the same suit that *neither* opponent can discard from the suit without "disguarding" it. Although the split guard has the form of a double guard involving both opponents, its inherent weakness makes it only a sheep in wolf's clothing.

Split guards fall into two sub-classifications, *balanced* and *unbalanced,* which terms refer to the numerical holdings of cards by opponents.

BALANCED SPLIT GUARD

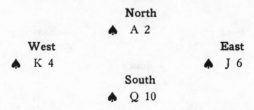

North
♠ A 2

West
♠ K 4

East
♠ J 6

South
♠ Q 10

In this guard West can not blank his King, nor can East blank his Jack lest South lead the Queen and pick it up by a scoop finesse. Here is another form overleaf.

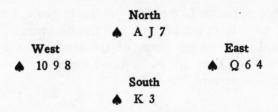

North
♠ A J 7

West
♠ 10 9 8

East
♠ Q 6 4

South
♠ K 3

In this guard if West "disguards" and East refuses to cover the lead of the Jack, the suit is blocked if North holds no side entry. Under these special local conditions, the guard may not be really split.

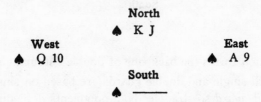

North
♠ K J

West
♠ Q 10

East
♠ A 9

South
♠ ———

In the quick or true squeezes the above guard must be accompanied by trumps. In their absence the squeeze may be equally effective, but it entails the loss of the lead after the squeeze has taken place, in order to establish the spade trick after East or West has been forced to disarm the suit. Without trumps the preliminary squeeze usually results in a strip ending.

UNBALANCED SPLIT GUARD

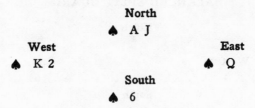

North
♠ A J

West
♠ K 2

East
♠ Q

South
♠ 6

Here West holds mass control while East defends finesse by discovery.

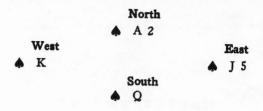

North
♠ A 2

West
♠ K

East
♠ J 5

South
♠ Q

If North has no side entry, West may discard his King with impunity. West defends rank control in this bizarre combination.

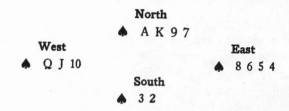

North
♠ A K 9 7

West
♠ Q J 10

East
♠ 8 6 5 4

South
♠ 3 2

If West "disguards" spades, East is found guarding them against the loss of another trick. This freak guard is the middle suit of Bonney's Squeeze, which see in Chapter Thirteen.

It may be seen from the above that split guards are the weakest defensive combinations of the three types in Bridge, because they are usually vulnerable simultaneously on both flanks.

The unbalanced split guard shown at the top of the page is the clash menace in what Chien-Hwa Wang calls clash squeezes that are special three-suit squeezes which he described in *Bridge Magazine* in 1956 and 1957. For example:

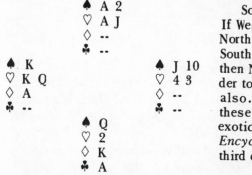

♠ A 2
♡ A J
◊ --
♣ --

♠ K
♡ K Q
◊ A
♣ --

♠ J 10
♡ 4 3
◊ --
♣ --

♠ Q
♡ 2
◊ K
♣ A

South leads his good club. If West shed his spade king, North casts off the heart jack, South scores his spade queen then North his heart ace in order to score the spade ace also. For other examples of these astronomically rare and exotic squeezes, turn to the *Encyclopedia of Bridge*, the third edition 1971, page 65.

CHAPTER TWELVE

FINESSE BY DISCOVERY

I N CHESS the term, "check by discovery," is used to denote the play of a piece to one side uncovering a direct line of attack upon the enemy's King, thereby "checking" it. In Bridge involving partners, a finesse may be discovered either by declarer, or by one defending partner whose bad discard discovers a finesse against his partner.

JETTISON SQUEEZE FINESSE

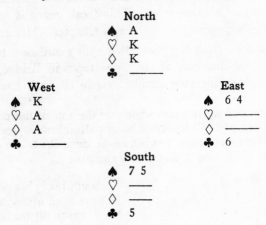

```
                        North
                    ♠  A
                    ♡  K
                    ◇  K
                    ♣  ———
    West                                East
  ♠  K                                ♠  6 4
  ♡  A                                ♡  ———
  ◇  A                                ◇  ———
  ♣  ———                              ♣  6
                        South
                    ♠  7 5
                    ♡  ———
                    ◇  ———
                    ♣  5
```

At notrump South wishing two tricks leads his losing club. As West can not part with either red Ace without establishing the King of its suit as a winner with North, West sheds his useless King of spades, and North *jettisons* the Ace of spades, discovering a winning spade finesse for South.

This endplay is purely hypothetical,—coming from a double dummy problem,—and it is so unnatural that no player has yet encountered it in an actual Bridge game, and probably never will.

It is the only offensive squeeze finesse wherein declarer himself discards in order to discover his winning finesse. Technically it is one of three general types of squeeze finesse, in spite of the fact that it is almost extinct as far as practical play is concerned.

In all squeeze finesses the preparation play must be a triple squeeze, except in the second general type based on a finesse "pick-up" or scoop position.

SQUEEZE PICK-UP

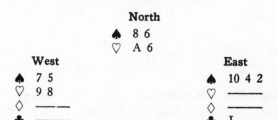

```
                    North
                  ♠ 8 6
                  ♡ A 6
    West                          East
  ♠ 7 5                         ♠ 10 4 2
  ♡ 9 8                         ♡ ———
  ◇ ———                         ◇ ———
  ♣ ———                         ♣ J
                    South
                  ♠ A 3
                  ♡ 3
                  ◇ 8
```

At notrump South, needing all four tricks, led his last good diamond to force a spade discard from West, and dummy shed a now useless heart. The Ace of hearts put dummy in to lead the eightspot of spades to finesse, while picking up West's now lone seven.   If East plays low, the eightspot wins; if East covers with the ten, South wins with his Ace and the six   of spades becomes the highest card in North America.   Here are the complete hands from a tournament:

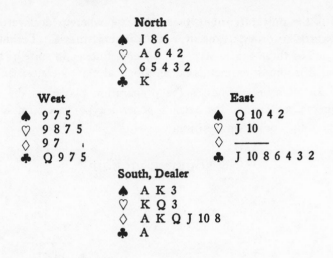

North
- ♠ J 8 6
- ♡ A 6 4 2
- ◇ 6 5 4 3 2
- ♣ K

West
- ♠ 9 7 5
- ♡ 9 8 7 5
- ◇ 9 7
- ♣ Q 9 7 5

East
- ♠ Q 10 4 2
- ♡ J 10
- ◇ ———
- ♣ J 10 8 6 4 3 2

South, Dealer
- ♠ A K 3
- ♡ K Q 3
- ◇ A K Q J 10 8
- ♣ A

With both sides vulnerable South dealt and bid two diamonds, North two hearts, and South seven notrump.

West's top-of-nothing opening lead of the nine of spades forced the Jack, Queen, and King in turn. By examination declarer noted identical symmetry distribution in the black suits with the only possibility for a squeeze in the majors. Five diamond leads drew club discards from opponents. Declarer laid down the Ace of clubs and followed with the King-Queen of hearts thereby discovering four hearts originally held by West when East's Jack and ten fell. Hence no automatic squeeze was possible against East, marked by the opening lead to hold the ten and at least two other spades. Declarer's only chance was to play West for the seven of spades. He led his last diamond forcing West to bare his seven of spades in the hope that declarer wouldn't try the pick-up finesse through East's ten.

A BASIC MANEUVER

At a national championship in Europe a bridge player was observed streaking down the grand-hotel upstairs corridor after a woman.

The card committee summoned the streaker for trial on "Improper attire and behaviour unbecoming to a gentleman and a life master." A conviction would terminate membership in the sponsoring league and revoke all master points of the accused. In Europe rules on dress are far stricter than in the American Contract Bridge League.

How would you rule? First decide, then see bottom of page 120.

By rearranging the original deal slightly, we get a variation of the squeeze scoop wherein both quick entries are in the same suit.

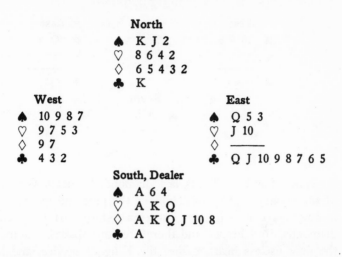

North
♠ K J 2
♡ 8 6 4 2
♢ 6 5 4 3 2
♣ K

West
♠ 10 9 8 7
♡ 9 7 5 3
♢ 9 7
♣ 4 3 2

East
♠ Q 5 3
♡ J 10
♢ ——
♣ Q J 10 9 8 7 6 5

South, Dealer
♠ A 6 4
♡ A K Q
♢ A K Q J 10 8
♣ A

With both sides vulnerable, South deals and bids two diamonds, North raises to three diamonds, and East overcalls at four clubs. Reckoning East's overcall to be based on the top clubs and North's diamond raise on the King-Queen of spades, South jumps to seven notrump.

West leads the four of clubs, clearly indicating at least eight clubs with East, as East would not have dared a vulnerable overcall for four by cards with fewer. South wins West's opening club lead, draw's West's diamonds in two leads, and gets the bad news when East sheds a club on the third round of hearts. South runs all but one diamond, noting the discards of the seven of spades and the trey and deuce of clubs by West, thereby showing eight clubs originally held by East. Of course, West might easily hold the Queen of spades if it weren't for the fact that East's vulnerable overcall at four clubs would be much too flimsy without that key card. Now the ending shapes up as follows:

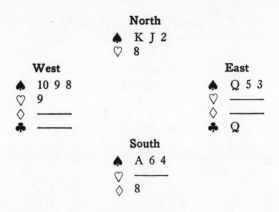

North
♠ K J 2
♡ 8

West
♠ 10 9 8
♡ 9
◇ ——
♣ ——

East
♠ Q 5 3
♡ ——
◇ ——
♣ Q

South
♠ A 6 4
♡ ——
◇ 8

When South leads his last diamond, he notes West's discard of the eightspot of spades showing the nine and ten also, as West is now marked with the original shape of three clubs, two diamonds, four hearts, and therefore four spades. Dummy sheds the now useless heart, cashes the King of spades, and leads the Jack to finesse through East's Queen while scooping up West's now lone ten.

Basic Difference

A squeeze scoop may be a simple squeeze in two suits, whereas a squeeze finesse must be a triple squeeze. The squeezed opponent need hold only one side guard to be forced to unguard the scoop finesse suit down to one card, whereas he must be forced to guard *two* side suits in order to be completely voided of the finesse suit at the end. This fundamental difference characterizes the second and third general types of forced finesse by discovery.

A BASIC MANEUVER (from page 118)

The card committee ruled that the accused was properly attired for the sport in which he was engaged at the time; case dismissed.

SQUEEZE FINESSE

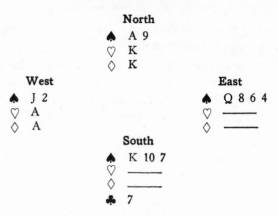

North
♠ A 9
♡ K
◇ K

West
♠ J 2
♡ A
◇ A

East
♠ Q 8 6 4
♡ —
◇ —

South
♠ K 10 7
♡ —
◇ —
♣ 7

When South, requiring all four tricks at notrump , leads his last good club, West must shed a spade to protect his red suits and North discards a red King. Picking up West's Jack of spades by North's King discovers the winning finesse through East's Queen.

Before we show more squeeze finesses, it is necessary to establish a simple system of terminology for complex squeezes, wherein one opponent is squeezed in three suits and his partner in two or three suits. We don't like to call such endplays triple double or triple triple squeezes, nor the higher squeezes wherein several preparation squeezes occur before the final squeezes. As a long string of triples and doubles wouldn't even be funny, we submit the

Coffin Point Count

Sportsmen habitually describe the beauty and size of their game by such loving appellations as "ten-point buck," so why can't Bridge game hunters use a similar easy system for their squeeze prey? In the Coffin Point System, the number of suits wherein an opponent is squeezed is the number of contact points of the squeeze. If the other opponent is also squeezed on the same lead, even in a suit or suits duplicated in both opponents' hands, the number of his squeezed suits is added to represent the total number of points of the compound squeeze. Thus a simple basic squeeze in two suits is called a "two-point squeeze," or simply a "2 squeeze," a triple squeeze is a "3 squeeze," a double triple squeeze is a "6 squeeze," etc. In intricate problem squeezes the point system is valuable to avoid such monstrous terms as triple triple triple double squeeze, which is simply written "3-3-3-4 squeeze." Only when opponents are forced to shed busy cards when forcing cards are led are these squeeze points counted.

In Chess, when both the uncovered piece and the uncovering piece simultaneously attack your opponent's King, you have the unique and frequently devastating advantage in your double threat known to that game as "double check." The Bridge analogy is the

JETTISON 5-POINT SQUEEZE FINESSE

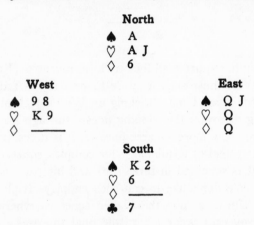

When South, requiring all four tricks at notrump , leads his good club and North jettisons a spade, West, automatically squeezed in two suits, must shed a spade, and East is automatically squeezed in three suits. East's best chance would be to shed a heart, hoping South won't dare risk the discovered finesse. In addition to discovering the heart finesse, leading the forcing club also attacks the spade suit, doubly guarded in both adverse hands.

These rare endings have been known to composers and solvers of double dummy problems for years. The author claims to be the first player to recognize and execute such an endplay in actual competition. It happened to be the third variety of the discovered finesse, wherein the finesse by discovery didn't actually materialize because the endplay concluded in a squeeze.

This grotesque deal occurred in a curious tournament,—a special match arranged by a team of twelve "certified" Bridge teachers who had challenged the Harvard Club of Boston. The professionals, however, soon discovered much to their chagrin that they had obtained more than they had bargained for when the Harvard Club, on whose team we played, defeated them by a large margin. But withal, the affair was a festive occasion, and "a good time was had by all."

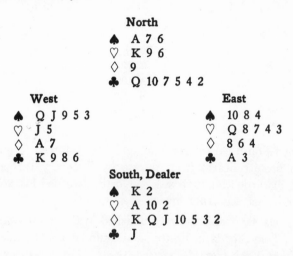

North
♠ A 7 6
♡ K 9 6
◊ 9
♣ Q 10 7 5 4 2

West
♠ Q J 9 5 3
♡ J 5
◊ A 7
♣ K 9 8 6

East
♠ 10 8 4
♡ Q 8 7 4 3
◊ 8 6 4
♣ A 3

South, Dealer
♠ K 2
♡ A 10 2
◊ K Q J 10 5 3 2
♣ J

Playing South we dealt and bid one diamond, West one spade, North two clubs, South three diamonds, North three notrump at which call the contract was made with overtricks at two other tables, and South jumped to five diamonds, primarily for the honors scored at total point play. At three tables five diamonds was defeated, but we made it!

Against our five diamond contract West opened with the Queen of spades which South's King won, and East signalled with his eightspot to show his partner the ten. West won South's second diamond lead, and continued spades, knocking out dummy's Ace. When dummy led a low club, East hopped up with the Ace while West played the nine to show the King also. East made the fatal error of blindly obeying West's peter and led a club which South trumped. East should have returned a spade in order to kill the impending squeeze,—a fine defensive play. Now South ran all but one trump to develop the five-point squeeze position, as follows:

THE HARVARD COUP

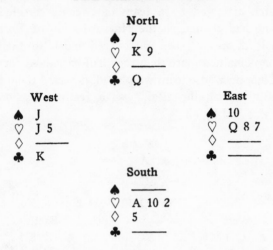

```
                        North
                        ♠ 7
                        ♡ K 9
                        ◊ ———
                        ♣ Q
        West                            East
        ♠ J                             ♠ 10
        ♡ J 5                           ♡ Q 8 7
        ◊ ———                           ◊ ———
        ♣ K                             ♣ ———
                        South
                        ♠ ———
                        ♡ A 10 2
                        ◊ 5
                        ♣ ———
```

When South led his last diamond, West, forced to guard clubs and to protect hearts from finesse by discovery through East's Queen, discarded his high spade, North discarded his now useless club, and East was truly squeezed *en masse!*

This classic deal was first published in the *West Coast Bridge Review*, Tom Stoddard, Editor; and again later by Samuel Wallace in the *New York Herald-Tribune.*

Queen fifth

CHAPTER THIRTEEN

THE SATURATION POINT

T HE threat of finesse by discovery in a squeeze ending may be
duplicated in two suits as follows:

HEXAGON SQUEEZE

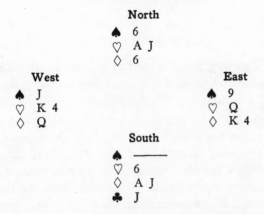

                        North
                    ♠ 6
                    ♡ A J
                    ◇ 6
    West   East
    ♠ J   ♠ 9
    ♡ K 4   ♡ Q
    ◇ Q   ◇ K 4
                        South
                    ♠ —
                    ♡ 6
                    ◇ A J
                    ♣ J

To win all four tricks at notrump   South leads his last good
club, triple-squeezing West out of his high spade, North discards
his now worthless diamond, and East is also triple squeezed.
East's best defence is to discard the Queen of hearts and to pray
that South will not take the discovered finesse through West's
King.

Note that we have called the above position a Hexagon
Squeeze because it is a true six-point squeeze. Similarly five-point
squeezes might be called Pentagon Squeezes, and so on, but we
use the geometric variation in terminology to indicate ultimate
saturation in squeezes,—*every suit is busy at all points*. These
grotesque squeezes are such rarities that there is only one on
record from actual play.

Edward T. Barco discovered and published it in the *Bridge World*, December, 1935.

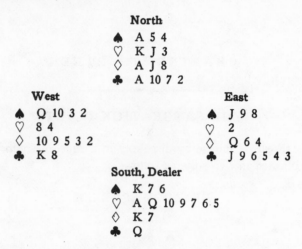

<pre>
                         North
                      ♠ A 5 4
                      ♡ K J 3
                      ◇ A J 8
                      ♣ A 10 7 2
      West   East
   ♠ Q 10 3 2   ♠ J 9 8
   ♡ 8 4   ♡ 2
   ◇ 10 9 5 3 2   ◇ Q 6 4
   ♣ K 8   ♣ J 9 6 5 4 3
                      South, Dealer
                      ♠ K 7 6
                      ♡ A Q 10 9 7 6 5
                      ◇ K 7
                      ♣ Q
</pre>

Mr. Barco playing South dealt and bid one heart, North three notrump , South six hearts, North seven hearts closing the auction, and West led a heart.

Curiously enough, by double dummy play the grand slam can be made by a one-way double squeeze. It is developed by transferring the opponents' diamond and club strength to opposite adverse hands with a Double Vienna Coup, that is, cashing all winners in both minor suits in order to unblock them for the double squeeze position. But as such play would require a good peek, declarer properly followed the only natural course open to him. Holding the diamond finesse in reserve as a last resort, declarer ran five trump tricks uncovering the

---

THE LAST WORD

Bo: If Two in One is shoe polish, and Three in One is oil, what is Four in One?

Mo: That's a schoolboy chestnut, five!

Bo: No, No! I said Four IN one, not four 'n one. Today Four in One is Coffin's Bridge Play Four Classics, *four books in one volume.*

Mo: But Coffin added his fifth book in the volume, Bridge Writer's Manual. *So four in one do make five!*

BARCO SQUEEZE

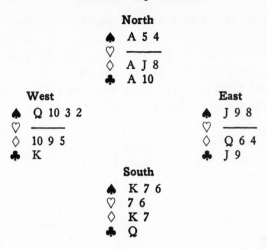

```
                    North
                  ♠ A 5 4
                  ♡ ──────
                  ◇ A J 8
                  ♣ A 10
   West                              East
 ♠ Q 10 3 2                        ♠ J 9 8
 ♡ ──────                          ♡ ──────
 ◇ 10 9 5                          ◇ Q 6 4
 ♣ K                               ♣ J 9
                    South
                  ♠ K 7 6
                  ♡ 7 6
                  ◇ K 7
                  ♣ Q
```

When South led a heart on which West and North each discarded a spade, East squeezed in three suits had to shed a spade
also; and when South led his last heart, West was fatally squeezed
in three suits. Note the weird combination of three double guards.

Only a few Hexagon Squeezes are known to exist at this writing. They are eight-card double dummy problems, one of which
was composed by the writer. See Chapter Twenty-one on problems, Coffin's Hex. Also, Alfred Sheinwold, a brilliant young
analyst and editor of the *Bridge World,* composed and published
therein several beauties in the July, August, September and October 1937 issues, offering cash prizes for solutions.

Actually the Barco Squeeze is unstable because a cook c a n
byepass it and resolve the position to a transfer and a simple
split squeeze. In the eight-card matrix above North wins his club
ace, leads the diamond jack that East then South must cover (to
transfer diamond control to West), then South cashes a heart
and North sheds a low spade. In the five-card ending South wins
his last heart, West must shed a spade to stop diamonds, N o r t h
sheds his now useless low diamond and East his d i a m o n d.
Finally North wins his diamond ace, squeezing East in the
black suits.

The New Hampshire Miracle

Without the threat of finesse by discovery, we used to believe that any squeeze of more than four points was an impossibility until Norman Bonney of Boston, Mass., former National Contract Champion (Goldman Trophy winner in the Easterns with W. Cleveland Coggswell in 1932), unearthed his freak squeeze when he won the first New Hampshire State Championships in 1933.

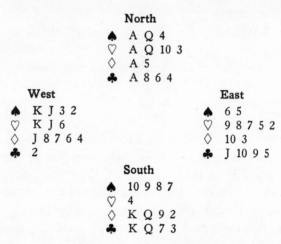

North
- ♠ A Q 4
- ♡ A Q 10 3
- ◇ A 5
- ♣ A 8 6 4

West
- ♠ K J 3 2
- ♡ K J 6
- ◇ J 8 7 6 4
- ♣ 2

East
- ♠ 6 5
- ♡ 9 8 7 5 2
- ◇ 10 3
- ♣ J 10 9 5

South
- ♠ 10 9 8 7
- ♡ 4
- ◇ K Q 9 2
- ♣ K Q 7 3

The deal is connected with an amusing incident showing the enthusiasm that a Bridge fan has for his game. North and South staggered into a ridiculous contract of seven notrump with South as declarer, West led the deuce of spades, and Mr. Bonney defended East. After the hand was fumbled and the contract defeated by two tricks, the South player turned to Mr. Bonney and asked, "Could I have made it?"

Mr. Bonney replied, "I think so, but I don't see just how at the moment." This happened in the afternoon Pairs event.

Before the evening play, one of the best players in New England who was a cripple without the use of his legs, W. Mark Noble, Jr. of Newton, Mass., arrived early, and requested help up the stairs into the card room.

As there were no men around at the time save Bonney and myself, we cradled the lame man in our arms and carried him up the long flight of stairs. On setting Mr. Noble down in his chair, however, Mr. Bonney, who has a weak heart, suddenly passed out. He was placed on a nearby sofa, rubbed, and cold water dashed into his face without avail. We became worried, because we didn't want the game to end in a funeral.

Suddenly Bonney came to and jumped up exclaiming, "By God! I can make seven notrump on that hand. And here's how you do it!" Somewhat shaky, he staggered over to a Bridge table and called for a pack of cards, which he laid out, not misplacing a single spot card!

He permitted West's opening lead of the deuce of spades to run to South's seven, finessed the Queen of Spades, then played the Ace of spades from dummy, played the Ace then Queen of clubs, and the Ace then Queen of diamonds, leaving this fantastic repeating squeeze ending:

BONNEY'S SQUEEZE

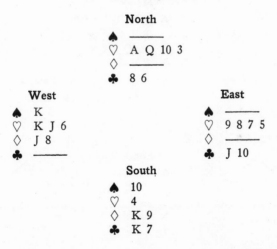

```
                    North
               ♠ ——
               ♡ A Q 10 3
               ◊ ——
               ♣ 8 6
   West                          East
♠ K                          ♠ ——
♡ K J 6                      ♡ 9 8 7 5
◊ J 8                        ◊ ——
♣ ——                         ♣ J 10
                    South
               ♠ 10
               ♡ 4
               ◊ K 9
               ♣ K 7
```

When South played his two Kings in either order on which dummy played two clubs, West had to release his third round control of hearts in order to avoid a repeated squeeze in hearts and spades, or in hearts and diamonds, and East had to yield a fourth round heart trick or a club trick! The technical name of this freak is the Triple-Double Automatic Repeating Squeeze, Bonney; but to give it a simple Latin name commemorating its discoverer, Norman Bonney, we might call it *Squeezum Bonniensis!*

CHAPTER FOURTEEN

DEFENCE AGAINST SQUEEZES

L ACKING any real defence against a squeeze, a player should discard so as not to disclose his weakness. Declarer often doesn't
know whether he has a real squeeze or not, particularly when he
has a choice between a squeeze and a finesse at the end. Take this
deal:

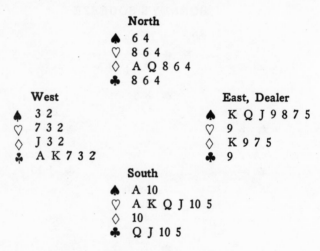

North
♠ 6 4
♡ 8 6 4
♢ A Q 8 6 4
♣ 8 6 4

West
♠ 3 2
♡ 7 3 2
♢ J 3 2
♣ A K 7 3 2

East, Dealer
♠ K Q J 9 8 7 5
♡ 9
♢ K 9 7 5
♣ 9

South
♠ A 10
♡ A K Q J 10 5
♢ 10
♣ Q J 10 5

East, vulnerable, deals and bids three spades, which preemptive
bid South overcalls at four hearts, and all pass.

West opens with the King of clubs, following with the Ace, and
a low club which East trumps. East leads the King of spades which
South wins with his Ace. South runs all his trumps and is faced
with this problem.

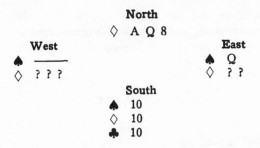

North

♢ A Q 8

West

♠ ——

♢ ? ? ?

East

♠ Q

♢ ? ?

South

♠ 10

♢ 10

♣ 10

Having lost three club tricks at the outset, South needs all three tricks for his contract. South leads his last club automatically squeezing East, as South thought, but East quickly discarded the nine of diamonds. Of course, South had marked East with the King of diamonds as a part of his opening vulnerable three bid, and East most certainly held the top spade. And yet,—South had had previous experiences with East's three bids sometimes based on only five probable tricks in play. After long thought South came to a decision.

"Must finesse," said South to himself as he finessed the Queen of diamonds up to East's lone King, and East delightedly scooped in another trick with his top spade, defeating the contract two tricks. Of course, putting up dummy's Ace of diamonds is the preferred play because it holds the loss down to a set of one trick if the guess is wrong, but the quick and unhesitating manner in which East discarded his nine   of diamonds fooled South. This situation is quite common and it warrants careful study.

There are three types of defense against a squeeze: bluff discarding as above, breaking up the impending squeeze position early in the play by killing quick vital entries, and/or squeeze cards as in Al Parrott's hand in Chapter Six and in the Harvard Coup in Chapter Twelve, and by the proper discarding against a false squeeze in order to keep it hopelessly false for declarer.

Defence Against False Squeezes

The most nerve-wracking defence in Bridge is to adjust your discards properly in order to ward off and defeat a false squeeze, particularly a false double squeeze. Absolute precision and accuracy in discarding, often aided by partner's signals and plays, are essential in order to keep declarer in his place with his false

squeeze. Be wary lest you unguard a key suit, thereby giving
declarer the whip hand. Tossing away an innocuous looking deuce
or trey may enable declarer to wreck your partner's hand completely.

Colossal Minutiae

It's bad enough when your partner gets squeezed naturally out
of a hand that looked beautiful before the pressure was applied,
but when you join forces with declarer, that's worse. Observe the
importance of spot cards in this deal:

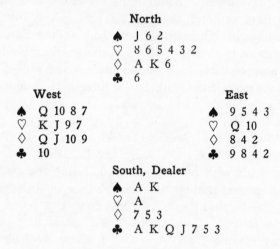

```
                        North
                        ♠ J 6 2
                        ♡ 8 6 5 4 3 2
                        ◇ A K 6
                        ♣ 6
        West                                East
        ♠ Q 10 8 7                          ♠ 9 5 4 3
        ♡ K J 9 7                           ♡ Q 10
        ◇ Q J 10 9                          ◇ 8 4 2
        ♣ 10                                ♣ 9 8 4 2
                        South, Dealer
                        ♠ A K
                        ♡ A
                        ◇ 7 5 3
                        ♣ A K Q J 7 5 3
```

In a tournament South bid two clubs and North showed the
hearts. South jumped to four clubs to show a solid suit, and since
the system used called for ace showing in this situation, North bid
four diamonds. South optimistically leaped to seven notrump
which West vociferously doubled.

West opened with the Queen of diamonds which dummy's
King won. Declarer ran all his clubs and West had to find four
discards before his partner could signal anything. West chose to
drop a low spade, two hearts, and the nine of diamonds. At his
first opportunity East rid himself of the four of diamonds, then a
low spade. West boldly discarded all his hearts on the club leads,
but when the Ace of hearts appeared, he had to trust to luck that
East held a third round diamond stopper and discarded the ten
of diamonds. And when South scored his thirteenth trick with

his seven of diamonds, the weeping and wailing and gnashing of teeth was heart-rending.

East moaned bitterly about West's double, little realizing that he, East, was the real culprit. His discard of the four of diamonds was fatal. He should have realized that West, holding honors in three suits, needed relief from pressure. All East had to do was to hang on like grim death to two diamonds and the Queen and ten of hearts, and West would have had no trouble.

A similar squeeze, only self-inflicted, can happen to declarer if he doesn't watch out. It is a fact well known by zoölogists that when a scorpion is cornered, he curls his flexible tail over his back and stings himself to death. This is exactly what we saw a player unthinkingly do in this deal:

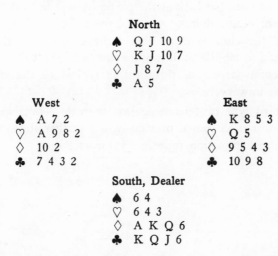

North
- ♠ Q J 10 9
- ♡ K J 10 7
- ◇ J 8 7
- ♣ A 5

West
- ♠ A 7 2
- ♡ A 9 8 2
- ◇ 10 2
- ♣ 7 4 3 2

East
- ♠ K 8 5 3
- ♡ Q 5
- ◇ 9 5 4 3
- ♣ 10 9 8

South, Dealer
- ♠ 6 4
- ♡ 6 4 3
- ◇ A K Q 6
- ♣ K Q J 6

In a rubber game South dealt and landed in a contract of three notrump after bidding the minor suits, North showed the majors. West led the deuce of hearts, dummy played the ten, and East won with the Queen. Seeing no future in hearts, East switched to the ten of clubs. All South had to do now was to set up a trick or two in the major suits and call it a day. But instead, he committed the most pitiful suicide squeeze we ever saw. He won the club return with dummy's Ace, ran four diamond tricks and two in clubs leaving this situation:

SUICIDE SQUEEZE

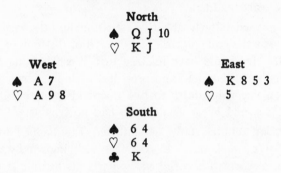

North
♠ Q J 10
♡ K J

West
♠ A 7
♡ A 9 8

East
♠ K 8 5 3
♡ 5

South
♠ 6 4
♡ 6 4
♣ K

Up to this point South had felt with smug assurance that the game was certain, but look at the pickle he was in! If he cashed the King of clubs, dummy would have no good discard; if he abandoned the club to avoid this pathetic self-inflicted squeeze, West would establish and capture the setting trick in hearts. The innocuous aspect of this deal is typical of the traps that waylay the unwary.

The third type of defence against squeezes,—breaking up the squeeze position as shown previously,—is further illustrated by a kind of false elimination squeeze known as the

A double
duck play ...

C.R.H.

INDUCED SQUEEZE

```
                    North
                  ♠ 8 6 4
                  ♡ 8 6 4
                  ◇ 6 4
                  ♣ A K J 6 4
  West                               East
♠ K Q J 10 9                       ♠ 3
♡ 10 7 5 3 2                       ♡ K Q 9
◇ 8 5 3                            ◇ J 10 9 7
♣ —                                ♣ Q 10 9 8 3
                    South, Dealer
                  ♠ A 7 5 2
                  ♡ A J
                  ◇ A K Q 2
                  ♣ 7 5 2
```

South dealt and bid one diamond. West overcalled at one spade and North said two clubs. East passed and South jumped to three notrump , satisfying West and North, but East, figuring that askew distribution in the minor suits would wreck South's contract, doubled for penalties, and all passed.

West led the King of spades which South let win, and West pushed out the ten of spades which South won with his Ace, East shed   a club. The hand is a pianola IF clubs split normally. Hence declarer led a low club toward dummy's King, hearing the bad news when West renounced with a heart. Dummy won the club and led a spade which West won, while East shed the heart nine. South hoped to *induce* West to run all his spades and squeeze East, whose double marked him with defence in three suits. West led another spade on which East shed the nine of clubs, leaving this situation:

Horse Play

One day in the pasture a foal said to his mother, "When I grow up, I will play bridge better than all those cookies like the world-champions, the Italians , The Aces and others. I will be the world's top bridger."

Replied his mother the mare, "Sorry, son. You're living in a foal's paradise. Such boasting is really foalish of you."

[135]

SUICIDE INVITATION DECLINED

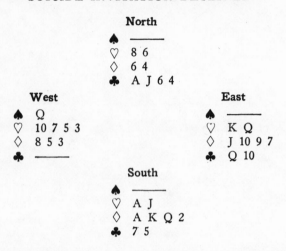

North
♠ ——
♡ 8 6
◊ 6 4
♣ A J 6 4

West
♠ Q
♡ 10 7 5 3
◊ 8 5 3
♣ ——

East
♠ ——
♡ K Q
◊ J 10 9 7
♣ Q 10

South
♠ ——
♡ A J
◊ A K Q 2
♣ 7 5

Had West continued at this point by grabbing his last spade trick, he would have initiated a repeating squeeze against East, which South could have concluded for two extra tricks for his contract. East's latest discards of the two nines were sharp advance warnings of labor pains. That East's next discard would have to be a vital honor or a diamond stopper became apparent to West. For a long time he fondled the Queen of spades in greedy meditation, but realizing that she might be the Black Widow Spider in Bridge as well as in Hearts, West thought better of it and switched to a low heart. East's King forced declarer's Ace. Declarer ran three diamond tricks and threw East in on the fourth round of diamonds in order to salvage one trick by forcing East to lead up to dummy's club tenace at the end, but East and West had won five tricks, defeating the contract.

The deal is a remarkable illustration of how declarer's invitation to commit suicide was declined by a defensive player. West advisedly avoided the venal vice of vaunting his last and vexatious spade trick, that would have eviscerated East in a vicious vise!

CHAPTER FIFTEEN

STRIP AND SQUEEZE

W E HAVE arrived at last in that realm of hybrid endplays where the process of stripping and squeezing go hand in hand. Technically, they fall into two separate groups, the Strip Squeezes, wherein elimination play paves the way for the squeeze, and the Squeeze Strips, wherein the luckless opponent is squeezed out of winners or essential exit cards before he is thrown in the lead.

In the deal just shown at the end of the last chapter, the squeeze by induction is really a kind of strip squeeze. The unwary opponent is partially stripped of exit cards and is thrown in the lead in the hope that he will fall into the trap of the false elimination and lead the wrong suit, squeezing his partner. But in a true strip squeeze, or the Forced Squeeze as it is called, the unfortunate opponent can not escape squeezing his partner,—he is *forced* to squeeze him. We submit the following example:

No Oil in the Snake Pit

In midwinter a lady snake crawled on the snow up to my door and said, "I am freezing to death, I am so cold."

I replied, "What are you doing in the open on such a cold day? You should be resting in a nice warm snake pit.

She replied, "To be honest I am broke from paying Arabian prices for oil,- so broke now that I cannot even afford a pit to hiss in."

So I invited the lady snake in and introduced her to a lamprey eel kept in my cellar. So this electric eel, like an electric blanket, kept both himself and the lady snake warm all the long cold winter. Of course, they played Honeymoon Bridge with Coffin's Silent Partner card racks in order to while away the time. (See page 160 in PERFECT PLAYS.)

Being modern, they were not married, quite shocking.

And come Spring the lady snake gave birth to 13 little sneels.

Mathematical Reproduction. *The lady snake had a married sister. Try as they might this sister and her husband could have no little snake, They could not multiply. You see, they were adders.*

But Love found the solution to have offspring. They found a hollow log in the forest to live in and practice log-a-rhythms. ----- 30 -----

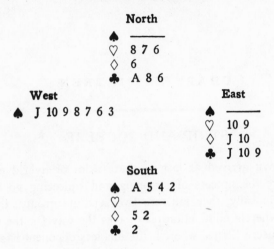

North
- ♠ ———
- ♡ 8 7 6
- ◇ 6
- ♣ A 8 6

West
- ♠ J 10 9 8 7 6 3

East
- ♠ ———
- ♡ 10 9
- ◇ J 10
- ♣ J 10 9

South
- ♠ A 5 4 2
- ♡ ———
- ◇ 5 2
- ♣ 2

At a contract of three notrump South has captured the first six tricks, and he is now faced with the apparently impossible problem of winning three tricks with his two black Aces supported by trash,—five positive losers. The possibility of a squeeze looks utterly hopeless by Culbertson's squeeze rule of "N minus 1," wherein N represents the number of required winners and 1 represents the number of losers allowed by the rule for a successful squeeze.

Geometry at the Bridge Table

A **square** is an honest bridge player, and four **squares** make a **square** game.

Definitions

A **circle** is created whenever a match-point duplicate bridge player *loses* all the points on a board.

A **cylinder** is a transparent object that frequents bridge tables, Whenever **circumscribing** transparent **cubes**, the liquids floating these cubes often dissolve good play.

A **hexagon** is a complete table of six rubber-bridge players wherein the two inactive players kibitz and **hex** the other four players.

Locus is a kind of loud buzzing insect that hangs around bridge clubs in the summertime and annoys the players.

A **pyramid** is the growing debt of a consistent loser unable to pay his losses. When he is barred from play for suspension of credit, the pyramid is said to be **truncated**.

Therefore, to eliminate idle cards South leads a low spade, throwing West in, while North sheds a heart and East a club. West is forced to continue spades and South holds up twice, leaving:

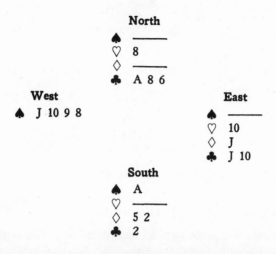

North
♠ ——
♡ 8
◊ ——
♣ A 8 6

West
♠ J 10 9 8

East
♠ ——
♡ 10
◊ J
♣ J 10

South
♠ A
♡ ——
◊ 5 2
♣ 2

When West makes his last spade lead, North sheds a low club and East is squeezed in three suits. In order to prevent South from winning all four tricks, East has to shed a heart or a club.

Theorem
When two husband-wife couples play against each other, and each couple is equal in skill, each to each and each to the other; with equal 52 **rectangular planes** the results are always equal.

Proof: Suppose that one couple gains a psychological advantage. This could happen only if one husband admits that he made an error in a bid or play, which is absurd.

From Am. Bridge Teachers' Ass'n *Quarterly*, Jan. 1963

The preliminary play of the complete hands is interesting:

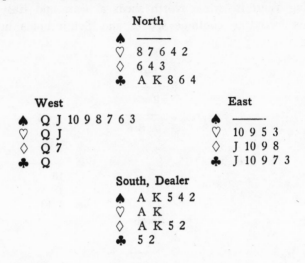

North
- ♠ ———
- ♡ 8 7 6 4 2
- ♢ 6 4 3
- ♣ A K 8 6 4

West
- ♠ Q J 10 9 8 7 6 3
- ♡ Q J
- ♢ Q 7
- ♣ Q

East
- ♠ ———
- ♡ 10 9 5 3
- ♢ J 10 9 8
- ♣ J 10 9 7 3

South, Dealer
- ♠ A K 5 4 2
- ♡ A K
- ♢ A K 5 2
- ♣ 5 2

South deals and bids two spades, pleasing West who passes, North three clubs, South three diamonds, North three hearts, and South three notrump , closing the auction.

West opens with the Queen of spades on which North sheds a diamond and East a club, and South wins with his King. Declarer sees eight quick tricks in his combined hands, four Aces and four Kings, ordinarily enough to score slam with fair distribution. As West is marked with eight spades originally, he holds five cards in the other three suits; and as their division is probably 2-2-1, declarer has slim hope of winning by direct establishment a single trick in addition to his eight barren quick tricks.

However, East is squeezed immediately in three suits. East can not shed a heart lest dummy's two club entries escort dummy's hearts to win tricks, and a diamond discard is similarly prohibitive. While East's actual club discard also seems dubious, it is the least of three evils.

Declarer runs two quick heart tricks to test the heart distribution, but the appearance of West's honors and East's peter proves the suit hopeless. Declarer lays down the King of diamonds to get a further count, and the situation looks brighter when West follows suit. As West now holds two minor suit cards, declarer probes further by playing the King of clubs, and when the Queen of Clubs falls, the game can be made if West holds a diamond. Dummy leads a diamond. If declarer ducks, the triple squeeze will develop, but declarer, not daring to let East in, plays the Ace. The fall of West's Queen of diamonds reveals the location of all adverse cards, and resolves the ending shown in the first diagram into a double dummy problem.

A true elimination may be combined with a strip squeeze to make some such combination as a fork strip forced automatic squeeze. We submit the forced squeeze ending with a slight alteration in the spade suit.

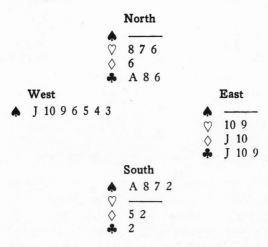

North
♠ ——
♡ 8 7 6
◊ 6
♣ A 8 6

West
♠ J 10 9 6 5 4 3

East
♠ ——
♡ 10 9
◊ J 10
♣ J 10 9

South
♠ A 8 7 2
♡ ——
◊ 5 2
♣ 2

At notrump South leads the seven of spades to win four tricks instead of three. West wins with the nine and continues with the Jack which South permits to win, and the remainder of the play proceeds as in the original diagram. The composer of double dummy problems frequently resorts to this method of superimposing one endplay on another to build up his complex problems.

Cook: In the deal on page 140 South can let West win the first spade trick.- Editor.

The Perkins Coup

The most famous strip squeeze in Bridge history was played by the author of "Vital Tricks," Frank K. Perkins of Boston, Mass., several years ago in the Filene Plaque Tournament.

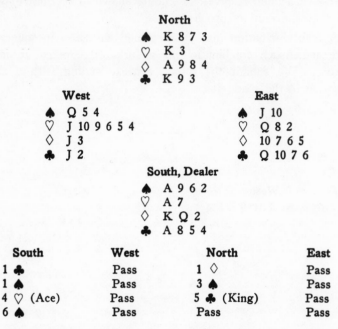

North
♠ K 8 7 3
♡ K 3
◇ A 9 8 4
♣ K 9 3

West
♠ Q 5 4
♡ J 10 9 6 5 4
◇ J 3
♣ J 2

East
♠ J 10
♡ Q 8 2
◇ 10 7 6 5
♣ Q 10 7 6

South, Dealer
♠ A 9 6 2
♡ A 7
◇ K Q 2
♣ A 8 5 4

South	West	North	East
1 ♣	Pass	1 ◇	Pass
1 ♠	Pass	3 ♠	Pass
4 ♡ (Ace)	Pass	5 ♣ (King)	Pass
6 ♠	Pass	Pass	Pass

The bidding was obviously optimistic. While North and South sported all the Aces and Kings, East and West held the secondary honors.

Against Mr. Perkins, playing South at six spades, West opened with the Jack of hearts. A losing trump and a losing club made the contract look sour. But, in the *Boston Herald*, Mr. Perkins did not reveal his identity as declarer, and he wrote, "South was a hard boiled player who gives nothing away, and is always looking for his chance!" He ran eight tricks immediately, two tops in each suit, leaving this endplay:

North
- ♠ 8 7
- ♡ ———
- ◇ 9 8
- ♣ 9

West
- ♠ Q
- ♡ 10 9 6 5
- ◇ ———
- ♣ ———

East
- ♠ ———
- ♡ Q
- ◇ 10 7
- ♣ Q 10

South
- ♠ 9 6
- ♡ ———
- ◇ Q
- ♣ 8 4

Requiring four of the last five tricks for his contract, South threw in West with a spade, while East informatively shed his heart. West had to lead a heart, North discarded his losing club while South trumped, and East was automatically squeezed. As East couldn't discard from diamonds without establishing them, East dropped a club. North trumped a club to draw East's last, and South scored the final trick with a club.

GIVING JOEY A JUMP RAISE IN MAMA'S OWN SUIT.

When the squeeze play is the preparation play for the elimination endplay, the compound is a Squeeze Strip. Note how the lead of the forcing card makes the adversary disgorge an established winner in order to guard another suit.

SQUEEZE STRIP

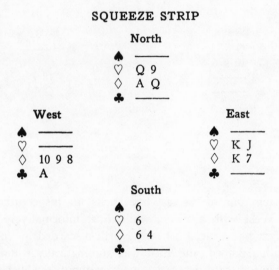

```
                      North
                   ♠ ——
                   ♡ Q 9
                   ◇ A Q
                   ♣ ——
     West                          East
  ♠ ——                          ♠ ——
  ♡ ——                          ♡ K J
  ◇ 10 9 8                      ◇ K 7
  ♣ A                           ♣ ——
                      South
                   ♠ 6
                   ♡ 6
                   ◇ 6 4
                   ♣ ——
```

With spades trumps South leads his last spade in order to win three tricks. Dummy sheds a heart, and East is squeezed out of a good heart, as he must defend his King of diamonds. South next throws East in with a heart. Note how this endplay is evolved from the complete deal in which it occurs.

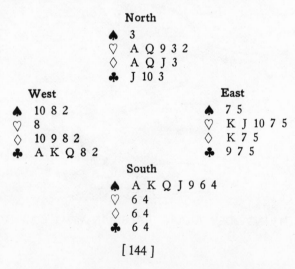

```
                      North
                   ♠ 3
                   ♡ A Q 9 3 2
                   ◇ A Q J 3
                   ♣ J 10 3
     West                          East
  ♠ 10 8 2                       ♠ 7 5
  ♡ 8                            ♡ K J 10 7 5
  ◇ 10 9 8 2                     ◇ K 7 5
  ♣ A K Q 8 2                    ♣ 9 7 5
                      South
                   ♠ A K Q J 9 6 4
                   ♡ 6 4
                   ◇ 6 4
                   ♣ 6 4
```

West deals and passes, North calls one heart pleasing East who passes, South one spade, West two clubs, North two diamonds, East passes again, and South jumps to four spades, finishing the auction. West leads the King then Queen of clubs, and as East fails to encourage the continuance of the suit by not petering, West switches to the eightspot of hearts. South stops to reflect. West's defensive bid must be based on five clubs; and as East did not echo in clubs, West must hold the Ace of clubs along with his King and Queen. Furthermore, if West holds either red King, he surely would have opened the bidding. Therefore East holds both red Kings, and the squeeze strip play is indicated. Dummy hops up with the Ace of hearts. Declarer runs all his trumps in order to squeeze East down to one heart and two diamonds, and to throw him in with the heart at the end.

Hexagon Squeeze Strip

We know of only one hexagon squeeze strip in existence, which is the basis of the famous Elks Misery Problem. See Chapter Twenty-one. also *Double Dummy Bridge,* Problem Number 209, (A-149),

Overtone Squeezes

In music, overtones are those minor vibrations in high octaves which are the natural offspring of certain basic chords. Similarly, certain preliminary squeezing operations may be considered the overtones of some final endplay positions. As in music, only the trained ear can detect these overtones. An amusing deal taken from a Pitt story by the author and published in the *Bridge World* illustrates the idea of a squeeze as an overtone.

Mushroom Roulette

Of wild mushrooms that you know not don't put any into your pot.
First have them checked by an expert, for if you don't heed this alert
And dare to eat a strange fungus, you may end missing from among us.-
Coffin's Law

TRIPLE SQUEEZE FORK STRIP

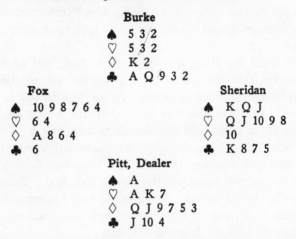

Burke
♠ 5 3 2
♡ 5 3 2
◇ K 2
♣ A Q 9 3 2

Fox
♠ 10 9 8 7 6 4
♡ 6 4
◇ A 8 6 4
♣ 6

Sheridan
♠ K Q J
♡ Q J 10 9 8
◇ 10
♣ K 8 7 5

Pitt, Dealer
♠ A
♡ A K 7
◇ Q J 9 7 5 3
♣ J 10 4

After each player had bid his longest suit, Pitt bought the contract for three notrump doubled by Sheridan. Fox opened with the ten of spades, and the Jack dropped the Ace. Unless spades are blocked, the contract is sewered. Even if Pitt can finesse clubs successfully for five tricks, he can win a total of only eight tricks before opponents run their spades. Hence diamonds must be set up and run before opponents can run all their spade tricks. Pitt led a low diamond which dummy's King won, and dummy returned another diamond whereon Sheridan sluffed a spade to unblock, and again Fox held up his Ace.

Fox thought to himself, "What a wonderful defensive play Sheridan has started, and will complete when he sheds his last blocking spade on my Ace of diamonds so that I can run down all my spades."

"Well, boys," announced Pitt, "three notrump is in the bag! I see through the plot, Fox. This hand is just another brain-child of yours! I'm supposed to lead another diamond so Sheridan can shake his last blocking spade, but I'm gonna fool ya!" So saying, Pitt abandoned the diamonds and finessed the Jack of clubs, and the poor flustered Sheridan grabbed the trick with his King, making game easy for Pitt.

Greatly annoyed, Fox chided Sheridan, "Don't you see, Ed? You're supposed to lay off that club. If Sam finesses again, still hold up your King and stop the run of the suit in the entryless dummy."

Said Pitt, "Well, I must say, Doc. Your defence is cooked. Even if Ed does hold up his King of clubs twice, I can still make my four club tricks for game. You forgot to give yourself more than two hearts headed by a high one. All I have to do now is to run the Ace, King, then a low heart throwing Ed in the lead, and after he takes two more heart tricks and a spade trick, he is down to naught but clubs, and perforce must lead one up to dummy's Ace-Queen."

"I take it you call the play a fork strip, Sam?" asked Sheridan.

"That is the final endplay," replied Pitt, "but it started as a triple squeeze!"

"Nuts! How do you get that way, Sam?" asked Fox.

"I can prove it. Very simple. If Sheridan sheds a club on my second diamond lead, he can not hold up twice with his King of clubs to shut out the suit; if he sheds a heart, I can lead a third diamond, forcing Fox to win with his Ace to hold me down to nine tricks, or else I can develop ten tricks by the original line of play."

While the preparatory squeeze play is usually thought of in conjunction with fork strips, it may also be valuable to develop an entry elimination.

DOUBLE SQUEEZE ENTRY STRIP

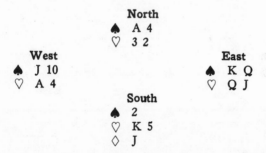

```
                    North
                 ♠  A 4
                 ♡  3 2
     West                        East
  ♠  J 10                     ♠  K Q
  ♡  A 4                      ♡  Q J
                    South
                 ♠  2
                 ♡  K 5
                 ◇  J
```

At notrump South, needing three tricks, leads his good diamond. West sheds a spade, North a heart, and East a heart. This manoeuvre completes the squeeze. North plays the Ace of spades to strip West of his last spade, and South plays his King of hearts! You'll find this one in the double dummy problems.

The squeeze strips may be accompanied by all the variations attendant upon pure strips. Mr. Arthur Brown, a well known Boston player, showed us a beauty.

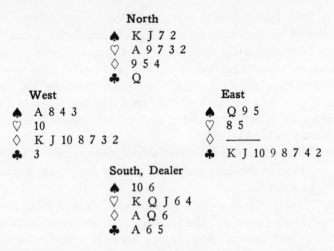

North
♠ K J 7 2
♡ A 9 7 3 2
♢ 9 5 4
♣ Q

West
♠ A 8 4 3
♡ 10
♢ K J 10 8 7 3 2
♣ 3

East
♠ Q 9 5
♡ 8 5
♢ ———
♣ K J 10 9 8 7 4 2

South, Dealer
♠ 10 6
♡ K Q J 6 4
♢ A Q 6
♣ A 6 5

Playing South Mr. Brown dealt and bid one heart, West two diamonds, North four hearts, and East five clubs. South persisted to five hearts, and West unwisely doubled, closing the auction.

West led his singleton club, and declarer alternately trumped clubs and led trumps, developing this endplay:

JETTISON EXIT SQUEEZE STRIP

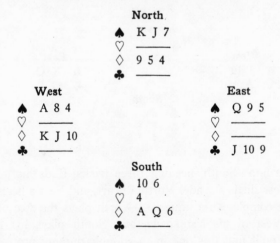

North
♠ K J 7
♡ ———
♢ 9 5 4
♣ ———

West
♠ A 8 4
♡ ———
♢ K J 10
♣ ———

East
♠ Q 9 5
♡ ———
♢ ———
♣ J 10 9

South
♠ 10 6
♡ 4
♢ A Q 6
♣ ———

South had the lead and required four of the last six tricks in order to fulfill his contract. South led his last trump on which the discards in turn were a spade, a diamond, and a club. South led a spade and West hopped up with his Ace and exited by returning the suit. But the timing was wrong for West. Dummy's King of spades won and a diamond was lost to West, who had to lead up to South's Ace-Queen, giving South his contract. Had West ducked the spade lead, dummy would have put up the King and thrown West in with his now bare Ace of spades with the same result.

As in Chess, a gambit play is an immediate sacrifice for future gains. Here unblocking to gain two tricks should havé been West's objective. Although South's clever squeeze elimination play was highly commendable, West could have defeated the contract. On the lead of the last heart West should have jettisoned his Ace of spades!

A somewhat similar ending caused plenty of fireworks in the New England Championships held at the Boston Art Club in February, 1935. In this freak deal all thirteen diamonds were held by one side, of which one partner held all four Aces!

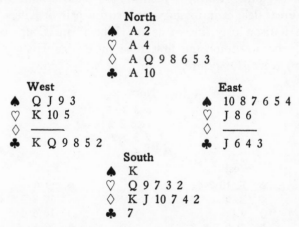

North
♠ A 2
♡ A 4
◇ A Q 9 8 6 5 3
♣ A 10

West
♠ Q J 9 3
♡ K 10 5
◇ ——
♣ K Q 9 8 5 2

East
♠ 10 8 7 6 5 4
♡ J 8 6
◇ ——
♣ J 6 4 3

South
♠ K
♡ Q 9 7 3 2
◇ K J 10 7 4 2
♣ 7

While six diamonds was the popular contract that was fulfilled at most tables, Mr. Lawrence Weiss of Boston playing North earned a clean top score at six notrump.

As West had bid clubs, East led the three of clubs, his proper fourth best opening, and West put up the Queen, forcing the Ace. Mr. Weiss ran two spade tricks and seven diamond tricks, squeezing West down to the King-ten of hearts and the King of clubs. Mr. Weiss pitched West in with a club, forcing him to lead away from his King of hearts.

Exit Squeeze Strip

While Mr. Weiss deservedly earned his top score, West was asleep at the switch. A simple matter of exiting, discarding his King of clubs, would have let East in with the Jack of clubs to lead a heart, killing dummy's Queen. As East discarded all his spades and two clubs, West can count North down to ♥ A-x accompanied by either the ten or Jack of clubs. In the first case East gets in with the Jack of clubs to lead a heart; in the second the club trick sacrificed is offset by a heart trick gained.

Fitzwilliam Coup

This is indeed a pretty handful of attack and defence, but we consider that our own play, a double-exit squeeze strip, "takes the cake." We have often wondered why most players enjoy playing the dummy rather than defending. Personally, we prefer the defensive game. Sitting West in the hand below, the writer found great delight in tossing overboard a pair of Kings, a classic double jettison play known as the Fitzwilliam Coup, because it actually occurred for the first time in Bridge History at Fitzwilliam, New Hampshire.

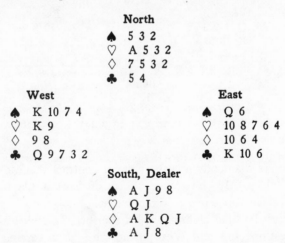

```
                    North
                 ♠  5 3 2
                 ♡  A 5 3 2
                 ◊  7 5 3 2
                 ♣  5 4
     West                          East
  ♠  K 10 7 4                   ♠  Q 6
  ♡  K 9                        ♡  10 8 7 6 4
  ◊  9 8                        ◊  10 6 4
  ♣  Q 9 7 3 2                  ♣  K 10 6
                  South, Dealer
                 ♠  A J 9 8
                 ♡  Q J
                 ◊  A K Q J
                 ♣  A J 8
```

South dealt and bid one diamond, North one heart, South two spades, North three diamonds, and South three notrump , closing the auction. Yours truly led the three of clubs and the fun was on.

Squeezed Double Exit

East's King forced the Ace. On the last round of diamonds we discarded the nine then King of hearts! We wished to protect the black suits and these discards were reasonably safe. Since South had bid spades and diamonds, it was fair to assume that he held no great heart length.

South, smiling pleasantly at this apparent gift of a heart trick, hastened to lay down his Queen and Jack of hearts. But our gift was Indian, for the Ace of hearts was frozen out. We discarded two low spades, because we realized that the only chance to defeat the contract was to find in East's hand either the Queen of spades or the Jack of clubs. In the latter case, a club discard might well hand declarer the game.

When declarer next laid down the Ace of spades it was obvious that East held the Queen, since otherwise declarer would have overtaken one of the heart honors to take the spade finesse. Foreseeing that South intended to throw us in on the next spade lead, we planted our second King under the Ace! Result, down one!

South could have won nine tricks in spite of our rather artistic defence. Instead of displaying such greedy haste in cashing the Queen and Jack of hearts, he should have paused to count the adverse distributions.

After the discard of the King of hearts, West is marked with an original holding of four red cards and nine black ones. The opening lead of the three of clubs indicated at most five clubs and at least four spades, thus marking East with at most two spades. South should have overtaken the first heart with dummy's Ace and led a low spade, finessing the eightspot. A spade return would have established a spade trick easily, and a club lead would have yielded the ninth trick at once!

Triple Squeeze Jettison Finesse

Terence Reese showed us the monster deal below with a gorgeous endplay. South opened four notrump on his ten rapid tricks, North raised to five notrump to show his trick in clubs, so South bid six notrump, end, hoping for his low spade to win trick twelve.

```
                    ♠ 6 5 3
                    ♡ 10 8 5 2
                    ◊ 10 6 5 2
                    ♣ K 7
    ♠ 10 9                          ♠ J 8 7 2
    ♡ J 9 7 6                       ♡ 4 3
    ◊ J 9 8 7                       ◊ 4 3
    ♣ Q J 10                        ♣ 8 5 4 3 2
                    ♠ A K Q 4
                    ♡ A K Q
                    ◊ A K Q
                    ♣ A 9 6
```

Against six notrump West led his queen of clubs to South's ace and South cashed his six red-suit winners but no red jack dropped to let dummy score a red ten for the twelfth trick. Next South won three top spade tricks but spades also failed to split 3-3. However, South's *third* spade trick triples squeezed West who, unable to spare a red jack, shed a club, dummy jettisoned his king of clubs and East scored his jack of spades. Down to ♣ 8 - 5, East led his five and South finessed his six to score his slam.

The deal has a simple cook. If South cashes his three top spades first, he triple squeezes West early. If West casts a club, South gets three club tricks straightaway. Reese admitted that the deal looks artificial, and we suspect that perhaps Reese cooked up the whole caper himself!

Oswald Jacoby wrote up the deal in his NEA Service newspaper column.

DIVISION THREE

Coups - Endplays of Time

THE MARTIEN COUP from Gay Paree

```
                        ♠ K 6
                        ♡ K Q 8 5 3
                        ◇ 9 2
    ♠ J 3               ♣ Q 7 6 4          ♠ 10 9 4
    ♡ 10 9 6 2                             ♡ J 7 4
    ◇ A K Q J 10 5                         ◇ 7 6
    ♣ J                                    ♣ K 10 9 5 2
                        ♠ A Q 8 7 5 2
                        ♡ A
                        ◇ 8 4 3
                        ♣ A 8 3
```

South	West	North	East
1 ♠	Double	Pass	2 ♣
2 ♠	3 ◇	3 ♡	Pass
3 ♠	Pass	4 ♠ (final bid)	

This deal from *Le Bridge* of June 1961 illustrates the new Martien coup. Note West's preference for the takeout double over bidding his diamonds first. A heart game is cold if East holds ♡A-K-Q-x, or less heart strength with compensating black-suit tricks.

In this deal reported as played by top French experts, West led his ◇K, ◇A then ◇Q on which dummy shed a club and East a heart. West shifted to the ♡2, won by South's ace. South won the ♠A then ♠K in dummy. Dummy won the ♡K but East trumped the ♡Q so South lost a club in the end for one down..

A lively autopsy ensued. Can declarer surely win ten tricks by ruffing the third diamond lead with the ♠K in dummy, cashing the ♡A, and throwing East on lead on the third round of spades?

East is stuck,- has to return a heart to dummy's ♡K-Q, or open his club tenace to let dummy's ♣Q win then a heart trick..

STOP! Before reading further, see if you can find an escape for East. For solution, please turn this book around 180 degrees.

East can slide out of the endplay trap by the Martien Coup! When dummy ruffs the third diamond lead with the ♠K, East simply discards a trump!

CHAPTER SIXTEEN

BASIC COUPS

THE TERM "coup" comes from the French *coup*, a blow. As *coup aux dames* means move in Checkers and *coup aux échecs* means move in Chess, in Bridge a coup might well mean any play or lead. In fact, Bridge players in certain sections heavily populated by Frenchmen, notably around Holyoke, Mass. and Manchester, New Hampshire, use its literal Anglicized form frequently. They say "cut" meaning to trump. Instead of trumping a club, you "cut" a club. As the French verb, *couper*, literally translated means to cut, it is apparent that a Bridge coup is definitely limited to plays of the trump suit. And as it is used mostly in the sense of its higher French use in *coup d'état*, it suggests a brilliant stroke, a strategic move, whether in defence or in attack.

But from the early days of Whist, the term coup has been used loosely in connection with any unusual play of significance. Such famous coups as the Bath Coup and Vienna Coup were named after the places where they first occurred, as in Bath, England, and Vienna, Austria. The Deschapelles Coup was named after a famous French Whist player, Guillaume le Breton Deschapelles, who first discovered and used it. And the Grand Coup is so called because it is a highly spectacular play wherein a player trumps his partner's plain suit winner in order to capture eventually an adverse trump honor. This type of play is based on the True Coup. The other Bridge coups, which have little or nothing at all to do with trumps, or endplays for that matter, are given in Chapter Twenty on Miscellaneous Coups.

Basic Position

The True Coup has been a teaser to name accurately and descriptively. We call it the

OVERRUFF FINESSE ENDPLAY

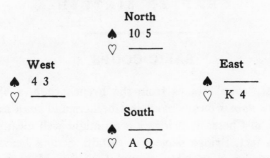

North
♠ 10 5
♡ ——

West
♠ 4 3
♡ ——

East
♠ ——
♡ K 4

South
♠ ——
♡ A Q

With hearts trumps South can't win both tricks unless North has the lead at the twelfth trick. North leads the plain suit, spades, forcing East to trump, and South overtrumps meanwhile finessing. Obviously, the play is an overtrumping finesse occurring at the end. Suppose the end position were:

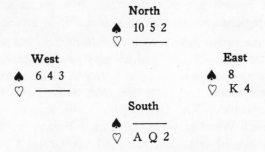

North
♠ 10 5 2
♡ ——

West
♠ 6 4 3
♡ ——

East
♠ 8
♡ K 4

South
♠ ——
♡ A Q 2

North leads his top spade, but South has couped himself and has to trump. In order to avoid getting locked in the lead prematurely, the stage for the coup is frequently set by the preliminary reducing of superfluous trumps. This peculiar phenomenon of the all-vital time element and other tricky preparatory plays in accurate time sequence account for the divisional classification of the True Coups as "Endplays of Time." The timing must be perfect. Whenever the dominant hand trumps partner's plain suit winners to keep this element of time in its proper sequence, the coup is said to be "grand."

Therefore, with superfluous trumps two steps are required to consummate a True Coup.

1. Declarer strips the hand down to a few cards, often by trumping, in order to rid himself of excess trumps to avoid the ending shown in the last diagram.

2. He captures an adverse trump honor by leading the plain suit at the end, as in the first diagram. He thus initiates the deadly overtrumping finesse in trumps to pick up the luckless adverse guarded trump honor, which it is impossible to envelop until the end, when its holder has been stripped of all his plain suit cards. Take the endplay in its popularly conceived form:

GRAND COUP

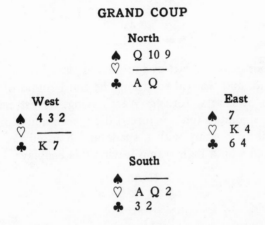

North
♠ Q 10 9
♡ ——
♣ A Q

West
♠ 4 3 2
♡ ——
♣ K 7

East
♠ 7
♡ K 4
♣ 6 4

South
♠ ——
♡ A Q 2
♣ 3 2

South, requiring all five tricks with hearts trumps, finesses the Queen of clubs. If North now cashes the Ace of clubs, the unfortunate ending shown in the second diagram of this chapter will develop. To avoid this catastrophe, South instead *trumps a good spade* (grand coup), and another club lead completes the correctly timed preparation for the endplay.

The Grand Coup is so rare that any player who makes one is entitled to pat himself on the back and join the Grand Coup Club, whose membership is more élite and exclusive than even the Hole-In-One-Club at Golf.

In twelve years of play the author has made only one Grand Coup, which follows:

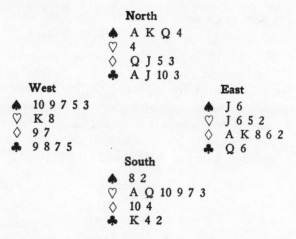

```
                        North
                    ♠ A K Q 4
                    ♡ 4
                    ◊ Q J 5 3
                    ♣ A J 10 3
    West                                East
♠ 10 9 7 5 3                        ♠ J 6
♡ K 8                               ♡ J 6 5 2
◊ 9 7                               ◊ A K 8 6 2
♣ 9 8 7 5                           ♣ Q 6
                        South
                    ♠ 8 2
                    ♡ A Q 10 9 7 3
                    ◊ 10 4
                    ♣ K 4 2
```

Against our final contract of four hearts played at South, West led a diamond, and we had to trump the third round of the suit with the ten of hearts, forcing West's King. West returned a club, and the dummy's ten   forced the Queen and King.

We reentered dummy with a spade and finessed the nine of trumps, and won a high trump leaving this endplay:

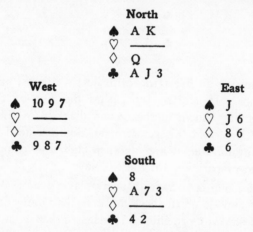

```
                        North
                    ♠ A K
                    ♡ ———
                    ◊ Q
                    ♣ A J 3
    West                                East
♠ 10 9 7                            ♠ J
♡ ———                               ♡ J 6
◊ ———                               ◊ 8 6
♣ 9 8 7                             ♣ 6
                        South
                    ♠ 8
                    ♡ A 7 3
                    ◊ ———
                    ♣ 4 2
```

Requiring all six tricks, we put North in with a club and *in effect we discarded our superfluous trump by ruffing the master diamond,* grand coup. We reentered the dummy with a spade,

and dummy led another spade. Had East trumped, we would
have overtrumped, pulled East's last trump, and won a club trick.
Hence East had to discard, so did we, and on dummy's club lead
we couped East's trumps.

The False Coups are positions resembling Coups, but alert
defence can defeat them by finding their weakness.

FALSE COUP

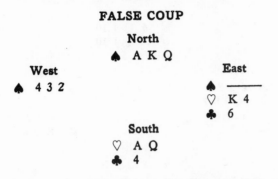

North
♠ A K Q

West
♠ 4 3 2

East
♠ ——
♡ K 4
♣ 6

South
♡ A Q
♣ 4

With hearts trumps North leads a good spade. East must
trump in order to score his club trick.

Exploded Theory

One well known writer calls coups "trump reducing plays,"
because he considers ruffing to reduce superfluous trumps their
typical characteristic. Calling a coup a trump reducing play is
inaccurate and misleading, because the trump reducing is only a
preparatory play. At times it is vital to plays of other groups,
especially in preparing for an elimination or a squeeze, or in the
reverse dummy type of hand. See Deal 48 on page 62 of *Vital
Tricks* by Frank K. Perkins. Mr. Perkins' fine book is complementary to *Endplays* because it thoroughly covers middlegame
plays with many beautiful hands. And again, in many coups
preliminary trump reducing is unnecessary or altogether wanting.
The basic manoeuvre of all True Coups is the winning trump
finesse against the enemy's higher trump at the end. *The lead
for the trump finesse is always from a plain suit* because the leader
holds no trump. As this characteristic phenomenon accounts for
the necessity of the endplay, every True Coup should properly be
called a plain suit trump finesse, or more simply, the Overruff
Finesse.

Furthermore, another preparatory play may embellish a coup, the continuous leading of plain suit winners through the opponent being couped so that they pin his trumps, until the endplay traps his trumps eventually. Note how embellishments are entirely wanting in the deal below.

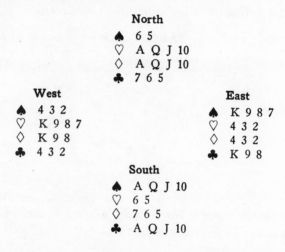

North
♠ 6 5
♡ A Q J 10
♢ A Q J 10
♣ 7 6 5

West
♠ 4 3 2
♡ K 9 8 7
♢ K 9 8
♣ 4 3 2

East
♠ K 9 8 7
♡ 4 3 2
♢ 4 3 2
♣ K 9 8

South
♠ A Q J 10
♡ 6 5
♢ 7 6 5
♣ A Q J 10

As the cards lie, a grand slam is a simple matter at notrump., or with either minor suit as trumps, but the grand slam with spades or hearts trumps can be made only by the simple Overruff Finesse without any frills. The hands are easily stripped down to the basic position, as in the example shown in the first diagram of this chapter.

Any coup, embellished by the continuous leads of plain suit winners through the opponent's trumps, is called a Continuous Coup. Two fine examples from actual play follow.

Mr. Lombard Williams, a famous real estate expert of Boston, Mass., and former New England Director of the United States Bridge Association, was the only player in the New England Championship at the Boston Art Club in February, 1935, to score a slam in the deal below. He made a True Coup, an Overruff Finesse.

North
- ♠ 7
- ♡ J 10 8
- ◇ A J
- ♣ Q J 6 5 4 3 2

West
- ♠ K Q 9 8 6 4 3
- ♡ 6 2
- ◇ 7 2
- ♣ K 9

East
- ♠ 10 5 2
- ♡ K 5 4 3
- ◇ Q 9 5 3
- ♣ 10 8

South
- ♠ A J
- ♡ A Q 9 7
- ◇ K 10 8 6 4
- ♣ A 7

At most tables South played the deal at four hearts, and won only nine or ten tricks. West led the King of spades invariably which South won with his Ace, and the majority of South players erred in hastening to trump spades and diamonds in dummy, or to draw trumps, or both.

Mr. Williams won twelve tricks for a clean top score by immediately establishing dummy's great club suit before touching trumps. After winning the spade opening, he played the Ace then low in clubs, throwing West in with the King. West returned the Queen of spades in order to shorten dummy's trumps and thus protect East's King of trumps against successive trump finesses. Dummy trumped and led the Jack then ten of hearts through East's King, on which East had to play low. Dummy switched to and continued the established clubs, and it mattered not when East trumped, as his guarded King of trumps was hopelessly caught in the mesh of master plain suit leads long before it finally fell prey to the cruel overruff finesse endplay.

Beautiful and choice endplays can not be found by active seeking. Like rare and exotic flowers they appear only by chance. If you go out to hunt them, you'll have no luck; but if you just wait patiently and keep your eyes open, they'll pop up of their own accord. During the proof reading of this work last August, we wandered up to the A. Marshall Jones' in Fitzwilliam, N. H., for an evening of "family Bridge." Partnered with Miss Beverly Jones, we enjoyed another Continuous Coup. The hand was so impressive that we published it in *Leisure Magazine,* and later worked it into a Pitt story in the *Bridge World,* which story we reproduce here.

The Killjoy Coup

Sam Pitt was kibitzing the play of Mrs. Katzenellengebogen one pleasant evening at a weekly neighborhood duplicate game. Mrs. Katzenellengebogen was fair, flush, and fifty, and really quite fat; but with all due respect to her, she was considered no back number as a Contract player.

"Oh Mr. Pitt," she giggled. "You should make *me* nervous, after all those fine lessons you've given me in the past. Why, I'd simply *adore* to have you watch." After adjusting himself comfortably in a plush chair, Pitt observed:

North, Dealer
♠ A J 10 8 7 5 4
♡ A J
◇ A J
♣ A J

West		East
♠ Q 9		♠ K 3 2
♡ Q		♡ 10 5 3 2
◇ Q 9 8 7 5		◇ K 10 3 2
♣ Q 9 8 7 5		♣ 3 2

South
♠ 6
♡ K 9 8 7 6 4
◇ 6 4
♣ K 10 6 4

North	East	South	West
1 ♠	Pass	2 ♡	Pass
3 ♠	Pass	4 ♡	Pass
4 NT	Pass	5 ♡	Pass
5 NT	Pass	6 ♣	Pass
7 ♡	Double	All pass	

During the bidding Pitt looked disgustedly at the ceiling when Mrs. Katzenellengebogen called six clubs. While West was huddling himself over his opening lead, Mrs. Katzenellengebogen turned and smiled at Pitt for his approval, but his face was expressionless,—like a Chinaman's.

West led the seven of diamonds, forcing dummy's Ace. South trumped the second round of spades, dummy cashed the Ace of hearts, felling West's lone Queen, and South trumped another spade, establishing dummy's spades. Dummy recaptured the lead with the Jack of hearts, and Pitt glanced at the ceiling again. Dummy led spades continuously through East, who simply discarded and discarded, first all his clubs then some diamonds, leaving:

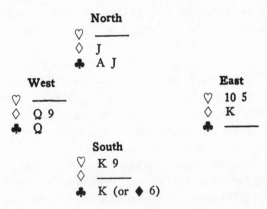

Mrs. Katzenellengebogen led the Ace of clubs from dummy, whereon East pounced with a trump, defeating the contract one trick.

"Mr. Pitt, I knew I was too weak to bid those clubs to show the King," moaned Mrs. Katzenellengebogen. Her face brightened, and she added, "Wasn't I smart to make six hearts by the coup play? But I couldn't have made seven!"

Pitt replied, "With your comment on the bidding I agree, but you had seven hearts all wrapped up to take home,—until you failed to cash the King of clubs before you made the Jack of hearts.

"Oh, Mr. Pitt! Why are you *always* such a killjoy?"

Pitt copied the deal and entered it in his collection under the title, "The Killjoy Coup."

Pitt's point is well taken. The proper development of many coup positions calls for precise timing to avoid going astray, as did poor Mrs. Katzenellengebogen.

Note carefully that, if North holds one more established spade to lead, declarer doesn't have to cash the King of clubs before the Jack of hearts to win the grand slam. In this case, the development would be identical with that in the preceding deal played by Mr. Lombard Williams. Compare carefully this difference of play in the two deals.

En Passant

In the game of Chess, the conventional way to capture an opponent's piece is to displace it from the square it occupies with your own piece, and to remove the enemy piece from the board out of action. The pawns, the little chessmen in front of the other pieces, may move directly forward only one square at a time, except that they have the special privilege of moving two squares on their first move. Another peculiarity of pawn play is that a pawn cannot capture an enemy's piece directly in front of it. To capture any piece, a pawn moves one square diagonally forward into the square occupied by the enemy's piece, and you remove the latter in the usual fashion from the chessboard out of play. *En Passant,* a French term applied to Chess, refers to capturing your opponent's pawn by moving your own pawn *into* the square *through which* his pawn passed in making its especially privileged double move, and by removing his pawn from the board, just as if it *had occupied* the square through which it had passed. The theory of this exceptional play is that the enemy's pawn really made *two separate moves* in the one privileged double move allowed on its opening play, and that you may capture it exactly as if it had progressed only the one square usually allowed by the rules.

This play in Chess has a counterpart in a unique Bridge endplay, a special kind of plain suit trump finesse wherein an otherwise losing trump wins a trick immediately, or becomes established for a trick later. It benefits from *two moves,* two privileged plays made on one trick when a loser is discarded on a loser, the enemy's master trump. A given mass in trumps scores an otherwise impossible trick against an equal adverse mass of higher rank.

EN PASSANT

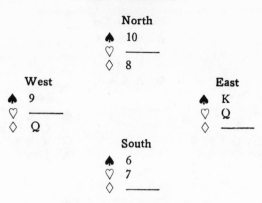

North
♠ 10
♡ ——
◇ 8

West
♠ 9
♡ ——
◇ Q

East
♠ K
♡ Q
◇ ——

South
♠ 6
♡ 7
◇ ——

Hearts are trumps and North leads a diamond in order to make South's trump good for a trick now or later, depending on whether East discards or trumps. The trump mass may be duplicated as follows:

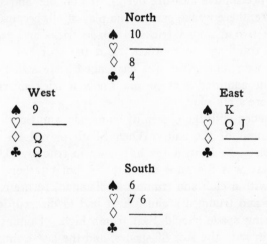

North
♠ 10
♡ ——
◇ 8
♣ 4

West
♠ 9
♡ ——
◇ Q
♣ Q

East
♠ K
♡ Q J
◇ ——
♣ ——

South
♠ 6
♡ 7 6
◇ ——
♣ ——

With hearts trumps North leads a diamond or a club to make up a trump trick for South. This endplay occurred in a friendly neighborhood duplicate game in this deal:

THE HOUDINI COUP

North, Dealer
- ♠ A 10 5 4
- ♡ 4
- ◇ 8 7 4 3
- ♣ A K 4 3

West
- ♠ 9 8 7 3
- ♡ 8
- ◇ Q J 10 9
- ♣ Q 9 8 5

East
- ♠ K Q J
- ♡ Q J 10 9
- ◇ A K 5
- ♣ J 10 7

South
- ♠ 6 2
- ♡ A K 7 6 5 3 2
- ◇ 6 2
- ♣ 6 2

North dealt and bid one club, East doubled, South bid two hearts as a preemptive measure over East's double, and all passed.

Of course, there was apparently no play at all, because declarer had to lose two diamond tricks, a spade trick, and two trump tricks, just fulfilling the contract. But the score of one South player who won nine tricks was challenged. He said he was no Houdini, but admitted that he *did* know a trick or two about Bridge. Here's his play.

West opened with the Queen of diamonds, and South trumped the third round of the suit. When South played the Ace and King of hearts, he learned the bad news in trumps. Up to this point the play was the same at all tables, but our hero next put dummy in with a club and trumped a diamond, reentered dummy with a club and trumped a club. East had to discard, lest South shed his losing spade should East trump high. Dummy was reentered again with the Ace of spades, and the last losing club led to promote that extra trick in trumps, *en passant.*

East was a dotard. He should have overtaken West's opening lead of the Queen of diamonds with his King, and switched to the Queen of trumps. In order to win his extra trick, South must trump four times; and as North holds only three entries, it is impossible for South to consummate all four ruffs if the defence deprives South of his precious extra ruff by stubbornly refusing to lead anything South can trump.

STEALING BASES

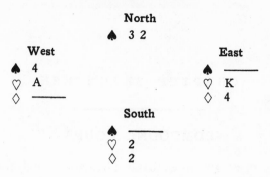

If declarer keeps a Poker face, he can sometimes make *en passant faux*. Dummy leads a spade, and if East doesn't have his wits about him, discarding a diamond instead of trumping, South steals a trick! Again, note a three-card variation:

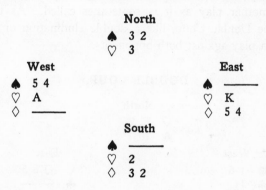

With hearts trumps North and South are entitled to one trick if either has the lead, but not to two. And yet, it is surprising the number of tricks we have stolen by the *en passant* plays. North leads a spade. If East passes, South trumps and leads a diamond, which West should trump. Of course, if West thinks East holds a trump and no diamond, West might pass.

As these *en passant* situations also occur quite frequently in the early play, their basic principle should be mastered thoroughly.

CHAPTER SEVENTEEN

COMPOUND COUPS

W HILE there are three basic eliminations and three basic squeezes, there is only one basic coup position as described in the last chapter. The *en passant* play is not a basic position, but simply a complementary middlegame play. Similarly, while eliminations and squeezes have many compounds, there are only two basic coup compounds, the Double Coup and the Forced Coup or smother play as it is sometimes called. As the name suggests, the Double Coup, like a double elimination or a double squeeze, is a play against both opponents.

DOUBLE COUP

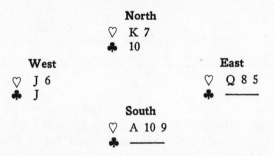

With hearts trumps the combination held by East and West is usually considered a sure trick winner. But note how their trump honors can be picked up if North leads a club. If East trumps low, South simply overruffs; and if East puts up the Queen of hearts, South plays the Ace and finesses through West's Jack on the return lead. The original deal from a rubber game caused a lot of excitement when declarer bid and made a grand slam in hearts.

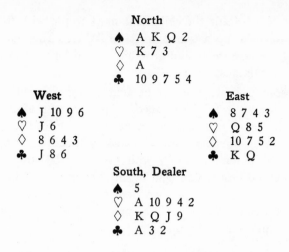

North
♠ A K Q 2
♡ K 7 3
◇ A
♣ 10 9 7 5 4

West
♠ J 10 9 6
♡ J 6
◇ 8 6 4 3
♣ J 8 6

East
♠ 8 7 4 3
♡ Q 8 5
◇ 10 7 5 2
♣ K Q

South, Dealer
♠ 5
♡ A 10 9 4 2
◇ K Q J 9
♣ A 3 2

South dealt and bid one heart, North two spades forcing to game, South three diamonds, North three hearts, South four notrump to show two Aces and the King of a bid suit, North five notrump to show the other two Aces, and South, trusting North for more solidity in hearts than he actually held, optimistically jumped to seven hearts. And declarer fulfilled his impossible looking contract! The notrump bids were Culbertson.

West opened with the Jack of spades, and South trumped the fourth round of the suit after discarding two clubs, played the Ace of clubs and Ace of diamonds, trumped a club, won two diamond tricks, and trumped a diamond to establish the double coup position at the end.

As North trumped a high diamond, he made a grand coup, so that the complete play was a Grand Double Coup!

The Double Coup has its false counterpart.

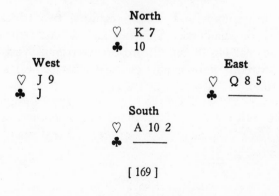

North
♡ K 7
♣ 10

West
♡ J 9
♣ J

East
♡ Q 8 5
♣ ———

South
♡ A 10 2
♣ ———

When North leads the club, East must trump with the Queen in order to make up a trump trick for West. This ending suggests that the defence should generally trump high when a double coup position is suspected.

The second basic coup compound is the Forced Coup, or smother play as it is often called. An opponent at the end of the hand is *forced* to make the trumpless trump lead for declarer, giving him the advantage of a revoke without revoking! The endplay enables him to catch with his singleton top trump the guarded second best trump held by an opponent. As this endplay depends on throwing in one opponent and forcing him to lead at the critical moment, in the early editions of "Endplays" this ending was called the Throwincoup.

FORCED COUP

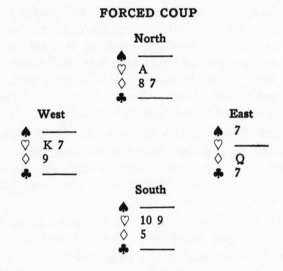

```
                    North
                 ♠ ———
                 ♡ A
                 ◇ 8 7
                 ♣ ———
    West                          East
 ♠ ———                          ♠ 7
 ♡ K 7                          ♡ ———
 ◇ 9                            ◇ Q
 ♣ ———                          ♣ 7
                    South
                 ♠ ———
                 ♡ 10 9
                 ◇ 5
                 ♣ ———
```

Hearts are trumps and South, requiring two tricks, throws East in with the diamond. This exit makes East return a black seven   so that North can discard or overtrump West and capture the apparently impregnably guarded King of hearts with the singleton Ace!

This ending is one of the most deceptive optical illusions in Bridge. It looks like, and in effect brings about, a result ordinarily obtainable only by a deliberate revoke. Yet the endplay is perfectly legitimate. It all looks perfectly simple, but show the original complete deal below to some friend not acquainted with the ending and see if he can find it.

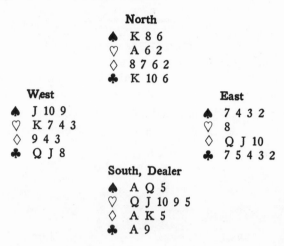

North
♠ K 8 6
♡ A 6 2
◇ 8 7 6 2
♣ K 10 6

West
♠ J 10 9
♡ K 7 4 3
◇ 9 4 3
♣ Q J 8

East
♠ 7 4 3 2
♡ 8
◇ Q J 10
♣ 7 5 4 3 2

South, Dealer
♠ A Q 5
♡ Q J 10 9 5
◇ A K 5
♣ A 9

South deals and bids one heart, North two hearts, South four notrump , and North, holding one Ace with some additional values, jumps to six hearts, closing the auction.

West leads the Jack of spades, which South wins. The Queen then Jack of hearts are finessed and win, but when East fails on the second heart lead, it looks as if dummy's Ace will never trap West's guarded King. South trumps the third round of clubs, runs two more spade tricks, and throws East in on the third round of diamonds, thereby making his impossible looking slam.

The hand has an amusing story connected with it. A well known Bridge teacher once thought she would try it on her duplicate players and slid the hand into one of her duplicate tournaments. When she discovered after the game that no one played the hand at hearts, but that several of her best customers actually bid and made six notrump by reason of a pretty automatic squeeze on West, was her face red!

CHAPTER EIGHTEEN

MULTIPLE COUPS

WHILE the double coups are Multiple Coups in a sense, this grouping of endplays refers to coups wherein the trump reducing preparatory play and/or the overruff finesse at the end is repeated. The Double Grand Coup involves repeated trump reducing.

```
                    North, Dealer
                    ♠ 8
                    ♡ A K 8 6
                    ◇ A K 4 2
                    ♣ Q J 10 2
       West                          East
       ♠ 7 5                         ♠ A J 6 4
       ♡ J 10 9                      ♡ Q 7 3
       ◇ J 7 6 5                     ◇ 10 9 8
       ♣ A K 9 4                     ♣ 8 6 5
                    South
                    ♠ K Q 10 9 3 2
                    ♡ 5 4 2
                    ◇ Q 3
                    ♣ 7 3
```

Playing South in the Monday Evening Duplicate at the Boston Chess Club, Sidney Wirt of Boston was the only player to score game at spades. North dealt and bid one club, South one spade; North two hearts, South two spades; North three diamonds, South three spades; North three notrump and South, counting on North for one spade, persisted to four spades, closing the auction.

West opened with the King, Ace, then low in clubs putting dummy in. Dummy's eightspot of spades coasted free winning the trick, South took the lead with the Queen of diamonds, and led the King of spades forcing East's Ace. East returned the ten of diamonds, and Mr. Wirt double-grand couped the deal for game by trumping twice and placing the lead in dummy when down to two cards, East held the Jack-six of spades under South's Queen-ten at the end.

The Triple Grand Coup wherein declarer "discards" three superfluous trumps is so rare that there is only one deal from actual play on record. In his "Auction Bridge Complete," 1926 edition, the late Milton C. Work wrote on page 396, "...mention was made of a Grand Coup Club; a Double Grand Coup Club which probably never has more than a dozen living members." Those were the good old days of Auction. Sidney Wirt is probably the charter member of the Double Grand Coup Club of Contract, and we have yet to find a contract player who played an original Triple Grand Coup. Here is Milton C. Work's from pages 396 and 397:

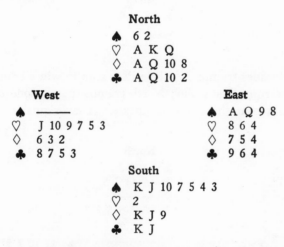

```
                        North
                    ♠  6 2
                    ♡  A K Q
                    ◇  A Q 10 8
                    ♣  A Q 10 2
        West                           East
    ♠  ——                          ♠  A Q 9 8
    ♡  J 10 9 7 5 3                 ♡  8 6 4
    ◇  6 3 2                        ◇  7 5 4
    ♣  8 7 5 3                      ♣  9 6 4
                        South
                    ♠  K J 10 7 5 4 3
                    ♡  2
                    ◇  K J 9
                    ♣  K J
```

Modern Contract bidding would be South one spade, North three clubs forcing, and South would eventually land in six spades.

West opens with the Jack of hearts which dummy wins. Dummy leads a spade and South's ten wins. Dummy reenters with a club and South's Jack of spades wins. (It would make no difference if East stepped in with his Ace at either trump lead.) South next trumps dummy's plain suit winners three times, triple grand coup, eventually trapping East's Ace-Queen of trumps at the end when North leads a plain suit from dummy at the twelfth trick.

The second type of Multiple Coup is the Repeating Coup, also called the Lydon Coup after John J. Lydon of Boston, Mass., who first discovered and made the play in an important tournament.

LYDON COUP

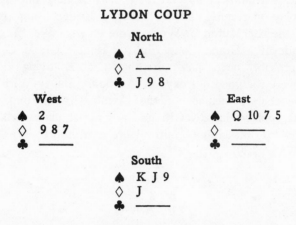

North
♠ A
♢ ――――
♣ J 9 8

West
♠ 2
♢ 9 8 7
♣ ――――

East
♠ Q 10 7 5
♢ ――――
♣ ――――

South
♠ K J 9
♢ J
♣ ――――

With spades trumps North leads a club to win all four tricks. South overruffs East's play, North trumps the diamond and leads a club to repeat the overruff finesse. The original deal was a freak.

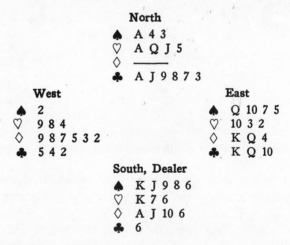

North
♠ A 4 3
♡ A Q J 5
♢ ――――
♣ A J 9 8 7 3

West
♠ 2
♡ 9 8 4
♢ 9 8 7 5 3 2
♣ 5 4 2

East
♠ Q 10 7 5
♡ 10 3 2
♢ K Q 4
♣ K Q 10

South, Dealer
♠ K J 9 8 6
♡ K 7 6
♢ A J 10 6
♣ 6

Playing South Mr. Lydon dealt and bid two spades, North six spades, and East doubled closing the auction. The Russell System, which Mr. Lydon was playing at the time, accounts for the peculiar bidding. This obsolete system was once recognized around Boston after it had been published in a volume called "Common Sense Contract" by Carlton Russell and Norman Bonney.

Against the contract of six spades West opened with the five of diamonds. Mr. Lydon alternately ruffed clubs and diamonds, and won three heart tricks, placing the lead in the dummy at the end to make a grand slam by his famous coup.

It should be noted that the Repeating Coups are not Double Coups. In the Repeating Coup the overruff finesse manoeuvre is *repeated* as above, while in a Double Coup one overruff finesse occurs involving *both opponents*. Furthermore, the term, "double," as applied to a double grand coup, does not refer to the coup proper, but simply indicates reducing trumps twice by ruffing plain suit winners.

William J. Huske of New York City unearthed a bizarre combination wherein both the trump reducing and the coup itself were repeated. He called it the Quadruple Grand Coup because four plain suit winners were trumped.

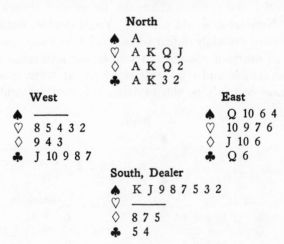

North
♠ A
♡ A K Q J
♢ A K Q 2
♣ A K 3 2

West
♠ ———
♡ 8 5 4 3 2
♢ 9 4 3
♣ J 10 9 8 7

East
♠ Q 10 6 4
♡ 10 9 7 6
♢ J 10 6
♣ Q 6

South, Dealer
♠ K J 9 8 7 5 3 2
♡ ———
♢ 8 7 5
♣ 5 4

South dealt and was not vulnerable. Fearing heart trouble from opponents, he preempted the situation by calling four spades. North, realizing that South's bid was based on utter trash but great length in spades, jumped to seven spades, and East gleefully doubled.

West opened with the Jack of clubs and South trumped North's four good hearts, reentering the dummy three times in diamonds. South entered dummy with his own last club and led a low club for the first coup. South just covered East's forced trump play, and dummy was put in again for the last time with the Ace of spades for the second coup against East. Note the slight difference between this ending and the Lydon Coup. In this endplay South led a *trump* to put North in for the final coup whereas Mr. Lydon led a *plain suit card* which the dummy trumped with the Ace of spades.

Suppose you deal yourself this hand:

♠ J 9 7 5 3 2
♥ A 7 5 3 2
♦ ———
♣ J 9

You pass, your partner opens at five diamonds, your right hand opponent overcalls at five notrump to show a powerhouse and to force his partner to declare his best suit. You pass, and his partner calls six spades, which the forcer now raises to seven spades. Now what would you do? You'd double, wouldn't you? You can most certainly defeat seven spades, and you can lay down the Ace of hearts if opponents try to escape into seven notrump . Well, you double and opponents stand pat at seven spades. You should most certainly be able to defeat this contract, and yet—

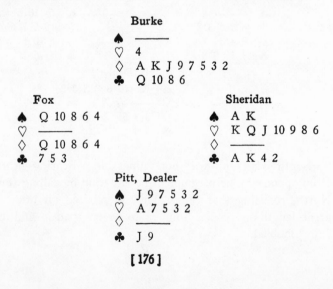

Burke
♠ ———
♥ 4
♦ A K J 9 7 5 3 2
♣ Q 10 8 6

Fox
♠ Q 10 8 6 4
♥ ———
♦ Q 10 8 6 4
♣ 7 5 3

Sheridan
♠ A K
♥ K Q J 10 9 8 6
♦ ———
♣ A K 4 2

Pitt, Dealer
♠ J 9 7 5 3 2
♥ A 7 5 3 2
♦ ———
♣ J 9

This deal was first published in *Judge Magazine,* September 1936, in one of the famous Pitt stories. Suppose the bidding proceed as indicated and you hold Pitt's cards. Well, as you probably suspect by now, you can't win a single trick!

As Sheridan advertised no diamond by calling seven spades, Burke led a club which Sheridan, now dummy, won. Fox led a heart equal from dummy, and trumped your Ace. Had you passed the heart lead, dummy would have simply continued to lead hearts. Dummy was reentered with another club, and Fox discarded his last club and three diamonds on dummy's four good hearts, leaving:

TRIPLE OVERRUFF FINESSE

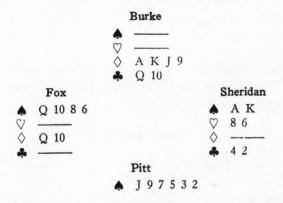

```
                        Burke
                        ♠ ──────
                        ♡ ──────
                        ◇ A K J 9
                        ♣ Q 10
        Fox                              Sheridan
    ♠ Q 10 8 6                           ♠ A K
    ♡ ──────                             ♡ 8 6
    ◇ Q 10                               ◇ ──────
    ♣ ──────                             ♣ 4 2
                        Pitt
                        ♠ J 9 7 5 3 2
```

Fox and Sheridan scored all their six trumps separately. Sheridan led a club, Fox overtrumped Pitt. Sheridan trumped a diamond and Fox overtrumped Pitt again. Sheridan trumped the last diamond to lead for the third and last coup!

PRAYER by Sturgis Coffin
Let the experts make slam cues,
Lay traps psychic in the thickets;
Signals, endplays, squeezes use;
But let me hold all the tickets!

CHAPTER NINETEEN

HYBRID COUPS

E NDPLAYS that can not be definitely classified as belonging
strictly to any one of the three great divisions, Eliminations,
Squeezes, or Coups; and endplays which are compounds or combinations of plays from two or three divisions, are hybrids. According to the first interpretation, the Forced Coup or smother play
is a hybrid, because it is practically an elimination. And yet, it is
an overruffing finesse.

The Coup Strips are really elimination plays preceded by trump
reducing. The Grand Coup Fork Strip given in Chapter Three is
a typical example. Here are some more.

COUP STRIP

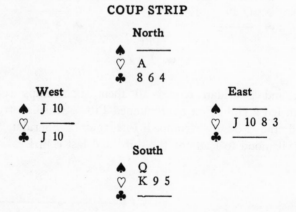

```
                    North
                 ♠ ———
                 ♡ A
                 ♣ 8 6 4
     West                        East
  ♠ J 10                      ♠ ———
  ♡ ———                       ♡ J 10 8 3
  ♣ J 10                      ♣ ———
                    South
                 ♠ Q
                 ♡ K 9 5
                 ♣ ———
```

Hearts are trumps and South, needing three tricks, trumps a
spade with dummy's Ace of hearts. Dummy leads a club. If East
does not split his equals South scores his nine of hearts immediately, and if East puts up the Jack or ten of hearts, South must
undertrump in order to establish a winning finesse over East's
trumps.

Here's the same thing in slightly different form:

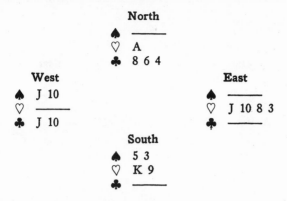

North
♠ ——
♡ A
♣ 8 6 4

West
♠ J 10
♡ ——
♣ J 10

East
♠ ——
♡ J 10 8 3
♣ ——

South
♠ 5 3
♡ K 9
♣ ——

The only difference is that South holds one more spade and one less trump, so that after North has trumped a spade and led a club, South *discards* a spade instead of undertrumping if East splits his equals. Discarding his losing spade while losing his anyway losing trump trick simultaneously on the same trick is known as discarding a loser on a loser. We might call the endplay the Telescoped Coup Strip, because two losing tricks were in effect *telescoped* into one.

It is idle to try to classify the different forms of the coup strips, because the endless variety of the minor details of arrangement leads to utter confusion. They are really only sub-species of one generic play. Here's still another form:

A Bridge Expert's Correspondence (strictly fiction)

Dear Mr. Bridge Expert:

I want to finesse the queen, but I don't even hold a tenspot. What should I do?

Sincerely yours,
Sam Swain

Dear Mr. Swain:

Lead a *DIAMOND* at all costs. If you play the *KNAVE*, her old man will make a *GRAND SLAM* with a *CLUB*, the sexton will *PLY* a *SPADE*, Gabriel will *TRUMPET*, and you will go down with *NO HONORS*.

Sincerely yours,
Bridge Expert

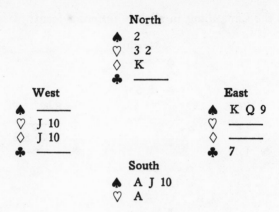

North
- ♠ 2
- ♡ 3 2
- ◊ K
- ♣ ——

West
- ♠ ——
- ♡ J 10
- ◊ J 10
- ♣ ——

East
- ♠ K Q 9
- ♡ ——
- ◊ ——
- ♣ 7

South
- ♠ A J 10
- ♡ A

Spades are trumps and North, wishing three tricks, leads the good diamond. If East discards so will South, giving South two spade tricks. So East trumps with an equal instead and South must undertrump! (Undertrumping Grand Coup!) As a trump return would give South the rest of the tricks by a finesse, East leads his club on which South discards his Ace of hearts and North trumps! Try to figure out a name for this one if you can! In the original edition of "Endplays" we called it the Undertrumping Grand Coup Fork Crossruff Strip. Since then we have given it plenty of other titles, and in desperation, we called it a few more things less technical and gave it up!

Here's a similar one expanded to six cards:

STRIP COUP

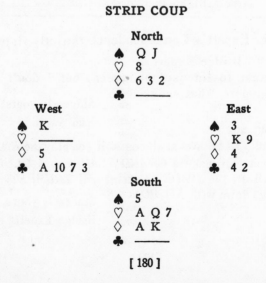

North
- ♠ Q J
- ♡ 8
- ◊ 6 3 2
- ♣ ——

West
- ♠ K
- ♡ ——
- ◊ 5
- ♣ A 10 7 3

East
- ♠ 3
- ♡ K 9
- ◊ 4
- ♣ 4 2

South
- ♠ 5
- ♡ A Q 7
- ◊ A K
- ♣ ——

Hearts are trumps and South, wanting five tricks, eliminates the diamond from West before throwing him in with a spade to force his club lead. When North trumps the club, South *under-trumps* to discard his superflous trump, so that North can lead the good spade and diamond through East's trumps.

Here's our old friend, the double coup from Chapter Seventeen, wearing a new cloak:

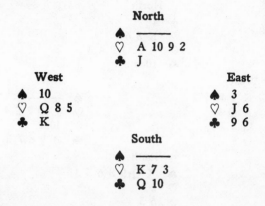

```
                       North
                    ♠ ——————
                    ♡ A 10 9 2
                    ♣ J
        West                           East
     ♠ 10                            ♠ 3
     ♡ Q 8 5                         ♡ J 6
     ♣ K                             ♣ 9 6
                       South
                    ♠ ——————
                    ♡ K 7 3
                    ♣ Q 10
```

South, wanting four tricks with hearts trumps, throws West in with the club. As West can not give up his tenace position in hearts, he leads a spade, North t r u m p s with the deuce of hearts and South overtrumps w i t h t h e t h r e e! Now leading the Queen of clubs pins East, while North can overtrump West.

THE ALCATRAZ COUP

Any type of deliberate cheating that gains a trick is called an *Alcatraz Coup.* For example:

Dummy ♡ A J 10   Looking for three tricks the
Declarer ♡ K 2   declarer calls the jack from
                     dummy, his R H O plays low,
                     then declarer discards! If LHO
plays low or plays the queen, declarer corrects his renounce and "kindly" lets LHO change his play, and finesses the right way!

Or dummy with ◊ 4-3-2 and declarer ◊ A-Q-10-8-7-6, he leads a low ◊ off dummy, RHO follows low and declarer ruffs! If L H O overruffs, declarer takes back his trump and finesses his ◊ 10!

Such a cheat play *could* occur innocently, but a director had better not believe it, adjust scores, and advise the rules committee.

Coup Gone Astray

In the Hamilton Trophy event for teams of four at the 47th annual congress of the American Whist League held in June, 1937, at Hanover, New Hampshire, we had the supreme pleasure of winning ten tricks against two Aces and K-J-10-7-2 in trumps held over us.

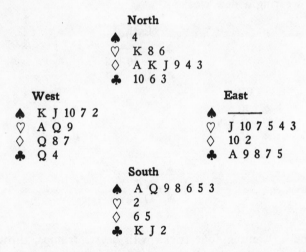

North
♠ 4
♡ K 8 6
◊ A K J 9 4 3
♣ 10 6 3

West
♠ K J 10 7 2
♡ A Q 9
◊ Q 8 7
♣ Q 4

East
♠ ———
♡ J 10 7 5 4 3
◊ 10 2
♣ A 9 8 7 5

South
♠ A Q 9 8 6 5 3
♡ 2
◊ 6 5
♣ K J 2

On the face of it this feat seemed impossible, but the answer was that the game was Whist whereat all four hands were played closed. Playing South, we turned the three of spades for trumps.

As there is no bidding in Whist to indicate distribution, West led the seven of spades, his fourth best trump to show at least five trumps, and East discarded a diamond. South won with the eight-spot and led his singleton heart. As second hand, West played low and North's King won. North played the King of diamonds to show his suit and returned a low heart for South to trump. South led a diamond, North finessed the Jack, as East's diamond discard showed weakness in the suit, and North cashed the Ace of diamonds whereon South discarded a low club. South trumped another heart and led the six of spades which West won with his ten leaving this situation:

COUP STRIP

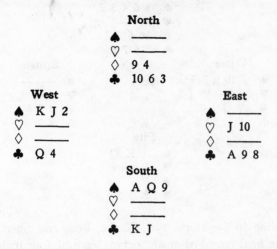

North
- ♠ ———
- ♡ ———
- ◇ 9 4
- ♣ 10 6 3

West
- ♠ K J 2
- ♡ ———
- ◇ ———
- ♣ Q 4

East
- ♠ ———
- ♡ J 10
- ◇ ———
- ♣ A 9 8

South
- ♠ A Q 9
- ♡ ———
- ◇ ———
- ♣ K J

At this point South had lost one trick, and actually lost only two more. West led the Queen of clubs which East finessed to South's King, and South returned the Jack forcing East's Ace. East led a heart, but it was too late. South played a lesser trump, West overtrumped, and West was endplayed.

West and East had a fine coup ending which they failed to capitalize. East should have won the club lead with his Ace and led a heart. South would have had to play a lesser trump which West would have overtrumped, and West would have exited in clubs to throw South in the lead. A totally different endplay at Contract Bridge enabled North to make five diamonds. See Chapter Four, page 42.

We were shown a deal some time ago, requiring a coup strip to score a slam that became a classic. At the time, we forwarded the deal to the late Milton C. Work, who published it in his syndicated newspaper Bridge column, and later we used it in one of our Pitt stories.

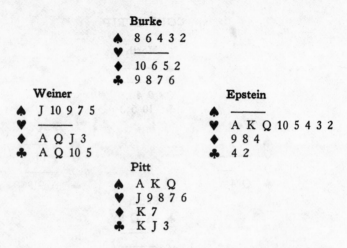

Burke
- ♠ 8 6 4 3 2
- ♥ ——
- ♦ 10 6 5 2
- ♣ 9 8 7 6

Weiner
- ♠ J 10 9 7 5
- ♥ ——
- ♦ A Q J 3
- ♣ A Q 10 5

Epstein
- ♠ ——
- ♥ A K Q 10 5 4 3 2
- ♦ 9 8 4
- ♣ 4 2

Pitt
- ♠ A K Q
- ♥ J 9 8 7 6
- ♦ K 7
- ♣ K J 3

According to the story, Pitt, Burke, Fox, and Sheridan were playing the final round of an important team-of-four match scored by total points against Weiner, Epstein, Soloski, and Nordblom.

In one room Pitt and Burke were not vulnerable, Weiner and Epstein vulnerable. Pitt dealt and bid one heart, Weiner doubled for a takeout, Burke passed, and Epstein, who could hardly believe his eyes, passed for penalties. Figuring that he had as good a chance to win tricks at hearts as at notrump , Pitt stood pat and passed also.

Against one heart doubled Weiner led the Jack of spades which Epstein trumped. Epstein led a club and Pitt's Jack fell prey to the Queen, Epstein trumped another spade, Weiner won another club finesse, and Epstein trumped a third spade. Epstein now put a diamond through Pitt, and discarded a diamond on the Ace of clubs. Weiner cashed the Ace of diamonds leaving:

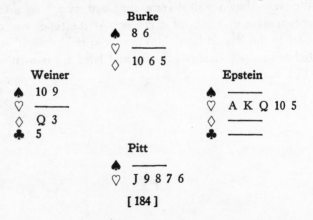

Burke
- ♠ 8 6
- ♡ ——
- ◇ 10 6 5

Weiner
- ♠ 10 9
- ♡ ——
- ◇ Q 3
- ♣ 5

Epstein
- ♠ ——
- ♡ A K Q 10 5
- ◇ ——
- ♣ ——

Pitt
- ♠ ——
- ♡ J 9 8 7 6

Epstein trumped Weiner's continuance with the five of hearts, forcing the now enraged Pitt to overtrump for his one and only trick. Result: Down six, doubled for 1100 points, and 100 in honors, or 1200 in all.

"This hand ought to win us the tournament," gloated Epstein, and Weiner gleefully agreed.

But the rebuttal at the other table knocked all the sunshine out of the incident for Weiner and Epstein. It seems that Soloski in the other room, playing Pitt's cards, had opened the bidding at one notrump, and after much spirited bidding, Sheridan, who held Epstein's hand, stumbled into a contract of six hearts, which Soloski doubled on his two sure trump tricks with 3½ honor-tricks on the side. Soloski opened with the King of spades, and Sheridan fulfilled his contract by the same endplay! And thus Sheridan won 1530 points (vulnerable slam 750, game bonus 500, tricks 180, and honors 100), which, compared to Pitt's loss of 1200 points, yielded a net gain of 330 points for Pitt's team! And Pitt's team-of-four also won the match!

Coup Squeeze

Practically every expert on endplays agreed on the hypothesis that it is impossible for a squeeze and a coup both to operate independently in the same hand,—until Jay J. Lennon exhibited his discovery in the *Bridge World* of October, 1937. On page 51 of the 1932 editions of Endplays we wrote:

" Alfred. Can you count? Say after Mamma; one two three."

"No problem, Mamma. One two three four five six seven eight nine ten jack queen king."

"A Coup Squeeze is a parallel squeeze because it is the *parallel* arrangement of a coup and a squeeze in the same deal. It is impossible for a coup and a squeeze to be compounded or combined in the same deal so that they both operate, but one or the other can produce one or two extra tricks, depending on the *biselective choice* in the discarding of the defence."

While the Lenz Thirteen*(Problem Number 3 in Chapter Twenty-one) conforms to this hypothesis, Mr. Lennon's findings have exploded it. Take the basic coup squeeze position.

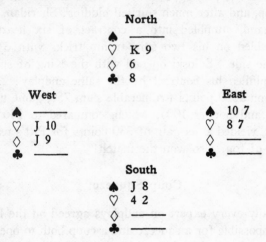

North
♠ —
♡ K 9
◇ 6
♣ 8

West
♠ —
♡ J 10
◇ J 9
♣ —

East
♠ 10 7
♡ 8 7
◇ —
♣ —

South
♠ J 8
♡ 4 2
◇ —
♣ —

Spades are trumps and North, requiring all four tricks, leads his good club. If East discards, so does South. North next plays the King of hearts and follows with anything, completing the simple coup. Hence the best defence is clear and East must trump the club lead immediately. South overtrumps and wins his second trump trick, squeezing West one way in the red suits. The squeeze supplies the extra plain suit winner necessary to consummate the coup.

As no squeeze develops if East delays trumping, Mr. Lennon points out that the ending is not a true squeeze coup. Admittedly, the sequence of endplays in the compound renders this fact true, because the coup occurs before the squeeze. But as the preferred defence is to trump North's club immediately, the compound endplay is certainly a true coup squeeze.

* See Andersson's *Sure Tricks*, No. 97.

But in order to have both a squeeze and a coup operate, regardless of the defence, Mr. Lennon resorts to combining an overtone squeeze with the above position, thereby proving conclusively that all endplay experts are liars through ignorance. Ask any endplay expert about the efficacy of the squeeze coup and he'll reply frankly, "They ain't no such animal." Mr. Lennon writes in the *Bridge World:*

"Nevertheless and notwithstanding, here it is! Step forward, ladies and gentlemen, and see the purple cow of Bridgedom,—a genuine squeeze coup!"

LENNON'S PURPLE COW

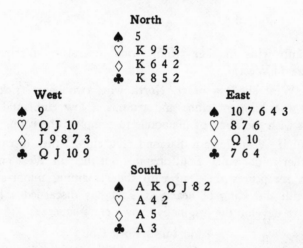

North
- ♠ 5
- ♡ K 9 5 3
- ◇ K 6 4 2
- ♣ K 8 5 2

West
- ♠ 9
- ♡ Q J 10
- ◇ J 9 8 7 3
- ♣ Q J 10 9

East
- ♠ 10 7 6 4 3
- ♡ 8 7 6
- ◇ Q 10
- ♣ 7 6 4

South
- ♠ A K Q J 8 2
- ♡ A 4 2
- ◇ A 5
- ♣ A 3

With neither side vulnerable, South bids two spades, North three notrump , and South seven spades, closing what Mr. Lennon refers to as the "leapy-jumpy" bidding. He observes, "If you must get to a contract of seven spades, it is probably as good a way as any."

West leads the Queen of hearts, which South wins with his Ace. South wins two trump tricks, finding West trumpless on the second. South scoops in two more tricks with his minor suit Aces, leaving the

SQUEEZE COUP

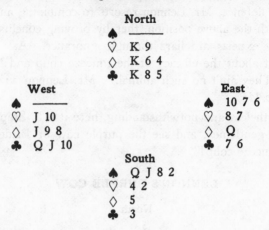

North
♠ —
♡ K 9
♢ K 6 4
♣ K 8 5

West
♠ —
♡ J 10
♢ J 9 8
♣ Q J 10

East
♠ 10 7 6
♡ 8 7
♢ Q
♣ 7 6

South
♠ Q J 8 2
♡ 4 2
♢ 5
♣ 3

South wins another trump trick, operating a triple squeeze on West!

If West sheds a heart, North wins two heart tricks, South scores the King of clubs and trumps a low club, and reenters North with the King of diamonds to complete the coup.

But if West sheds a diamond or a club, North discards from the other minor suit. South trumps out the suit West unguarded. North recaptures the lead with the remaining minor-suit King (or with the King of hearts if East has discarded a heart) in order to develop the originally shown coup squeeze.

Morton's Fork Coup

Cardinal Morton, Chancellor of King Henry VII, collected the royal taxes *two* ways; from the ostentatious because they could afford to pay and from the frugal because they had hoarded their savings and could pay. See Dorothy Hayden Truscott's example in the *Bridge Encyclopedia*, third edition 1971, page 288. Also see *Perfect Plays* No. 128 on page 89. And below in the world pair championship of 1970 in Stockholm, South was usually in 6 ♡ and West led his ♢ 4. One South finessed, later shed two low ♠s on dummy's ♢ A-K. Better is to win trick one *in dummy*, draw the trumps, then try to guess who has the ace of clubs.

♠ 9 4 3　♡ A 10 8 2　♢ A K 7　♣ K 8 4

♠ 8 6 2　♡ 9 5　♢ Q 9 5 4 2　♣ J 5　2⊕♠ Q J 10　♡ 4　♢ 10 8 6 3　♣ A 10 9

♠ A K 7 5　♡ K Q J 7 6 3　♢ J　♣ Q 7　　/ 6 3

If South or dummy snatches the first club lead, South ditches his second club on dummy's second diamond trick and loses only one trick,- in spades later. If a defender second hand scores his club ace, South gets *two* club tricks and sheds two spade losers.

CHAPTER TWENTY

MISCELLANEOUS COUPS

A LL THOSE plays not based on the overruff finesse endplay that have been dubbed coups on account of their unusual significance are discussed in this chapter. Many miscellaneous coups do not even involve endplay. They appear in this work only by sufferance, because they have traditional value.

Eliminations Dubbed Coups

Any double exit play in two suits is called a Fitzwilliam Coup after the beautiful little New England village of Fitzwilliam, New Hampshire, where this famous coup first occurred in an actual game. The original hand is a classic and it is in Chapter Fifteen, on page 150. Walter Wyman of Arlington, Mass., later played a Double Fitzwilliam Coup wherein he exited *twice* in each of two suits. See the second deal in Chapter Two, page 17.

Squeezes Dubbed Coups

A Vienna Coup is a squeeze complicated by a preliminary un-blocking manoeuvre. Declarer must cash a quick winner, thereby establishing a winner for an opponent, only to squeeze that opponent in that and in another suit later. Several Vienna Coups have already been shown in the chapters on squeezes. The play takes its name from a famous old double dummy Whist problem that made its first appearance in Vienna, Austria. See Chapter Ten, page 103.

The Harvard Coup, shown in Chapter Twelve on Finesse by Discovery, is a special complicated squeeze. In the future, any squeeze involving finesse by discovery will be a Harvard Coup.

The Perkins Coup, given in Chapter Fifteen on Strip and Squeeze, is the phenomenal crossruff strip trump squeeze, involving the double use of trumps. The endplay is distinctive for its rarity and beauty. See page 142.

Ostrich Coup

An Ostrich Coup is thrusting one's head into the Bridge sand,— running one's immediate winners without regard to dire consequences. For example, suppose that a player with the opening lead against a notrump contract holds this hand:

♠ A 6   ♡ A 6   ◊ K Q J 10 9 8 6   ♣ A 6.

More frequently than not, a beginner, usually the commonest type of Bridge Ostrich, will lay down his three Aces first, thereby decapitating the Goose that lays the Golden Eggs,—in diamonds. Playing declarer at a trump contract, a beginner too often plays the Ostrich Coup by disastrously forcing his own hand to trump too much, needlessly giving opponents trump control. A beginner doesn't seem to realize that his l o w trumps will win tricks anyway by reason of their trump suit length. The term, Ostrich Coup, is Ely Culbertson's.

Monte Carlo Coup

Approximately in 1870 an enterprising individual in Monte Carlo published a satirical postal card of that world famous gambling house. It depicted a dead man hanging from a scaffold with the brief epithet,

"Le Rouge gagne et le Noir gagne, mais la Banque gagne toujours."

This postal card enjoyed a good sale, but it was brief because the city fathers, fearful lest business be ruined and their tax revenue be correspondingly reduced, suppressed the edition. While many who lose their all at Monte Carlo commit suicide, the house tries to prevent such "accidents." If a destitute player is seen moping about the premises, a guard slips a few hundred francs into his pocket with the friendly advice to book passage on the next boat out.

Similarly, a certain honor among professional gamblers directs them not to fleece their victims completely. If a gambler wins all a man's money, he makes a point of losing a bit before concluding play, so that his victim won't be left destitute.

[190]

Whenever a host at Bridge defeats his guests overwhelmingly, he deliberately loses the last rubber to them to salve their feelings and self esteem. Gentlemen in all sports often follow this principle. It is the Unwritten Law of Sportsmanship. Any deliberate losing bid or play made guardedly for this purpose we call a Monte Carlo Coup.

Traditional Coups

Another well known modern coup is the Culbertson Coup. It is the best finessing procedure favored by the mathematical laws of chance to win three tricks, occasionally four, from A-Q-10-9-8 of a suit with the Ace and Queen at least doubly guarded in separate friendly hands.

CULBERTSON COUP

North

♣ A 10 6 4

South

♣ Q 9 8 7

With this combination lead the Queen. If West plays low, North should play low also. If East gobbles up the trick with the King, finesse thru the Jack on the second round.

While two tricks will be lost if East holds K-J-x, they will be offset by the loss of two tricks if you first play your Ace and West shows up with K-J-x. Although the Culbertson Coup unnecessarily loses a trick whenever West holds the lone King, again this loss is counterbalanced by South's ability to pick up East's lone Jack on the original Queen lead.

The main purpose of the coup is to eliminate guessing. If you first play the Ace and lead low toward the Queen and adversaries follow suit with l o w cards, you have to *guess* whether to finesse a spot card against the Jack or to put up the Queen. If you first lead the Queen, planning to finesse on the second round thru the Jack, the odds are about three to one that you will win three tricks, because the adverse King and Jack will lie favorably about three-quarters of the time, either divided in both opponents' hands, King and Jack or Jack and King, or both massed with West.

A Frenchman taught Ely Culbertson this coup over twenty years ago in Europe when the latter was just a beginner at Bridge! It was the only good play this particular Frenchman knew in Bridge, and he imparted his meagre but valuable knowledge to our modern Hoyle.

Le Coup En Blanc

A simple ducking play wherein no finesse position is involved fifty million Frenchmen call Le Coup en Blanc.

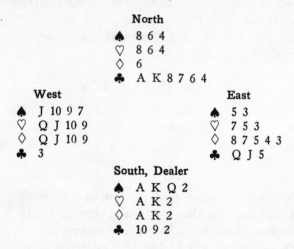

```
                      North
                   ♠  8 6 4
                   ♡  8 6 4
                   ◇  6
                   ♣  A K 8 7 6 4
     West                              East
  ♠  J 10 9 7                       ♠  5 3
  ♡  Q J 10 9                       ♡  7 5 3
  ◇  Q J 10 9                       ◇  8 7 5 4 3
  ♣  3                              ♣  Q J 5
                   South, Dealer
                   ♠  A K Q 2
                   ♡  A K 2
                   ◇  A K 2
                   ♣  10 9 2
```

South deals and bids one spade, North two clubs, South four notrump , North six clubs, and South six notrump.

West leads a red Queen which South wins, and in order to fulfill his contract, South must duck the first or second round of clubs in dummy, that is, play a low card then and permit East to win a trick, so that the suit will be established at a time when South still holds a card therein.

While this ducking play will lose a trick whenever the adverse clubs are evenly divided, ducking is a safety play in this case to ensure twelve tricks in case they aren't divided evenly. Playing for the drop will cost three tricks, if it fails as above.

Of course, in the hand above the safety play becomes marked on the second round of clubs when West renounces, but this safety play isn't completely safe unless declarer ducks the first round of clubs to guard against finding Q-J-5-3 with West.

Counting House Coup

A player is frequently vexed by the problem of finessing or playing for a drop of adverse high cards. Postponing the decision as long as possible sometimes enables a player to get an accurate count of adverse shapes and high cards by a special kind of endplay, which we call the Counting House Coup.

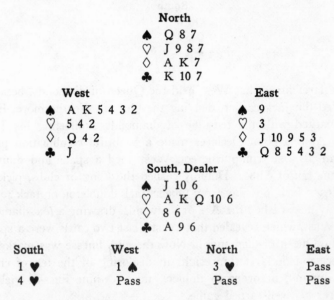

North
- ♠ Q 8 7
- ♡ J 9 8 7
- ◇ A K 7
- ♣ K 10 7

West
- ♠ A K 5 4 3 2
- ♡ 5 4 2
- ◇ Q 4 2
- ♣ J

East
- ♠ 9
- ♡ 3
- ◇ J 10 9 5 3
- ♣ Q 8 5 4 3 2

South, Dealer
- ♠ J 10 6
- ♡ A K Q 10 6
- ◇ 8 6
- ♣ A 9 6

South	West	North	East
1 ♥	1 ♠	3 ♥	Pass
4 ♥	Pass	Pass	Pass

Against South's contract of four hearts, West ran the King then Ace of spades, following with a low spade which East trumped. South, observing another losing trick in clubs, moaned about his rough treatment with nine laydown tricks staring him in the face at notrump. To Trick Four East returned the Jack of Diamonds, forcing dummy's King. Dummy led a trump, revealing East's two major suit singletons when East discarded a club. East was now marked with eleven minor suit cards. Hoping to squeeze East, South ran three more trump tricks, leaving this blind situation:

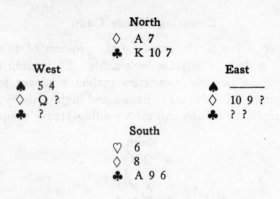

North
◇ A 7
♣ K 10 7

West
♠ 5 4
◇ Q ?
♣ ?

East
♠ ——
◇ 10 9 ?
♣ ? ?

South
♡ 6
◇ 8
♣ A 9 6

Declarer knew that West held the Queen of diamonds, because East led the Jack earlier, denying the Queen. Furthermore, East was marked with the ten-nine of diamonds supporting his Jack lead. At this point Declarer made a beautiful combination play. He ran his last trump whereon West shed a spade and dummy shed the *ten* of clubs. Dummy cashed the King of clubs, picking up West's Jack, possibly from Queen-Jack doubleton or Jack *solus*. Dummy next cashed the Ace of diamonds, drawing a *low* diamond from West, which revealed that West's last two cards were a spade and the Queen of diamonds! Now the club finesse was marked a winner, and declarer's foresight in disposing of the ten of clubs from dummy, in order to unblock the Ace-nine finesse, yielded Declarer his well-earned game.

Eliminating suits in order to obtain a count of the adverse distributions might be a fourth great division of Endplays,—a special group involving concealment of forces. It is not true endplay in the mechanical sense from the point of view of double dummy play, and therefore it falls into that general class of pseudo or false endplays, all based on concealment of forces.

Old Whist Coups

The Bath Coup is named after that historic watering place, Bath, England, where the coup was first discovered and made. The Bath Coup is made by holding up the Ace when you hold A-J-x on the lead of your left hand opponent's King in order to induce him to fall into your trap and continue the suit.

North
♠ 8 7
♡ 8 7 5
♢ 3 2
♣ A 8 7 5 4 2

West
♠ K Q 10 9 5
♡ K Q 10 4
♢ K Q 10 7
♣ ———

East
♠ 6 4 3
♡ 9 6 2
♢ 9 8 6 5
♣ Q 6 3

South
♠ A J 2
♡ A J 3
♢ A J 4
♣ K J 10 9

South plays the deal at three notrump doubled by West. The opening lead is the King of spades, and South permits West to win with his three Kings, Triple Bath Coup, to insure game, as the club suit is blocked if East's Queen is not allowed to win also.

The Dewey Coup

The Dewey Coup is any special play pinioning on a key entry card. The two diametrically opposed types are well exemplified by the historic entry-creating Deschapelles Coup and its blood-cousin, the entry-destroying Merrimac Coup. These coups are classified after Commodore George Dewey* on account of their similarity to the destruction of two Spanish fleets in the Spanish War. In the Deschapelles Coup declarer's adversaries make a daring raid into the enemy's heavily fortified Manila Bay, apparently against superior forces, and, unscathed, run out of the fray their victorious fleet of long suit tricks. The Merrimac

---

*By strange coincidences, the author married Elizabeth White Dewey on 29 June 1935, when her first cousin, Thomas E. Dewey, now famous for his ability to squash rackets, gave her away, and on the same day was appointed special district attorney in New York City. Both Deweys are related to Commodore George Dewey. Her birthday falls on Dewey Day, the First of May, when the Commodore won his great battle in Manila Bay!—*Publisher.*

Coup, however, bottles up the long suit of one's opponent by sinking his only entry card, just as the young and dashing Lieut. Richard P. Hobson sank the *Merrimac* in Santiago Harbor to bottle up the Spanish fleet.

Deschapelles Coup

The Deschapelles Coup was invented and named after that famous French Whist player of bygone days, Guillaume le Breton Deschapelles. The play consists of leading a King or other high card when the next lower ranking card of the same suit is absent from the leader's hand, for the purpose of creating an entry with the leader's partner, whom it is vital to get in the lead. Usually, it is a defending player who takes his life in his hands and makes the mad-looking lead of an unsupported King or Queen through or up to an exposed Ace, often accompanied by its Knave. This play is daring enough in Contract Bridge. But in Whist, whereat only master card-reading, unaided by bidding and exposed dummy, could penetrate the thick veil of concealment of card distribution and dispersion, the Deschapelles Coup was little short of pure. genius.

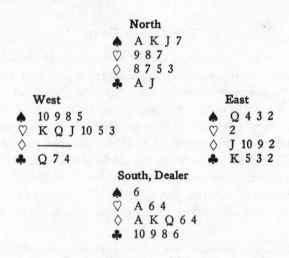

```
                        North
                    ♠  A K J 7
                    ♡  9 8 7
                    ◇  8 7 5 3
                    ♣  A J
      West                                East
  ♠  10 9 8 5                         ♠  Q 4 3 2
  ♡  K Q J 10 5 3                     ♡  2
  ◇  ———                              ◇  J 10 9 2
  ♣  Q 7 4                            ♣  K 5 3 2
                    South, Dealer
                    ♠  6
                    ♡  A 6 4
                    ◇  A K Q 6 4
                    ♣  10 9 8 6
```

At a progressive party South had won a game, and he dealt and bid one diamond. West jumped to three hearts. This over-bid of nearly four tricks was justified only by honors and lack of vulnerability. North called three spades, East passed, and South called three notrump , concluding the auction.

West opened with the King of hearts, which South passed. West continued with the ten of hearts which South topped with his Ace. The game looked 90% sure, until West discarded a spade when South led a diamond honor. In order to preserve a diamond entry to his own hand and thus to score his long diamond later, South played another honor then low in diamonds, throwing in East. At this point East made the Deschapelles Coup,—he led. his unsupported King of clubs up to the teeth of dummy's Ace-Jack. Naively believing this lead to be from King-Queen, declarer won the trick with dummy's Ace of clubs (it would have done him no good to duck), and, in order to set up all his own clubs, he returned the dummy's Jack. But West pounced thereon with the Queen, and scored four more heart tricks, de-feating the contract by three tricks.

The entry-creating Deschapelles Coup has an entry-destroy-ing counterpart, the Merrimac Coup. In his excellent *Redbook* on page 255, Ely Culbertson aptly titled this coup after the manner in which a player sinks the opponent's Ace or other single entry like the *Merrimac*, to bottle up the opponent's fleet of long suit ·tricks.

From page 210

No. 6 (A-149) DD 209 **ELKS' MISERY PROBLEM** WIN 12

```
              ♠ K 3  ♡ Q 9 5  ◇ Q 8 5 3 2  ♣ K J 8
♠ J 6 4                                        ♠ Q 10 9 8 7
♡ J 8 7 6                                      ♡ K 10 3
◇ J 6 4                                        ◇ K
♣ 10 9 6                                       ♣ Q 7 5 3
              ♠ A 5 2  ♡ A 4 2  ◇ A 10 9 7  ♣ A 4 2
```

At notrump West leads the ♡6. Can North and South win 12 tricks against the best defense ?   By George S. Coffin.

This is the original version of the famous Elks' Misery Prob-lem in *Elks Magazine* of June 1935. Many years after it was pub-lished someone discovered a killing defense,- East keeps clubs. A new perfected version is No. 209 in *Double Dummy Bridge.*

MERRIMAC COUP

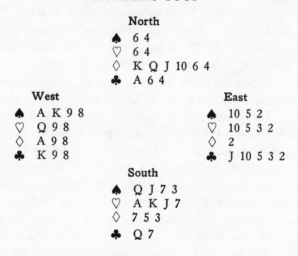

North
- ♠ 6 4
- ♡ 6 4
- ◊ K Q J 10 6 4
- ♣ A 6 4

West
- ♠ A K 9 8
- ♡ Q 9 8
- ◊ A 9 8
- ♣ K 9 8

East
- ♠ 10 5 2
- ♡ 10 5 3 2
- ◊ 2
- ♣ J 10 5 3 2

South
- ♠ Q J 7 3
- ♡ A K J 7
- ◊ 7 5 3
- ♣ Q 7

West deals and bids one spade, North two diamonds, East passes, and South bids two hearts. Finding himself minced in between strong opponents advertising all the missing high card strength, West passes, North rebids his diamonds at three, and South optimistically calls three notrump. West doubles and all pass.

Against three notrump West opens with the King of spades to have a look at the dummy. South feels pleased with his contract because another spade lead will give him at least one more spade trick, which with two hearts, a club, and five diamonds within one lead of establishment will yield, without a finesse, his precariously bid game.

But West is thinking about the way dummy's diamonds can plough through the defence, once they get started. West now makes a Merrimac Coup,—he leads the King of clubs to knock out and sink dummy's Ace, giving South a nasty turn. But South recovers and permits the King of clubs to hold the trick! West leads another club, this time scuttling declarer's ship for good. South's club doubleton spells his undoing. South wins the club trick with his now lone Queen, and struggles on, but West holds up his Ace of diamonds until the third round of the suit, forever closing the temple doors to dummy's sacred diamonds.

Pitt Coup

The Pitt Coup is an unblocking manoeuvre. Declarer jettisons the high trump on the opponent's plain suit lead, in order to retain a l o w trump and to lead through the left hand opponent's tenace minor in trumps to pick them up, and score an otherwise unavailable plain suit winner in partner's hand. Curiously enough, Pitt had nothing to do with the coup. An anonymous French Whist writer used Pitt as one of four fictitious names for the four players around the Whist table, instead of A and C versus B and D then in vogue (analagous to our North and South versus East and West and analagous to the English use of A and B versus Y and Z). These same four Whist players, Pitt, Burke, Fox, and Sheridan have been revived in the modern Pitt stories in the *Bridge World* and in *Judge Magazine*.

PITT COUP

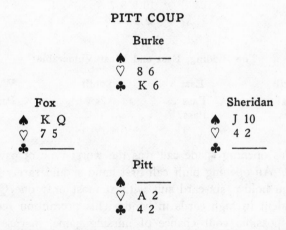

Burke

♠ ———
♡ 8 6
♣ K 6

Fox

♠ K Q
♡ 7 5
♣ ———

Sheridan

♠ J 10
♡ 4 2
♣ ———

Pitt

♠ ———
♡ A 2
♣ 4 2

With hearts trumps Fox led a spade, according to the Frenchman's original Whist textbook, on which Burke discarded a club, and the fictitious Pitt made his famous coup. He trumped with his Ace of hearts in order to unblock the trump suit and to lead his deuce of hearts through Fox, thereby winning all four tricks for his side.

The Contract Bridge analogy of the Pitt Coup came up in an amusing hand in a rubber game, as follows:

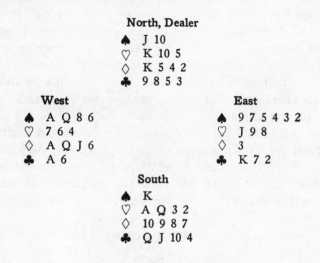

North, Dealer
♠ J 10
♡ K 10 5
◇ K 5 4 2
♣ 9 8 5 3

West
♠ A Q 8 6
♡ 7 6 4
◇ A Q J 6
♣ A 6

East
♠ 9 7 5 4 3 2
♡ J 9 8
◇ 3
♣ K 7 2

South
♠ K
♡ A Q 3 2
◇ 10 9 8 7
♣ Q J 10 4

The Bidding, East and West Vulnerable:

North	East	South	West
1 ♠!	Pass	2 ♥	Pass!
Pass	Pass?		

North's opening spade call was the worst type of psychic bid we know. An opening bluff call first hand should rarely be tried, unless you hold a six-card suit with at most only one Queen or its equivalent in high cards in hand. This precaution reduces as much as possible your chance of missing game, in case partner should make a forcing takeout which you unconventionally pass. Such a psychic bid has been used successfully by S. Garton Churchill, which he describes and exemplifies in his fine book, *Contract Bidding Tactics at Match Point Play.* Of that work, see pages 114, 115, 276 to 279 inclusive, and 297.

East and West have a laydown game at spades,—unless South happens to make the unnatural opening lead of a heart and continues the suit through its fourth round to establish the setting trick in trumps,—but these considerations in no way condone North's psychic. East was napping when he passed South's bid of two hearts. Had North had a legitimate opening bid, he would

[200]

not have passed the bid of two hearts according to the modern suit-over-suit forcing principle followed by good players. Hence North's original call became marked as a "phoney," and East should have backed in with a call of two spades, which West would have unceremoniously jumped to four spades.

Against two hearts West, not desiring to give up his tenace position in any plain suit, led the seven of hearts, forcing the ten, Jack, and Queen. South led a club, which West passed to East's King. East led his lone diamond, which West won with his Ace, and West returned the Queen, forcing the King and a trump from East. East returned a low spade which West won with the Ace. West cashed his high diamond, and let East trump the fourth round of diamonds. East led a spade, forcing South to trump, and South led another club, leaving this situation:

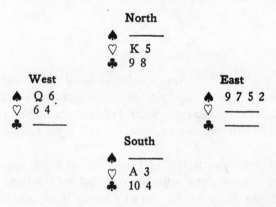

```
                    North
                ♠  ———
                ♡  K 5
                ♣  9 8

      West                        East
  ♠  Q 6                      ♠  9 7 5 2
  ♡  6 4                      ♡  ———
  ♣  ———                      ♣  ———

                    South
                ♠  ———
                ♡  A 3
                ♣  10 4
```

West's only chance to score his six of hearts was to lead a spade, hoping Declarer would block himself by trumping low in either friendly hand. South, however, had seen East trump with the eightspot and nine, denying the six. South trumped the spade with his Ace, and finessed the five of trumps to win the balance of tricks, going down only two.

Simon says, *"You play money bridge fairly well but you think that you are better than you really are. Your bidding is adequate, but your defense is shocking. You like to win but you don't keep accounts. You tell everybody that you are about all square on the year.*

"You lie and you know it." From **Why you LOSE at bridge,** by Simon.

Simon says, *(In Washington DC, 3 October 1974) "The ship of state is leaking at the top."*

That Grand Old Maestro of Bridge, Sidney S. Lenz, showed in his beautiful book on play entitled *How's Your Bridge?* a hand illustrating the Pitt Coup in double form:

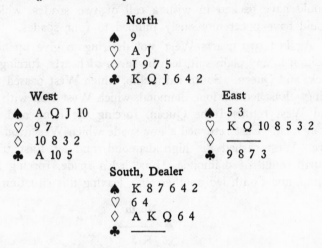

```
                          North
                    ♠ 9
                    ♡ A J
                    ◇ J 9 7 5
                    ♣ K Q J 6 4 2
      West                                  East
  ♠ A Q J 10                            ♠ 5 3
  ♡ 9 7                                 ♡ K Q 10 8 5 3 2
  ◇ 10 8 3 2                            ◇ ───────
  ♣ A 10 5                              ♣ 9 8 7 3
                        South, Dealer
                    ♠ K 8 7 6 4 2
                    ♡ 6 4
                    ◇ A K Q 6 4
                    ♣ ───────
```

South dealt and bid one spade, pleasing West who passed, North two clubs, and East, not vulnerable, stuck in a risky preemptive bid of three hearts. South bid four diamonds, West four hearts, and North five diamonds which call West doubled, and all passed.

Against five diamonds West led the nine of hearts which North, now dummy, won with the Ace and led the King of clubs, whereon South discarded his anyway losing heart, and West won with the Ace. West returned a heart and South properly trumped with an honor. When South led a trump honor, the wisdom of his first Pitt Coup became clear when East failed. Dummy next finessed the seven of diamonds and South trumped a low club with his last trump honor, the second Pitt Coup, and the dummy, after finessing trumps again and drawing all West's trumps, led his two top clubs, felling East's nine and eightspot, so that dummy's clubs were all run and one spade trick was lost at the end.

Had declarer tried to establish spade ruffs in the dummy at Trick Two, excessive forces in his own hand would have eventually held him down to ten tricks.

Coffin Coup

The Coffin Coup is a gambit play,—the deliberate sacrifice of a trump trick to gain a *tempo* that is essential to score several tricks later. We claim to be the first actually to discover and use this unique play in tournament competition.

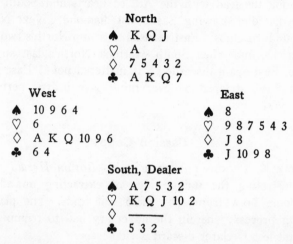

North
- ♠ K Q J
- ♡ A
- ◇ 7 5 4 3 2
- ♣ A K Q 7

West
- ♠ 10 9 6 4
- ♡ 6
- ◇ A K Q 10 9 6
- ♣ 6 4

East
- ♠ 8
- ♡ 9 8 7 5 4 3
- ◇ J 8
- ♣ J 10 9 8

South, Dealer
- ♠ A 7 5 3 2
- ♡ K Q J 10 2
- ◇ ———
- ♣ 5 3 2

This deal came up in a Boston Chess Club tournament in the early days of the then newly reorganized club, when it held forth at the Hotel Lenox in Boston. Playing South we dealt and bid one spade, West two diamonds, North four clubs forcing to game, we bid four hearts, North bid four notrump to show two Aces and the King of a bid suit, and with one Ace and extra values we jumped to six hearts, and North changed the bid back to spades at six, closing the auction.

West led the King of diamonds and a grand slam looked as "easy as pie" when the dummy was spread. We trumped the· diamond opening and won two rounds of trumps in the dummy. When East failed to follow suit on the second round, we didn't feel so sorry about stopping at six spades. We played the dummy's Ace of hearts and then made our famous coup. We led dummy's last trump and *overtook* it with the Ace, thereby promoting West's ten of trumps to the rank of top trump. But we didn't care, as we simply ran our hearts, then clubs, permitting West to trump in for his only trick whenever he felt like taking it!

The proper contract of six spades was defeated at other tables, and many South players were so unfortunate as to play the hand at six hearts where they were unmercifully beaten.

One North player did well at six clubs by a simple entry elimination play. East led the Jack of diamonds which South trumped. North took the lead with the Ace of hearts and South trumped another diamond drawing East's last diamond. Next North ran three rounds of clubs. East refused to trump North's two winning spade tricks, and when South overtook North's last spade with the Ace, East again discarded. It mattered not if East trumped, because East, stripped of everything save hearts, perforce had to lead one!

Passion Coup!

Frank K. Perkins published in his *Boston Herald* column a deal illustrating the unique idea of extracting an adversary's bothersome l o w trumps by plain suit leads. The play was a stripping process, wherein the adversary had to trump dummy's plain suit lest Declarer discard a vital loser.

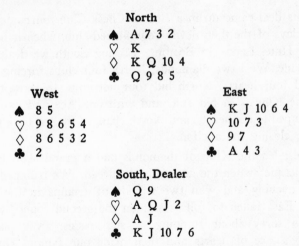

```
                        North
                        ♠ A 7 3 2
                        ♡ K
                        ◇ K Q 10 4
                        ♣ Q 9 8 5
          West                              East
          ♠ 8 5                             ♠ K J 10 6 4
          ♡ 9 8 6 5 4                       ♡ 10 7 3
          ◇ 8 6 5 3 2                       ◇ 9 7
          ♣ 2                               ♣ A 4 3
                        South, Dealer
                        ♠ Q 9
                        ♡ A Q J 2
                        ◇ A J
                        ♣ K J 10 7 6
```

South dealt and bid one club, North one diamond, and East one spade. South next bid two hearts, North four clubs, South four notrump , North five spades to show the Ace, South six clubs, and all passed.

West led the eightspot of spades, which dummy's Ace won. South then North each won a diamond trick, and North led a third high diamond. This play was a lethal caress that forced East to give up a l o w trump, instead of discarding or trumping with his Ace, lest South discard his dead spade. South over-trumped, North recaptured the lead with the King of hearts and administered to East's last low trump another fatal dose of dia-monds. Again East had to trump low and South had to over-trump. South next ran three more hearts whereon dummy shed all three low spades. The last heart lead was the kiss of death that forced East to complete submission. East was able to dis-card, or to win the one and only trick immediately with the Ace of trumps.

Coup Without A Name

Norman Bonney showed us the famous Rainbow Hand from an important tournament in Boston. It is considered to be one of the most remarkable hands that ever came up in tournament competition.

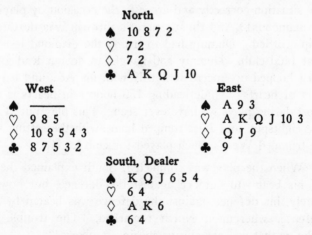

North
♠ 10 8 7 2
♡ 7 2
◇ 7 2
♣ A K Q J 10

West
♠ ———
♡ 9 8 5
◇ 10 8 5 4 3
♣ 8 7 5 3 2

East
♠ A 9 3
♡ A K Q J 10 3
◇ Q J 9
♣ 9

South, Dealer
♠ K Q J 6 5 4
♡ 6 4
◇ A K 6
♣ 6 4

South dealt and bid one spade, North two clubs, East four hearts, South four spades, and East doubled, closing the auction.

West led the nine of hearts, and after examining the dummy, East realized, after a long huddle, that his only chance to defeat the contract was to score a ruff of clubs in addition to his two heart tricks and the Ace of trumps. Therefore, holding a quick trump stopper, he overtook the nine of hearts with the ten and immediately switched to the nine of clubs which dummy won.

South next went into an introspective huddle. East's club lead was obviously a singleton. That being so, he would win the first trump lead and get his partner in with a heart and trump a club. Finally South evolved a plan to thwart this marked line of defence. If he could discard dummy's certain losing heart on the third round of diamonds while throwing *East* in the lead, East would be unable to get the lead back into West's hand in hearts. Hence, declarer couldn't afford to touch trumps until he had severed this threatening liaison between East and West. He led a low diamond from dummy.

Now it was East's turn to go into a huddle again. Foreseeing the impending diamond throwin play, East exited by playing his Jack of diamonds which South's Ace won. South laid down the King of diamonds and East continued to exit by dropping the Queen of diamonds thereunder. South led his last diamond, still hoping to toss East in with the ten or ninespot.

Now it was West's turn to huddle. Finally he, too, analysed the situation correctly and arose to the occasion by playing his ten of diamonds! And thus declarer's throwin was defeated and his ship scuttled. Dummy had to trump the diamond lest West lead that fatal club. Dummy had naught to do but lead a spade and East hopped up unceremoniously with his Ace, and led the *three-spot* of hearts! Underleading 150 honors in hearts is one of the most daring plays we have ever seen. This play put West in with the eightspot, and East romped home with the setting trick when he trumped West's much played for club lead!

When the play was completed, South explained the technique of his beautiful defence against the defence, but how, unfortunately, his defence against the defence was beaten by unbeatable defence, whereupon North remarked, "The trouble with you, John, is that you are always chasing rainbows!"

CHAPTER TWENTY-ONE

FAMOUS PROBLEMS

A S DOUBLE dummy problems have fascinated students of Whist and Bridge since time immemorial, this master edition of *Endplays* would be incomplete without offering a few choice problems for the reader to solve. Unlike a bidding problem, a sound double dummy problem has only one correct solution. As in Chess problems, all the pieces are exposed to view so that each player with complete knowledge of all the cards in the other three hands can play to his best possible advantage.

As in Chess problems, when a double dummy problem contains an alternative solution that is independent of the defence, the problem is considered to be unsound or "cooked" as it is called. Unfortunately Bridge columnists publish many hands from play that are "cooked." "A Hand a Day" by Frank K. Perkins in the *Boston Herald* and *Traveler* contains the best series of hands from play in any American newspaper. After four years of careful study we have failed to find a single "cooked" hand in his column! This phenomenal record has never been equalled in the history of Bridge! Other newspaper Bridge columns contain from one to fifteen percent "cooked" hands, and one well known writer disgraced himself by publishing in *Collier's Magazine* an article including twelve deals, of which six were "cooked." True in 1938, today's columns are superior.

Another type of unsound problem is the problem based on an absurd condition, often called the "fairy problem." We saw one such problem wherein West was prohibited from playing or leading his King of spades at any time. But Alfred Sheinwold, Editor of the *Bridge World Magazine,* tells us that he is going to compose the fairy problem *par excellence,* the condition w a s that tricks be won alternately by black and red cards!

Robert F. Foster, that fine old gentleman of Whist and Bridge, distinguished himself for his famous work, *Vanity Fair's Bridge Problems*. The book contains a collection of one hundred double dummy problems selected for their beauty and difficulty of solution, including some problems used by Sidney S. Lenz in his *Judge Magazine* contests for prizes. The book was the only publication on this department of the game in 1938.

Over a period of forty years Mr. Foster published these problems in *Vanity Fair Magazine* and in the *New York Sun*. The original Foster collection of 500 problems, all the work of other authors, included 250 "cooked" problems, of which a couple accidentally crept into his book. While Mr. Foster thoughtfully gave the name of the composer of each problem, many Bridge writers fail in the courtesy of giving proper credit to the source of these problems, which they plagiarize freely in their columns, thereby laying themselves open to lawsuits for infringement of the copyright laws!

We recently purchased from Ivar Andersson of Stockholm, Sweden, his collection of 150 problems for future publication, if there is enough demand for them. We published them in 1948.

Since the publication of the original Foster collection, many fine new problems have been composed, of which we present the most beautiful, including what we consider the three most difficult Bridge problems in the world.

You have noted elsewhere in this work how one Bridge ending can be superimposed upon another. A Bridge problem composer works backwards. On a basic endplay, the cornerstone of the problem, he lays his leads and plays and fastens them securely with the mortar of timing to erect his beautiful Castle of Cards. The solver has to worm his way through a maze of super squeezes and other preliminary manoeuvres in proper sequence to uncover this cornerstone,—to drive the defence to retreat into a hopeless endplay trap whence there is no escape.

While we have purposely omitted solutions, they will be mailed on request, if you send us a self-addressed and properly stamped envelope.

We received recently a letter referring to one of our problems. It read, ". . . I never knew a Coffin could spread so much cheer," signed Mrs. J. E. Morner, Hamilton, Ohio. We hope she's right!

In the third edition 1938 we offered six numbered full-pack double dummy problems. Duckworth in the fourth and fifth editions in 1950 and 1957 deleted number two, the "Merry-Go-Round", and renumbered the others two to five. We gave then as now, no solution; but we will be happy to furnish solutions for 25¢ coin or postage stamps to cover mailing costs. Be sure to renumber the solutions if using a Duckworth edition. In this sixth edition we have reverted to the original 1938 numbering, 1 thru 6.

No. 1   THE OMNIBUS PROBLEM   WIN 12

♠ K J 7 3 2   ♡ J 10 3   ◊ J 3 2   ♣ 10 3

♠ Q
♡ Q 9 8 7 5
◊ K Q 10 9 8 5
♣ 9

♠ 10 8 6 4
♡ 6 4
◊ 6 4
♣ K 7 6 4 2

♠ A 9 5   ♡ A K 2   ◊ A 7   ♣ A Q J 8 5

At notrump West leads his ◊K. N & S must win NINE tricks against any defense. This problem was discovered in actual play by Norman J. Bonney. It is unsound, having several cooks, that is, different winning lines of play independent of the defense. The idea is to find *all* the different kinds of endplays in order to solve it. This problem is a veritable omnibus of endplays.

No. 2 (A-99)   THE MERRY-GO-ROUND   ♠ WIN 13

♠ 8 7 5 4   ♡ K J 7 5 2   ◊ A 5 3 2   ♣ --

♠ --
♡ 10 9 8 3
◊ Q J 10 9
♣ A Q 10 5 3

♠ K 6
♡ A Q 6 4
◊ 8 6 4
♣ 8 6 4 2

♠ A Q J 10 9 3 2   ♡ --   ◊ K 7   ♣ K J 9 7

With spades trumps West leads his ◊ Q. N & S must win ALL 13 tricks against any defense. This problem is pretty, not difficult. By George S. Coffin.

Note: In (A-99) the "A" refers to *Sure Tricks* by Ivar Andersson, Problem 99; and "DD" refers to *Double Dummy Bridge.*

A diamond may be forever, but a coffin is forever and forever. - Coffin's Law.

No. 3 (A-97) THE LENZ THIRTEEN   ♡ WIN 13

♠ 5 ♡ 8 5 ◇ A K 7 ♣ A K 8 5 4 3 2

♠ K 10 7	♠ 8 6 4 3 2
♡ 9	♡ Q 7 6 2
◇ Q 10 8 3	◇ J 6 2
♣ Q J 10 9 7	♣ 6

♠ A Q J 9 ♡ A K J 10 4 3 ◇ 9 5 4 ♣ --

With hearts trumps West leads the ♣ Q. N & S must win ALL 13 tricks against any defense. This problem by grand old maestro Sidney S. Lenz, is the famous Vaniva Shaving Cream hand pub‑ lished in 1928, when money was easy and stocks were high. Of 20,000 solutions received, only 550 were correct.

No. 4 (A-42) DD 217 COFFIN'S HEX   ♠ WIN 13

♠ 10 9 3 2 ♡ A Q 5 ◇ A Q 5 ♣ A K 2

♠ --	♠ Q J
♡ J 10 9 8 7	♡ K 4 3 2
◇ J 10 9 8 7	◇ K 4 3 2
♣ Q J 10	♣ 9 8 7

♠ A K 8 7 6 5 4 ♡ 6 ◇ 6 ♣ 6 5 4 3

With spades trumps West leads the ♣ Q. N & S must win ALL 13 tricks against any defense. By George S. Coffin. Of the original eight-card ending of this problem, "Quart Major" in the *Brisbane Courier* in Queensland, Australia circa 1933 wrote, ". . . laid with the maximum of openness and minimum trickiness of any problem I have seen,'" shows the beauty of the *hexagon squeeze*. In 1934 Perkins published it in the *Boston Herald*. And in 1935 it appeared again in the February *Elks' Magazine*.

No. 5. (A-83) THE WHIST PLAYER'S HEARTBREAKER

♠ 4 3 ♡ Q 8 7 5 ◇ A 9 8 ♣ K J 8 7

♠ A 10 5 2	♠ J 8 6
♡ 10 4 2	♡ K 9 6 3
◇ K Q	◇ 7 6 5
♣ 10 9 5 2	♣ Q 6 3

♠ K Q 9 7 ♡ A J ◇ J 10 4 3 2 ♣ A 4

Hearts are trumps and S leads. N & S must win NINE tricks against any defense. This is an antique whist problem. This may account for the fact that South leads instead of West.

No. 6 (A-149) DD 209. Please turn to page 197..

BIBLIOGRAPHY

Since the material of *Endplays* was originally new, the only authentic bibliography was the author's own articles in bridge magazines before the first edition in 1932. So the books cited below are "after the fact" for supplementary reading.

Andersson, Ivar (of Stockholm) - *Sure Tricks*, 200 double dummy problems and 73 sure tricks, Coffin 1948; plus 7 new sure tricks and revisions, David McKay 1950.

Bergholt, Ernest - *Double Dummy Bridge*, Thomas De La Rue 1906.

Bonney, Norman J. - *The Play of the Cards* in Carlton Russell's *Common Sense Bridge,*- Auction - Contract; Russell 1935.

Cioffi, Raphael - *Bridge Endings* (24 endplay deals and 50 double dummy problems by Andersson) Coffin 1953.

Coffin - *Double Dummy Bridge* , 1966, second revised edition, 1975.

Darwen, Hugh - *Bridge Magic* (89 double dummy problems plus 11 others), Faber & Faber 1973.*

Downes, E. Hall --*Eliminations, Squeezes and Coups*, circa 1935.

Eng, Fook H. -*Bridge Squeezes Illustrated,* pub. by author 1973.*

Foster, Robert F. - *Vanity Fair's Bridge Problems* (100 miniature double dummy problems) Horace Liveright 1932.

Love, Dr. Clyde E. (mathematics professor at University of MI, Ann Arbor) - *Squeeze Play in Bridge,* Richard R. Smith 1951; *Bridge Squeezes Complete* (second revised edition) Sterling, 1959, Dover 1968.*

Romanet, Dr. Bertrand - *Le Squeeze au Bridge,* Grasset, 1954.

Rosencrans, FNU - *Squeezes, Coups & End Plays.* Author 1954

MONTHLY MAGAZINES ON BRIDGE

Bridge Magazine, Milton C. Work, editor, "Eliminations at Bridge Explained," November 1971.

Bridge Magazine of Great Britain, A. E. Manning-Foster, editor. "Squeezes at Bridge Explained," September 1931 and "Eliminations at Bridge Explained," October 1931.*

Bridge World, Ely Culbertson, editor. "Coups at Bridge Explained" November 1931, "Some New Endplays" March 1936.*

* *Currently available. Unmarked items are out of print.*

[211]

A CATALOGUE OF
SELECTED DOVER BOOKS
IN ALL FIELDS OF INTEREST

A CATALOGUE OF SELECTED DOVER
BOOKS IN ALL FIELDS OF INTEREST

RACKHAM'S COLOR ILLUSTRATIONS FOR WAGNER'S RING. Rackham's finest mature work—all 64 full-color watercolors in a faithful and lush interpretation of the *Ring*. Full-sized plates on coated stock of the paintings used by opera companies for authentic staging of Wagner. Captions aid in following complete Ring cycle. Introduction. 64 illustrations plus vignettes. 72pp. 8⅝ x 11¼. 23779-6 Pa. $6.00

CONTEMPORARY POLISH POSTERS IN FULL COLOR, edited by Joseph Czestochowski. 46 full-color examples of brilliant school of Polish graphic design, selected from world's first museum (near Warsaw) dedicated to poster art. Posters on circuses, films, plays, concerts all show cosmopolitan influences, free imagination. Introduction. 48pp. 9⅜ x 12¼. 23780-X Pa. $6.00

GRAPHIC WORKS OF EDVARD MUNCH, Edvard Munch. 90 haunting, evocative prints by first major Expressionist artist and one of the greatest graphic artists of his time: *The Scream, Anxiety, Death Chamber, The Kiss, Madonna*, etc. Introduction by Alfred Werner. 90pp. 9 x 12. 23765-6 Pa. $5.00

THE GOLDEN AGE OF THE POSTER, Hayward and Blanche Cirker. 70 extraordinary posters in full colors, from Maitres de l'Affiche, Mucha, Lautrec, Bradley, Cheret, Beardsley, many others. Total of 78pp. 9⅜ x 12¼. 22753-7 Pa. $5.95

THE NOTEBOOKS OF LEONARDO DA VINCI, edited by J. P. Richter. Extracts from manuscripts reveal great genius; on painting, sculpture, anatomy, sciences, geography, etc. Both Italian and English. 186 ms. pages reproduced, plus 500 additional drawings, including studies for *Last Supper*, Sforza monument, etc. 860pp. 7⅞ x 10¾. (Available in U.S. only) 22572-0, 22573-9 Pa., Two-vol. set $15.90

THE CODEX NUTTALL, as first edited by Zelia Nuttall. Only inexpensive edition, in full color, of a pre-Columbian Mexican (Mixtec) book. 88 color plates show kings, gods, heroes, temples, sacrifices. New explanatory, historical introduction by Arthur G. Miller. 96pp. 11⅜ x 8½. (Available in U.S. only) 23168-2 Pa. $7.95

UNE SEMAINE DE BONTÉ, A SURREALISTIC NOVEL IN COLLAGE, Max Ernst. Masterpiece created out of 19th-century periodical illustrations, explores worlds of terror and surprise. Some consider this Ernst's greatest work. 208pp. 8⅛ x 11. 23252-2 Pa. $5.00

DRAWINGS OF WILLIAM BLAKE, William Blake. 92 plates from Book of Job, *Divine Comedy, Paradise Lost,* visionary heads, mythological figures, Laocoon, etc. Selection, introduction, commentary by Sir Geoffrey Keynes. 178pp. 8⅛ x 11.　　　　　　　　　22303-5 Pa. $4.00

ENGRAVINGS OF HOGARTH, William Hogarth. 101 of Hogarth's greatest works: *Rake's Progress, Harlot's Progress, Illustrations for Hudibras, Before and After, Beer Street and Gin Lane,* many more. Full commentary. 256pp. 11 x 13¾.　　　　　　　　　　　22479-1 Pa. $12.95

DAUMIER: 120 GREAT LITHOGRAPHS, Honore Daumier. Wide-ranging collection of lithographs by the greatest caricaturist of the 19th century. Concentrates on eternally popular series on lawyers, on married life, on liberated women, etc. Selection, introduction, and notes on plates by Charles F. Ramus. Total of 158pp. 9⅜ x 12¼.　　　23512-2 Pa. $5.50

DRAWINGS OF MUCHA, Alphonse Maria Mucha. Work reveals drafts-man of highest caliber: studies for famous posters and paintings, render-ings for book illustrations and ads, etc. 70 works, 9 in color; including 6 items not drawings. Introduction. List of illustrations. 72pp. 9⅜ x 12¼. (Available in U.S. only)　　　　　　　　　　23672-2 Pa. $4.00

GIOVANNI BATTISTA PIRANESI: DRAWINGS IN THE PIERPONT MORGAN LIBRARY, Giovanni Battista Piranesi. For first time ever all of Morgan Library's collection, world's largest. 167 illustrations of rare Piranesi drawings—archeological, architectural, decorative and visionary. Essay, detailed list of drawings, chronology, captions. Edited by Felice Stampfle. 144pp. 9⅜ x 12¼.　　　　　　　　　23714-1 Pa. $7.50

NEW YORK ETCHINGS (1905-1949), John Sloan. All of important American artist's N.Y. life etchings. 67 works include some of his best art; also lively historical record—Greenwich Village, tenement scenes. Edited by Sloan's widow. Introduction and captions. 79pp. 8⅜ x 11¼.　　　　　　　　　　　　　　　23651-X Pa. $4.00

CHINESE PAINTING AND CALLIGRAPHY: A PICTORIAL SURVEY, Wan-go Weng. 69 fine examples from John M. Crawford's matchless private collection: landscapes, birds, flowers, human figures, etc., plus calligraphy. Every basic form included: hanging scrolls, handscrolls, album leaves, fans, etc. 109 illustrations. Introduction. Captions. 192pp. 8⅞ x 11¾.　　　　　　　　　　　　　　23707-9 Pa. $7.95

DRAWINGS OF REMBRANDT, edited by Seymour Slive. Updated Lipp-mann, Hofstede de Groot edition, with definitive scholarly apparatus. All portraits, biblical sketches, landscapes, nudes, Oriental figures, classical studies, together with selection of work by followers. 550 illustrations. Total of 630pp. 9⅛ x 12¼.　　21485-0, 21486-9 Pa., Two-vol. set $15.00

THE DISASTERS OF WAR, Francisco Goya. 83 etchings record horrors of Napoleonic wars in Spain and war in general. Reprint of 1st edition, plus 3 additional plates. Introduction by Philip Hofer. 97pp. 9⅜ x 8¼.　　　　　　　　　　　　　　　21872-4 Pa. $3.75

THE EARLY WORK OF AUBREY BEARDSLEY, Aubrey Beardsley. 157 plates, 2 in color: *Manon Lescaut, Madame Bovary, Morte Darthur, Salome,* other. Introduction by H. Marillier. 182pp. 8⅛ x 11. 21816-3 Pa. $4.50

THE LATER WORK OF AUBREY BEARDSLEY, Aubrey Beardsley. Exotic masterpieces of full maturity: *Venus and Tannhauser, Lysistrata, Rape of the Lock, Volpone,* Savoy material, etc. 174 plates, 2 in color. 186pp. 8⅛ x 11. 21817-1 Pa. $4.50

THOMAS NAST'S CHRISTMAS DRAWINGS, Thomas Nast. Almost all Christmas drawings by creator of image of Santa Claus as we know it, and one of America's foremost illustrators and political cartoonists. 66 illustrations. 3 illustrations in color on covers. 96pp. 8⅜ x 11¼. 23660-9 Pa. $3.50

THE DORÉ ILLUSTRATIONS FOR DANTE'S DIVINE COMEDY, Gustave Doré. All 135 plates from Inferno, Purgatory, Paradise; fantastic tortures, infernal landscapes, celestial wonders. Each plate with appropriate (translated) verses. 141pp. 9 x 12. 23231-X Pa. $4.50

DORÉ'S ILLUSTRATIONS FOR RABELAIS, Gustave Doré. 252 striking illustrations of *Gargantua and Pantagruel* books by foremost 19th-century illustrator. Including 60 plates, 192 delightful smaller illustrations. 153pp. 9 x 12. 23656-0 Pa. $5.00

LONDON: A PILGRIMAGE, Gustave Doré, Blanchard Jerrold. Squalor, riches, misery, beauty of mid-Victorian metropolis; 55 wonderful plates, 125 other illustrations, full social, cultural text by Jerrold. 191pp. of text. 9⅜ x 12¼. 22306-X Pa. $7.00

THE RIME OF THE ANCIENT MARINER, Gustave Doré, S. T. Coleridge. Dore's finest work, 34 plates capture moods, subtleties of poem. Full text. Introduction by Millicent Rose. 77pp. 9¼ x 12. 22305-1 Pa. $3.50

THE DORE BIBLE ILLUSTRATIONS, Gustave Doré. All wonderful, detailed plates: Adam and Eve, Flood, Babylon, Life of Jesus, etc. Brief King James text with each plate. Introduction by Millicent Rose. 241 plates. 241pp. 9 x 12. 23004-X Pa. $6.00

THE COMPLETE ENGRAVINGS, ETCHINGS AND DRYPOINTS OF ALBRECHT DURER. "Knight, Death and Devil"; "Melencolia," and more—all Dürer's known works in all three media, including 6 works formerly attributed to him. 120 plates. 235pp. 8⅜ x 11¼. 22851-7 Pa. $6.50

MAXIMILIAN'S TRIUMPHAL ARCH, Albrecht Dürer and others. Incredible monument of woodcut art: 8 foot high elaborate arch—heraldic figures, humans, battle scenes, fantastic elements—that you can assemble yourself. Printed on one side, layout for assembly. 143pp. 11 x 16. 21451-6 Pa. $5.00

THE COMPLETE WOODCUTS OF ALBRECHT DURER, edited by Dr. W. Kurth. 346 in all: "Old Testament," "St. Jerome," "Passion," "Life of Virgin," Apocalypse," many others. Introduction by Campbell Dodgson. 285pp. 8½ x 12¼.   21097-9 Pa. $7.50

DRAWINGS OF ALBRECHT DURER, edited by Heinrich Wolfflin. 81 plates show development from youth to full style. Many favorites; many new. Introduction by Alfred Werner. 96pp. 8⅛ x 11.   22352-3 Pa. $5.00

THE HUMAN FIGURE, Albrecht Dürer. Experiments in various techniques—stereometric, progressive proportional, and others. Also life studies that rank among finest ever done. Complete reprinting of Dresden Sketchbook. 170 plates. 355pp. 8⅜ x 11¼.   21042-1 Pa. $7.95

OF THE JUST SHAPING OF LETTERS, Albrecht Dürer. Renaissance artist explains design of Roman majuscules by geometry, also Gothic lower and capitals. Grolier Club edition. 43pp. 7⅞ x 10¾   21306-4 Pa. $3.00

TEN BOOKS ON ARCHITECTURE, Vitruvius. The most important book ever written on architecture. Early Roman aesthetics, technology, classical orders, site selection, all other aspects. Stands behind everything since. Morgan translation. 331pp. 5⅜ x 8½.   20645-9 Pa. $4.50

THE FOUR BOOKS OF ARCHITECTURE, Andrea Palladio. 16th-century classic responsible for Palladian movement and style. Covers classical architectural remains, Renaissance revivals, classical orders, etc. 1738 Ware English edition. Introduction by A. Placzek. 216 plates. 110pp. of text. 9½ x 12¾.   21308-0 Pa. $10.00

HORIZONS, Norman Bel Geddes. Great industrialist stage designer, "father of streamlining," on application of aesthetics to transportation, amusement, architecture, etc. 1932 prophetic account; function, theory, specific projects. 222 illustrations. 312pp. 7⅞ x 10¾.   23514-9 Pa. $6.95

FRANK LLOYD WRIGHT'S FALLINGWATER, Donald Hoffmann. Full, illustrated story of conception and building of Wright's masterwork at Bear Run, Pa. 100 photographs of site, construction, and details of completed structure. 112pp. 9¼ x 10.   23671-4 Pa. $5.50

THE ELEMENTS OF DRAWING, John Ruskin. Timeless classic by great Viltorian; starts with basic ideas, works through more difficult. Many practical exercises. 48 illustrations. Introduction by Lawrence Campbell. 228pp. 5⅜ x 8½.   22730-8 Pa. $3.75

GIST OF ART, John Sloan. Greatest modern American teacher, Art Students League, offers innumerable hints, instructions, guided comments to help you in painting. Not a formal course. 46 illustrations. Introduction by Helen Sloan. 200pp. 5⅜ x 8½.   23435-5 Pa. $4.00

THE ANATOMY OF THE HORSE, George Stubbs. Often considered the great masterpiece of animal anatomy. Full reproduction of 1766 edition, plus prospectus; original text and modernized text. 36 plates. Introduction by Eleanor Garvey. 121pp. 11 x 14¾. 23402-9 Pa. $6.00

BRIDGMAN'S LIFE DRAWING, George B. Bridgman. More than 500 illustrative drawings and text teach you to abstract the body into its major masses, use light and shade, proportion; as well as specific areas of anatomy, of which Bridgman is master. 192pp. 6½ x 9¼. (Available in U.S. only) 22710-3 Pa. $3.50

ART NOUVEAU DESIGNS IN COLOR, Alphonse Mucha, Maurice Verneuil, Georges Auriol. Full-color reproduction of *Combinaisons ornementales* (c. 1900) by Art Nouveau masters. Floral, animal, geometric, interlacings, swashes—borders, frames, spots—all incredibly beautiful. 60 plates, hundreds of designs. 9⅜ x 8-1/16. 22885-1 Pa. $4.00

FULL-COLOR FLORAL DESIGNS IN THE ART NOUVEAU STYLE, E. A. Seguy. 166 motifs, on 40 plates, from *Les fleurs et leurs applications decoratives* (1902): borders, circular designs, repeats, allovers, "spots." All in authentic Art Nouveau colors. 48pp. 9⅜ x 12¼. 23439-8 Pa. $5.00

A DIDEROT PICTORIAL ENCYCLOPEDIA OF TRADES AND INDUSTRY, edited by Charles C. Gillispie. 485 most interesting plates from the great French Encyclopedia of the 18th century show hundreds of working figures, artifacts, process, land and cityscapes; glassmaking, papermaking, metal extraction, construction, weaving, making furniture, clothing, wigs, dozens of other activities. Plates fully explained. 920pp. 9 x 12. 22284-5, 22285-3 Clothbd., Two-vol. set $40.00

HANDBOOK OF EARLY ADVERTISING ART, Clarence P. Hornung. Largest collection of copyright-free early and antique advertising art ever compiled. Over 6,000 illustrations, from Franklin's time to the 1890's for special effects, novelty. Valuable source, almost inexhaustible.
Pictorial Volume. Agriculture, the zodiac, animals, autos, birds, Christmas, fire engines, flowers, trees, musical instruments, ships, games and sports, much more. Arranged by subject matter and use. 237 plates. 288pp. 9 x 12. 20122-8 Clothbd. $14.50

Typographical Volume. Roman and Gothic faces ranging from 10 point to 300 point, "Barnum," German and Old English faces, script, logotypes, scrolls and flourishes, 1115 ornamental initials, 67 complete alphabets, more. 310 plates. 320pp. 9 x 12. 20123-6 Clothbd. $15.00

CALLIGRAPHY (CALLIGRAPHIA LATINA), J. G. Schwandner. High point of 18th-century ornamental calligraphy. Very ornate initials, scrolls, borders, cherubs, birds, lettered examples. 172pp. 9 x 13. 20475-8 Pa. $7.00

ART FORMS IN NATURE, Ernst Haeckel. Multitude of strangely beautiful natural forms: Radiolaria, Foraminifera, jellyfishes, fungi, turtles, bats, etc. All 100 plates of the 19th-century evolutionist's *Kunstformen der Natur* (1904). 100pp. 9⅜ x 12¼.   22987-4 Pa. $5.00

CHILDREN: A PICTORIAL ARCHIVE FROM NINETEENTH-CENTURY SOURCES, edited by Carol Belanger Grafton. 242 rare, copyright-free wood engravings for artists and designers. Widest such selection available. All illustrations in line. 119pp. 8⅜ x 11¼.
23694-3 Pa. $3.50

WOMEN: A PICTORIAL ARCHIVE FROM NINETEENTH-CENTURY SOURCES, edited by Jim Harter. 391 copyright-free wood engravings for artists and designers selected from rare periodicals. Most extensive such collection available. All illustrations in line. 128pp. 9 x 12.
23703-6 Pa. $4.50

ARABIC ART IN COLOR, Prisse d'Avennes. From the greatest ornamentalists of all time—50 plates in color, rarely seen outside the Near East, rich in suggestion and stimulus. Includes 4 plates on covers. 46pp. 9⅜ x 12¼.   23658-7 Pa. $6.00

AUTHENTIC ALGERIAN CARPET DESIGNS AND MOTIFS, edited by June Beveridge. Algerian carpets are world famous. Dozens of geometrical motifs are charted on grids, color-coded, for weavers, needleworkers, craftsmen, designers. 53 illustrations plus 4 in color. 48pp. 8¼ x 11. (Available in U.S. only)   23650-1 Pa. $1.75

DICTIONARY OF AMERICAN PORTRAITS, edited by Hayward and Blanche Cirker. 4000 important Americans, earliest times to 1905, mostly in clear line. Politicians, writers, soldiers, scientists, inventors, industrialists, Indians, Blacks, women, outlaws, etc. Identificatory information. 756pp. 9¼ x 12¾.   21823-6 Clothbd. $40.00

HOW THE OTHER HALF LIVES, Jacob A. Riis. Journalistic record of filth, degradation, upward drive in New York immigrant slums, shops, around 1900. New edition includes 100 original Riis photos, monuments of early photography. 233pp. 10 x 7⅞.   22012-5 Pa. $7.00

NEW YORK IN THE THIRTIES, Berenice Abbott. Noted photographer's fascinating study of city shows new buildings that have become famous and old sights that have disappeared forever. Insightful commentary. 97 photographs. 97pp. 11⅜ x 10.   22967-X Pa. $5.00

MEN AT WORK, Lewis W. Hine. Famous photographic studies of construction workers, railroad men, factory workers and coal miners. New supplement of 18 photos on Empire State building construction. New introduction by Jonathan L. Doherty. Total of 69 photos. 63pp. 8 x 10¾.
23475-4 Pa. $3.00

CATALOGUE OF DOVER BOOKS

THE DEPRESSION YEARS AS PHOTOGRAPHED BY ARTHUR ROTH-STEIN, Arthur Rothstein. First collection devoted entirely to the work of outstanding 1930s photographer: famous dust storm photo, ragged children, unemployed, etc. 120 photographs. Captions. 119pp. 9¼ x 10¾.
23590-4 Pa. $5.00

CAMERA WORK: A PICTORIAL GUIDE, Alfred Stieglitz. All 559 illustrations and plates from the most important periodical in the history of art photography, Camera Work (1903-17). Presented four to a page, reduced in size but still clear, in strict chronological order, with complete captions. Three indexes. Glossary. Bibliography. 176pp. 8⅜ x 11¼.
23591-2 Pa. $6.95

ALVIN LANGDON COBURN, PHOTOGRAPHER, Alvin L. Coburn. Revealing autobiography by one of greatest photographers of 20th century gives insider's version of Photo-Secession, plus comments on his own work. 77 photographs by Coburn. Edited by Helmut and Alison Gernsheim. 160pp. 8⅛ x 11.
23685-4 Pa. $6.00

NEW YORK IN THE FORTIES, Andreas Feininger. 162 brilliant photographs by the well-known photographer, formerly with Life magazine, show commuters, shoppers, Times Square at night, Harlem nightclub, Lower East Side, etc. Introduction and full captions by John von Hartz. 181pp. 9¼ x 10¾.
23585-8 Pa. $6.00

GREAT NEWS PHOTOS AND THE STORIES BEHIND THEM, John Faber. Dramatic volume of 140 great news photos, 1855 through 1976, and revealing stories behind them, with both historical and technical information. Hindenburg disaster, shooting of Oswald, nomination of Jimmy Carter, etc. 160pp. 8¼ x 11.
23667-6 Pa. $5.00

THE ART OF THE CINEMATOGRAPHER, Leonard Maltin. Survey of American cinematography history and anecdotal interviews with 5 masters—Arthur Miller, Hal Mohr, Hal Rosson, Lucien Ballard, and Conrad Hall. Very large selection of behind-the-scenes production photos. 105 photographs. Filmographies. Index. Originally Behind the Camera. 144pp. 8¼ x 11.
23686-2 Pa. $5.00

DESIGNS FOR THE THREE-CORNERED HAT (LE TRICORNE), Pablo Picasso. 32 fabulously rare drawings—including 31 color illustrations of costumes and accessories—for 1919 production of famous ballet. Edited by Parmenia Migel, who has written new introduction. 48pp. 9⅜ x 12¼.
(Available in U.S. only)
23709-5 Pa. $5.00

NOTES OF A FILM DIRECTOR, Sergei Eisenstein. Greatest Russian filmmaker explains montage, making of Alexander Nevsky, aesthetics; comments on self, associates, great rivals (Chaplin), similar material. 78 illustrations. 240pp. 5⅜ x 8½.
22392-2 Pa. $4.50

HOLLYWOOD GLAMOUR PORTRAITS, edited by John Kobal. 145 photos capture the stars from 1926-49, the high point in portrait photography. Gable, Harlow, Bogart, Bacall, Hedy Lamarr, Marlene Dietrich, Robert Montgomery, Marlon Brando, Veronica Lake; 94 stars in all. Full background on photographers, technical aspects, much more. Total of 160pp. 8⅜ x 11¼. 23352-9 Pa. $6.00

THE NEW YORK STAGE: FAMOUS PRODUCTIONS IN PHOTO-GRAPHS, edited by Stanley Appelbaum. 148 photographs from Museum of City of New York show 142 plays, 1883-1939. *Peter Pan, The Front Page, Dead End, Our Town,* O'Neill, hundreds of actors and actresses, etc. Full indexes. 154pp. 9½ x 10. 23241-7 Pa. $6.00

DIALOGUES CONCERNING TWO NEW SCIENCES, Galileo Galilei. Encompassing 30 years of experiment and thought, these dialogues deal with geometric demonstrations of fracture of solid bodies, cohesion, leverage, speed of light and sound, pendulums, falling bodies, accelerated motion, etc. 300pp. 5⅜ x 8½. 60099-8 Pa. $4.00

THE GREAT OPERA STARS IN HISTORIC PHOTOGRAPHS, edited by James Camner. 343 portraits from the 1850s to the 1940s: Tamburini, Mario, Caliapin, Jeritza, Melchior, Melba, Patti, Pinza, Schipa, Caruso, Farrar, Steber, Gobbi, and many more—270 performers in all. Index. 199pp. 8⅜ x 11¼. 23575-0 Pa. $6.50

J. S. BACH, Albert Schweitzer. Great full-length study of Bach, life, background to music, music, by foremost modern scholar. Ernest Newman translation. 650 musical examples. Total of 928pp. 5⅜ x 8½. (Available in U.S. only) 21631-4, 21632-2 Pa., Two-vol. set $11.00

COMPLETE PIANO SONATAS, Ludwig van Beethoven. All sonatas in the fine Schenker edition, with fingering, analytical material. One of best modern editions. Total of 615pp. 9 x 12. (Available in U.S. only) 23134-8, 23135-6 Pa., Two-vol. set $15.00

KEYBOARD MUSIC, J. S. Bach. Bach-Gesellschaft edition. For harpsichord, piano, other keyboard instruments. English Suites, French Suites, Six Partitas, Goldberg Variations, Two-Part Inventions, Three-Part Sinfonias. 312pp. 8⅛ x 11. (Available in U.S. only) 22360-4 Pa. $6.95

FOUR SYMPHONIES IN FULL SCORE, Franz Schubert. Schubert's four most popular symphonies: No. 4 in C Minor ("Tragic"); No. 5 in B-flat Major; No. 8 in B Minor ("Unfinished"); No. 9 in C Major ("Great"). Breitkopf & Hartel edition. Study score. 261pp. 9⅜ x 12¼. 23681-1 Pa. $6.50

THE AUTHENTIC GILBERT & SULLIVAN SONGBOOK, W. S. Gilbert, A. S. Sullivan. Largest selection available; 92 songs, uncut, original keys, in piano rendering approved by Sullivan. Favorites and lesser-known fine numbers. Edited with plot synopses by James Spero. 3 illustrations. 399pp. 9 x 12. 23482-7 Pa. $9.95

PRINCIPLES OF ORCHESTRATION, Nikolay Rimsky-Korsakov. Great classical orchestrator provides fundamentals of tonal resonance, progression of parts, voice and orchestra, tutti effects, much else in major document. 330pp. of musical excerpts. 489pp. 6½ x 9¼.   21266-1 Pa. $7.50

TRISTAN UND ISOLDE, Richard Wagner. Full orchestral score with complete instrumentation. Do not confuse with piano reduction. Commentary by Felix Mottl, great Wagnerian conductor and scholar. Study score. 655pp. 8⅛ x 11.   22915-7 Pa. $13.95

REQUIEM IN FULL SCORE, Giuseppe Verdi. Immensely popular with choral groups and music lovers. Republication of edition published by C. F. Peters, Leipzig, n. d. German frontmaker in English translation. Glossary. Text in Latin. Study score. 204pp. 9⅜ x 12¼.
23682-X Pa. $6.00

COMPLETE CHAMBER MUSIC FOR STRINGS, Felix Mendelssohn. All of Mendelssohn's chamber music: Octet, 2 Quintets, 6 Quartets, and Four Pieces for String Quartet. (Nothing with piano is included). Complete works edition (1874-7). Study score. 283 pp. 9⅜ x 12¼.
23679-X Pa. $7.50

POPULAR SONGS OF NINETEENTH-CENTURY AMERICA, edited by Richard Jackson. 64 most important songs: "Old Oaken Bucket," "Arkansas Traveler," "Yellow Rose of Texas," etc. Authentic original sheet music, full introduction and commentaries. 290pp. 9 x 12.   23270-0 Pa. $7.95

COLLECTED PIANO WORKS, Scott Joplin. Edited by Vera Brodsky Lawrence. Practically all of Joplin's piano works—rags, two-steps, marches, waltzes, etc., 51 works in all. Extensive introduction by Rudi Blesh. Total of 345pp. 9 x 12.   23106-2 Pa. $14.95

BASIC PRINCIPLES OF CLASSICAL BALLET, Agrippina Vaganova. Great Russian theoretician, teacher explains methods for teaching classical ballet; incorporates best from French, Italian, Russian schools. 118 illustrations. 175pp. 5⅜ x 8½.   22036-2 Pa. $2.50

CHINESE CHARACTERS, L. Wieger. Rich analysis of 2300 characters according to traditional systems into primitives. Historical-semantic analysis to phonetics (Classical Mandarin) and radicals. 820pp. 6⅛ x 9¼.
21321-8 Pa. $10.00

EGYPTIAN LANGUAGE: EASY LESSONS IN EGYPTIAN HIERO-GLYPHICS, E. A. Wallis Budge. Foremost Egyptologist offers Egyptian grammar, explanation of hieroglyphics, many reading texts, dictionary of symbols. 246pp. 5 x 7½. (Available in U.S. only)
21394-3 Clothbd. $7.50

AN ETYMOLOGICAL DICTIONARY OF MODERN ENGLISH, Ernest Weekley. Richest, fullest work, by foremost British lexicographer. Detailed word histories. Inexhaustible. Do not confuse this with Concise Etymological Dictionary, which is abridged. Total of 856pp. 6½ x 9¼.
21873-2, 21874-0 Pa., Two-vol. set $12.00

A MAYA GRAMMAR, Alfred M. Tozzer. Practical, useful English-language grammar by the Harvard anthropologist who was one of the three greatest American scholars in the area of Maya culture. Phonetics, grammatical processes, syntax, more. 301pp. 5⅜ x 8½.   23465-7 Pa. $4.00

THE JOURNAL OF HENRY D. THOREAU, edited by Bradford Torrey, F. H. Allen. Complete reprinting of 14 volumes, 1837-61, over two million words; the sourcebooks for *Walden*, etc. Definitive. All original sketches, plus 75 photographs. Introduction by Walter Harding. Total of 1804pp. 8½ x 12¼.   20312-3, 20313-1 Clothbd., Two-vol. set $50.00

CLASSIC GHOST STORIES, Charles Dickens and others. 18 wonderful stories you've wanted to reread: "The Monkey's Paw," "The House and the Brain," "The Upper Berth," "The Signalman," "Dracula's Guest," "The Tapestried Chamber," etc. Dickens, Scott, Mary Shelley, Stoker, etc. 330pp. 5⅜ x 8½.   20735-8 Pa. $4.50

SEVEN SCIENCE FICTION NOVELS, H. G. Wells. Full novels. *First Men in the Moon, Island of Dr. Moreau, War of the Worlds, Food of the Gods, Invisible Man, Time Machine, In the Days of the Comet.* A basic science-fiction library. 1015pp. 5⅜ x 8½. (Available in U.S. only)
20264-X Clothbd. $8.95

ARMADALE, Wilkie Collins. Third great mystery novel by the author of *The Woman in White* and *The Moonstone.* Ingeniously plotted narrative shows an exceptional command of character, incident and mood. Original magazine version with 40 illustrations. 597pp. 5⅜ x 8½.
23429-0 Pa. $6.00

MASTERS OF MYSTERY, H. Douglas Thomson. The first book in English (1931) devoted to history and aesthetics of detective story. Poe, Doyle, LeFanu, Dickens, many others, up to 1930. New introduction and notes by E. F. Bleiler. 288pp. 5⅜ x 8½. (Available in U.S. only)
23606-4 Pa. $4.00

FLATLAND, E. A. Abbott. Science-fiction classic explores life of 2-D being in 3-D world. Read also as introduction to thought about hyperspace. Introduction by Banesh Hoffmann. 16 illustrations. 103pp. 5⅜ x 8½.
20001-9 Pa. $2.00

THREE SUPERNATURAL NOVELS OF THE VICTORIAN PERIOD, edited, with an introduction, by E. F. Bleiler. Reprinted complete and unabridged, three great classics of the supernatural: *The Haunted Hotel* by Wilkie Collins, *The Haunted House at Latchford* by Mrs. J. H. Riddell, and *The Lost Stradivarious* by J. Meade Falkner. 325pp. 5⅜ x 8½.
22571-2 Pa. $4.00

AYESHA: THE RETURN OF "SHE," H. Rider Haggard. Virtuoso sequel featuring the great mythic creation, Ayesha, in an adventure that is fully as good as the first book, *She.* Original magazine version, with 47 original illustrations by Maurice Greiffenhagen. 189pp. 6½ x 9¼.
23649-8 Pa. $3.50

UNCLE SILAS, J. Sheridan LeFanu. Victorian Gothic mystery novel, considered by many best of period, even better than Collins or Dickens. Wonderful psychological terror. Introduction by Frederick Shroyer. 436pp. 5⅜ x 8½.   21715-9 Pa. $6.00

JURGEN, James Branch Cabell. The great erotic fantasy of the 1920's that delighted thousands, shocked thousands more. Full final text, Lane edition with 13 plates by Frank Pape. 346pp. 5⅜ x 8½.
                                                     23507-6 Pa. $4.50

THE CLAVERINGS, Anthony Trollope. Major novel, chronicling aspects of British Victorian society, personalities. Reprint of Cornhill serialization, 16 plates by M. Edwards; first reprint of full text. Introduction by Norman Donaldson. 412pp. 5⅜ x 8½.   23464-9 Pa. $5.00

KEPT IN THE DARK, Anthony Trollope. Unusual short novel about Victorian morality and abnormal psychology by the great English author. Probably the first American publication. Frontispiece by Sir John Millais. 92pp. 6½ x 9¼.   23609-9 Pa. $2.50

RALPH THE HEIR, Anthony Trollope. Forgotten tale of illegitimacy, inheritance. Master novel of Trollope's later years. Victorian country estates, clubs, Parliament, fox hunting, world of fully realized characters. Reprint of 1871 edition. 12 illustrations by F. A. Faser. 434pp. of text. 5⅜ x 8½.   23642-0 Pa. $5.00

YEKL and THE IMPORTED BRIDEGROOM AND OTHER STORIES OF THE NEW YORK GHETTO, Abraham Cahan. Film *Hester Street* based on *Yekl* (1896). Novel, other stories among first about Jewish immigrants of N.Y.'s East Side. Highly praised by W. D. Howells—Cahan "a new star of realism." New introduction by Bernard G. Richards. 240pp. 5⅜ x 8½.   22427-9 Pa. $3.50

THE HIGH PLACE, James Branch Cabell. Great fantasy writer's enchanting comedy of disenchantment set in 18th-century France. Considered by some critics to be even better than his famous *Jurgen*. 10 illustrations and numerous vignettes by noted fantasy artist Frank C. Pape. 320pp. 5⅜ x 8½.   23670-6 Pa. $4.00

ALICE'S ADVENTURES UNDER GROUND, Lewis Carroll. Facsimile of ms. Carroll gave Alice Liddell in 1864. Different in many ways from final Alice. Handlettered, illustrated by Carroll. Introduction by Martin Gardner. 128pp. 5⅜ x 8½.   21482-6 Pa. $2.00

FAVORITE ANDREW LANG FAIRY TALE BOOKS IN MANY COLORS, Andrew Lang. The four Lang favorites in a boxed set—the complete *Red, Green, Yellow* and *Blue* Fairy Books. 164 stories; 439 illustrations by Lancelot Speed, Henry Ford and G. P. Jacomb Hood. Total of about 1500pp. 5⅜ x 8½.   23407-X Boxed set, Pa. $14.95

HOUSEHOLD STORIES BY THE BROTHERS GRIMM. All the great Grimm stories: "Rumpelstiltskin," "Snow White," "Hansel and Gretel," etc., with 114 illustrations by Walter Crane. 269pp. 5⅜ x 8½.
21080-4 Pa. $3.50

SLEEPING BEAUTY, illustrated by Arthur Rackham. Perhaps the fullest, most delightful version ever, told by C. S. Evans. Rackham's best work. 49 illustrations. 110pp. 7⅞ x 10¾. 22756-1 Pa. $2.50

AMERICAN FAIRY TALES, L. Frank Baum. Young cowboy lassoes Father Time; dummy in Mr. Floman's department store window comes to life; and 10 other fairy tales. 41 illustrations by N. P. Hall, Harry Kennedy, Ike Morgan, and Ralph Gardner. 209pp. 5⅜ x 8½. 23643-9 Pa. $3.00

THE WONDERFUL WIZARD OF OZ, L. Frank Baum. Facsimile in full color of America's finest children's classic. Introduction by Martin Gardner. 143 illustrations by W. W. Denslow. 267pp. 5⅜ x 8½.
20691-2 Pa. $3.50

THE TALE OF PETER RABBIT, Beatrix Potter. The inimitable Peter's terrifying adventure in Mr. McGregor's garden, with all 27 wonderful, full-color Potter illustrations. 55pp. 4¼ x 5½. (Available in U.S. only)
22827-4 Pa. $1.25

THE STORY OF KING ARTHUR AND HIS KNIGHTS, Howard Pyle. Finest children's version of life of King Arthur. 48 illustrations by Pyle. 131pp. 6⅛ x 9¼. 21445-1 Pa. $4.95

CARUSO'S CARICATURES, Enrico Caruso. Great tenor's remarkable caricatures of self, fellow musicians, composers, others. Toscanini, Puccini, Farrar, etc. Impish, cutting, insightful. 473 illustrations. Preface by M. Sisca. 217pp. 8⅜ x 11¼. 23528-9 Pa. $6.95

PERSONAL NARRATIVE OF A PILGRIMAGE TO ALMADINAH AND MECCAH, Richard Burton. Great travel classic by remarkably colorful personality. Burton, disguised as a Moroccan, visited sacred shrines of Islam, narrowly escaping death. Wonderful observations of Islamic life, customs, personalities. 47 illustrations. Total of 959pp. 5⅜ x 8½.
21217-3, 21218-1 Pa., Two-vol. set $12.00

INCIDENTS OF TRAVEL IN YUCATAN, John L. Stephens. Classic (1843) exploration of jungles of Yucatan, looking for evidences of Maya civilization. Travel adventures, Mexican and Indian culture, etc. Total of 669pp. 5⅜ x 8½. 20926-1, 20927-X Pa., Two-vol. set $7.90

AMERICAN LITERARY AUTOGRAPHS FROM WASHINGTON IRVING TO HENRY JAMES, Herbert Cahoon, et al. Letters, poems, manuscripts of Hawthorne, Thoreau, Twain, Alcott, Whitman, 67 other prominent American authors. Reproductions, full transcripts and commentary. Plus checklist of all American Literary Autographs in The Pierpont Morgan Library. Printed on exceptionally high-quality paper. 136 illustrations. 212pp. 9⅛ x 12¼. 23548-3 Pa. $12.50

AN AUTOBIOGRAPHY, Margaret Sanger. Exciting personal account of hard-fought battle for woman's right to birth control, against prejudice, church, law. Foremost feminist document. 504pp. 5⅜ x 8½.
20470-7 Pa. $5.50

MY BONDAGE AND MY FREEDOM, Frederick Douglass. Born as a slave, Douglass became outspoken force in antislavery movement. The best of Douglass's autobiographies. Graphic description of slave life. Introduction by P. Foner. 464pp. 5⅜ x 8½.   22457-0 Pa. $5.50

LIVING MY LIFE, Emma Goldman. Candid, no holds barred account by foremost American anarchist: her own life, anarchist movement, famous contemporaries, ideas and their impact. Struggles and confrontations in America, plus deportation to U.S.S.R. Shocking inside account of persecution of anarchists under Lenin. 13 plates. Total of 944pp. 5⅜ x 8½.
22543-7, 22544-5 Pa., Two-vol. set $12.00

LETTERS AND NOTES ON THE MANNERS, CUSTOMS AND CONDITIONS OF THE NORTH AMERICAN INDIANS, George Catlin. Classic account of life among Plains Indians: ceremonies, hunt, warfare, etc. Dover edition reproduces for first time all original paintings. 312 plates. 572pp. of text. 6⅛ x 9¼.   22118-0, 22119-9 Pa.. Two-vol. set $12.00

THE MAYA AND THEIR NEIGHBORS, edited by Clarence L. Hay, others. Synoptic view of Maya civilization in broadest sense, together with Northern, Southern neighbors. Integrates much background, valuable detail not elsewhere. Prepared by greatest scholars: Kroeber, Morley, Thompson, Spinden, Vaillant, many others. Sometimes called Tozzer Memorial Volume. 60 illustrations, linguistic map. 634pp. 5⅜ x 8½.
23510-6 Pa. $7.50

HANDBOOK OF THE INDIANS OF CALIFORNIA, A. L. Kroeber. Foremost American anthropologist offers complete ethnographic study of each group. Monumental classic. 459 illustrations, maps. 995pp. 5⅜ x 8½.
23368-5 Pa. $13.00

SHAKTI AND SHAKTA, Arthur Avalon. First book to give clear, cohesive analysis of Shakta doctrine, Shakta ritual and Kundalini Shakti (yoga). Important work by one of world's foremost students of Shaktic and Tantric thought. 732pp. 5⅜ x 8½. (Available in U.S. only)
23645-5 Pa. $7.95

AN INTRODUCTION TO THE STUDY OF THE MAYA HIEROGLYPHS, Syvanus Griswold Morley. Classic study by one of the truly great figures in hieroglyph research. Still the best introduction for the student for reading Maya hieroglyphs. New introduction by J. Eric S. Thompson. 117 illustrations. 284pp. 5⅜ x 8½.   23108-9 Pa. $4.00

A STUDY OF MAYA ART, Herbert J. Spinden. Landmark classic interprets Maya symbolism, estimates styles, covers ceramics, architecture, murals, stone carvings as artforms. Still a basic book in area. New introduction by J. Eric Thompson. Over 750 illustrations. 341pp. 8⅜ x 11¼.
21235-1 Pa. $6.95

CATALOGUE OF DOVER BOOKS

GEOMETRY, RELATIVITY AND THE FOURTH DIMENSION, Rudolf Rucker. Exposition of fourth dimension, means of visualization, concepts of relativity as Flatland characters continue adventures. Popular, easily followed yet accurate, profound. 141 illustrations. 133pp. 5⅜ x 8½.

23400-2 Pa. $2.75

THE ORIGIN OF LIFE, A. I. Oparin. Modern classic in biochemistry, the first rigorous examination of possible evolution of life from nitrocarbon compounds. Non-technical, easily followed. Total of 295pp. 5⅜ x 8½.

60213-3 Pa. $4.00

PLANETS, STARS AND GALAXIES, A. E. Fanning. Comprehensive introductory survey: the sun, solar system, stars, galaxies, universe, cosmology; quasars, radio stars, etc. 24pp. of photographs. 189pp. 5⅜ x 8½. (Available in U.S. only)

21680-2 Pa. $3.75

THE THIRTEEN BOOKS OF EUCLID'S ELEMENTS, translated with introduction and commentary by Sir Thomas L. Heath. Definitive edition. Textual and linguistic notes, mathematical analysis, 2500 years of critical commentary. Do not confuse with abridged school editions. Total of 1414pp. 5⅜ x 8½.   60088-2, 60089-0, 60090-4 Pa., Three-vol. set $18.50

Prices subject to change without notice.

Available at your book dealer or write for free catalogue to Dept. GI, Dover Publications, Inc., 180 Varick St., N.Y., N.Y. 10014. Dover publishes more than 175 books each year on science, elementary and advanced mathematics, biology, music, art, literary history, social sciences and other areas.